LANDSCAPE PROFESSIONAL PRACTICE

Graduate of the Royal Botanic Gardens, Kew, Chartered Landscape Architect, MBA and Barrister, Gordon Rowland Fraser draws upon 30 years of project management, professional practice and teaching experience to provide an uncomplicated and intuitive guide to the business aspects of the landscape profession. An indispensable reference for seasoned professionals, the book will enable the student or novice practitioner to turn their drawing board inspiration into reality without being overwhelmed or afraid of overseeing the implementation of their proposals.

Guided by the Landscape Institute's 2013 Pathway to Chartership syllabus, this structured, step-by-step, narrative guide sets out the documentation commonly used within the landscape profession and makes accessible a logical and sequential understanding of contractual relationships; procurement strategies; processes of preparing client estimates and obtaining competitive quotations; of preparing contract documentation and administering formal contracts; general concepts of law as they relate to land management and the landscape profession; of business administration, market appraisal and positioning; and of the landscape consultant's appointment.

As an understanding of professional practice is intrinsic to all Landscape Institute accredited courses, this is an essential text for every landscape architecture student during their education and their subsequent journey into professional practice. Those undertaking Garden Design Diplomas will similarly find the book invaluable as they venture into the world of creativity and commerce, while the seasoned practitioner will find it a comprehensive point of reference to add to their bookshelf.

Landscape Professional Practice

Gordon Rowland Fraser
Chartered Landscape Architect, MBA, Barrister

ASHGATE

© Gordon Rowland Fraser 2015

All rights reserved. No part of this publication may be reproduced, stored in a retrieval system or transmitted in any form or by any means, electronic, mechanical, photocopying, recording or otherwise without the prior permission of the publisher.

Gordon Rowland Fraser has asserted his right under the Copyright, Designs and Patents Act, 1988, to be identified as the author of this work.

Published by
Ashgate Publishing Limited
Wey Court East
Union Road
Farnham
Surrey, GU9 7PT
England

Ashgate Publishing Company
110 Cherry Street
Suite 3-1
Burlington, VT 05401-3818
USA

www.ashgate.com

British Library Cataloguing in Publication Data
A catalogue record for this book is available from the British Library

Library of Congress Cataloging-in-Publication Data
Fraser, Gordon Rowland.
  Landscape professional practice / by Gordon Rowland Fraser.
    pages cm
  Includes bibliographical references and index.
    ISBN 978-1-4724-4121-8 (hardback: alk. paper)—ISBN 978-1-4724-4122-5 (ebook) — ISBN 978-1-4724-4123-2 (epub)
    1. Landscape architecture—Study and teaching (Higher) 2. Landscaping industry—Management—Study and teaching (Higher) 3. Landscape contracting—Study and teaching (Higher) 4. Industrial management—Study and teaching (Higher) I. Title.
  SB469.4.F73 2015
  712.076—dc23
                                                                                            2014028397
ISBN: 9781472441218 (hbk)
ISBN: 9781472441225 (ebk – PDF)
ISBN: 9781472441232 (ebk –ePUB)

Printed in the United Kingdom by Henry Ling Limited, at the Dorset Press, Dorchester, DT1 1HD

Contents

List of Figures	*xiii*
Table of Cases	*xv*
Biographical Note	*xviii*
Foreword	*xix*
Acknowledgements	*xxi*

Introduction		1
Section I	**Professional Judgment Ethics and Values**	
1	**Professional Association**	**11**
1.1	The Landscape Institute	11
1.2	Standards of Conduct and Practice for Landscape Professionals	13
1.2.1	To preserve the character and quality of the environment	13
1.2.2	To uphold the reputation and dignity of the profession	14
1.2.3	To actively promote the code of conduct	14
1.2.4	To actively promote and further the Landscape Institute objectives	15
1.2.5	To act with integrity consistent with professional obligations	15
1.2.6	To only undertake professional work for which competent	17
1.2.7	To maintain and promote professional competence	17
1.2.8	To organise professional work responsibly with regard to clients	18
1.2.9	To carry out professional work with care and to relevant standards	18
1.2.10	To promote professional services in a truthful and responsible manner	19

1.2.11 To ensure personal and professional finances are managed prudently 20
1.2.12 To maintain adequate and appropriate professional indemnity insurance 20
1.2.13 To deal with professional complaints promptly and appropriately 21
1.3 Continuing Professional Development 22

Section II Organisation and Management

2 The Law of Contract 27

2.1 Invitation to Treat 28
2.2 Offer 28
2.3 Acceptance 29
2.4 Consideration 31
2.5 Contract Terms 32
2.6 Privity of Contract 33
2.7 Agency 34
2.8 Discharge of Contracts 34
2.9 Remedies for Breach of Contract 35
2.10 Misrepresentation 37

3 The Tort of Professional Negligence 41

3.1 Legal Duty of Care 41
3.2 Breach of Duty 43
3.3 Causation 44
3.4 Remoteness of Damage 45
3.5 Defences 46
   3.5.1 Willing assumption of risk 47
   3.5.2 Exclusion of liability 47
   3.5.3 Contributory negligence 48
3.6 Remedies 49
3.7 Negligent Misrepresentation 50
3.8 Professional Indemnity Insurance 51

4 Health and Safety Legislation 53

4.1 Health and Safety at Work Act 54
4.2 The Management of Health and Safety at Work Regulations 55
4.3 Method Statements 57
4.4 The Control of Substances Hazardous to Health Regulations (COSHH) 57
4.5 The Reporting of Injuries, Diseases and Dangerous Occurrences Regulations (RIDDOR) 58
   4.5.1 Death or major injuries 58
   4.5.2 Over-three-day injuries 59

		4.5.3	Work-related diseases	59
		4.5.4	Dangerous occurrences	59
	4.6	Enforcement		59

5 Business Performance and Development — 63

- 5.1 The Transformation Process — 63
- 5.2 Comparison of Goods and Services — 65
- 5.3 Performance Analysis — 66
  - 5.3.1 Quality — 66
  - 5.3.2 Speed — 67
  - 5.3.3 Dependability — 67
  - 5.3.4 Flexibility — 67
  - 5.3.5 Cost — 67
  - 5.3.6 Historical performance — 68
  - 5.3.7 Target performance — 68
  - 5.3.8 Competitor benchmarking — 69
- 5.4 The Business Environment — 70
  - 5.4.1 Legal — 70
  - 5.4.2 Political — 71
  - 5.4.3 Economic — 71
  - 5.4.4 Social — 72
  - 5.4.5 Technological — 72
- 5.5 Market Appraisal — 73
  - 5.5.1 Resources — 73
  - 5.5.2 Resource markets — 74
  - 5.5.3 Customers — 74
  - 5.5.4 Competitors — 74
- 5.6 Business Promotion — 75

6 Business Management — 77

- 6.1 Private Sector Organisations — 77
  - 6.1.1 Sole trader — 77
  - 6.1.2 Partnership — 78
  - 6.1.3 Limited company — 79
  - 6.1.4 Public limited company — 79
- 6.2 Not-for-Profit Organisations — 80
  - 6.2.1 Charitable incorporated organisation — 80
  - 6.2.2 Company limited by guarantee — 81
  - 6.2.3 Consumer co-operative society — 81
  - 6.2.4 Workers co-operative — 81
- 6.3 Public Sector Organisations — 82
- 6.4 Financial Accounting — 83
  - 6.4.1 Profit and loss accounts — 83
  - 6.4.2 Balance sheets — 85
  - 6.4.3 Cash flow forecasting — 85

7	**Engaging a Landscape Professional**		89
	7.1	Scope of Services	89
	7.2	Form of Agreement	90
	7.3	The Landscape Consultant's Appointment	91
	7.4	The Professional Practitioner's Fees	93
		7.4.1 Calculating professional fees	93
		7.4.2 Percentage fees	96
		7.4.3 Time charged fees	97
		7.4.4 Lump sum fees	97
		7.4.5 Expenses and disbursements	98

Section III Legislative Bases of Assessment and Analysis

8	**Development Control and Environmental Management**	103
	8.1 Permitted Development	105
	8.2 Environmental Impact Assessment	107
	8.3 Tree Preservation Orders	112
	8.4 Conservation Areas	114
	8.5 Forestry Regulations	114
	8.6 Hedgerows Regulations	116
	8.7 Habitats Regulations	118

Section IV Project Implementation

9	**Understanding Contractual Relationships**		123
	9.1	Roles and Responsibilities	123
		9.1.1 The role of the client	123
		9.1.2 The role of the contractor	125
		9.1.3 The role of the professional practitioner	126
	9.2	Procurement Strategies	129
		9.2.1 Traditional procurement	130
		9.2.2 Design and build procurement	133
		9.2.3 Management procurement	137

10	**Construction Design and Management Regulations**	141
	10.1 The Requirement for Notification	142
	10.2 Obligations of the Client	143
	10.3 Obligations of the Construction Design and Management Coordinator	145
	10.4 Obligations of Designers/Professional Practitioners	146
	10.5 Obligations of the Principal Contractor	148
	10.6 Obligations of All Contractors and the Self-Employed	149
	10.7 Competence and Training	151

11	**Estimating Project Budgets**	155
	11.1 Measurement	158

11.2	Formulating a Schedule	158
11.3	Attributing Rates	161
11.4	Sources of Rates	162
	11.4.1 Previously quoted schemes	163
	11.4.2 Manufacturer's or supplier's costs	163
	11.4.3 Indicative quotations from contractors	163
	11.4.4 Spon's Landscape and External Works Price Book	164

12 Specification Fundamentals 169

12.1	Contract Documentation	169
12.2	Building Information Modelling	171
12.3	Specification Structure	171
12.4	The Common Arrangement of Work Sections	173
12.5	Preliminaries/General Conditions	174
	12.5.1 Project particulars	174
	12.5.2 Drawings	174
	12.5.3 The site/existing buildings	174
	12.5.4 Description of the work	174
	12.5.5 Conditions of contract	175
	12.5.6 Employer's requirements: tendering sub-letting & supply	175
	12.5.7 Employer's requirements; management of the works	175
	12.5.8 Employer's requirements: quality standards/control	176
	12.5.9 Employer's requirements: security/safety/protection	176
	12.5.10 Employer's requirements: facilities/temporary work/services	176
12.6	Materials and Workmanship	177
	12.6.1 Materials	177
	12.6.2 Workmanship	177
	12.6.3 Quality assurance	178
	12.6.4 British Standards	178
	12.6.5 Specification by type	178
	12.6.6 Specification by proprietary name	179
	12.6.7 Specification by minimum standard	179
	12.6.8 Specification by supplier	179
	12.6.9 Specification by method	180
	12.6.10 Specification by finished effect	180
12.7	Standard Specification Clauses	180
	12.7.1 NBS Landscape	181
	12.7.2 National Plant Specification	181
	12.7.3 Code of Practice for Handling & Establishing Landscape Plants	183
	12.7.4 Other sources	184

13 Conditions of Contract 187

13.1	Sub-Contracts	188
13.2	Forms of Agreement	189
13.3	The JCLI Conditions of Contract	191

	13.3.1	Details of the parties	192
	13.3.2	Nature and location of the works	192
	13.3.3	The contract documents	192
	13.3.4	The contract sum	192
	13.3.5	Professional practitioner's details	193
	13.3.6	The Construction Design and Management Regulations	193
	13.3.7	Dispute resolution	194
	13.3.8	Construction Industry Scheme	195
	13.3.9	Supplemental provisions	196
	13.3.10	Construction Design and Management planning period	197
	13.3.11	Duration of the works	197
	13.3.12	Liquidated damages	197
	13.3.13	Defects and establishment of plants	198
	13.3.14	Theft or malicious damage	199
	13.3.15	Retentions	200
	13.3.16	Supply of documents	201
	13.3.17	Contribution, levy and tax changes	201
	13.3.18	Contractor's liability insurance	202
	13.3.19	Insurance of the works	202
	13.3.20	Attestation	203

14 Single Stage Selective Tendering — 205

14.1	Pre-Tender Evaluation	206
14.2	Preliminary Enquiry	209
14.3	Invitation to Tender	210
14.4	Tender Evaluation	211
14.5	Tender Outcome	213

15 Contract Administration — 215

15.1	Certification		216
	15.1.1	Landscape Architect's/Contract Administrator's Instruction	217
	15.1.2	Interim Payment Certificate	218
	15.1.3	Payless Notice(s) (Type 1)	220
	15.1.4	Payless Notice(s) (Type 2)	220
	15.1.5	Certificate of Practical Completion	221
	15.1.6	Certificate of Making Good	222
	15.1.7	Final Certificate	223
15.2	Drawing Office Records		224
	15.2.1	Job lists	224
	15.2.2	Contract documentation	225
	15.2.3	Valuations, certificates and variations	225
	15.2.4	Correspondence	225
	15.2.5	Practice timesheets and invoices	226

16 Alternative Dispute Resolution Procedures — 229

- 16.1 Major Forms of Alternative Dispute Resolution — 230
  - 16.1.1 Mediation — 231
  - 16.1.2 Arbitration — 233
  - 16.1.3 Adjudication — 234
- 16.2 Changes in Civil Litigation — 235
- 16.3 Alternative Dispute Resolution Clauses — 236
- 16.4 Alternative Dispute Resolution v Litigation — 237
  - 16.4.1 Predictability — 238
  - 16.4.2 Reliability — 238
  - 16.4.3 Expediency — 239
  - 16.4.4 Public scrutiny — 239
  - 16.4.5 Future relations — 240
  - 16.4.6 Expense — 240
  - 16.4.7 Desired outcomes — 240
  - 16.4.8 Sociology — 241
- 16.5 Conclusions — 241

List of References — 245
Index — 249

List of Figures

5.1	The Transformation Model	64
5.2	Transformation in Context	65
6.1	Sample Profit and Loss Account	84
6.2	Sample Balance Sheet	86
7.1	Worked Example of Calculating Professional Fees	95
9.1	Traditional Procurement	131
9.2	Design & Build Procurement	134
11.1	Conventional Format for Schedule of Operations	159
11.2	*Spon's Landscape and External Works Price Book* 'Measured Works'	165
12.1	Contract Documentation	170
12.2	Worked Example of Tree Pit Specification	178
12.3	Worked Example of Specification for Paving Sample	179
12.4	Worked Example of Tree Staking Specification	181
12.5	Sample Screen Shot of NBS Landscape	182
13.1	Contract Documentation	188
14.1	Worked Example of Invitation to Tender Letter	211

Table of Cases

Adams v Lindsell [1818] 1 B&Ald 681 KB

Addis v Gramophone Ltd [1909] AC 488 HL

Anglia Television Ltd v Reed [1972] 1 QB 60 CA

Ashton v Turner [1981] QB 137

Barnett v Chelsea & Kensington Hospital Management Committee [1969] 1 QB 428

Blyth v Birmingham Waterworks [1856] 11 Ex. 781

Bolam v Friern Hospital Management Committee [1957] 1 WLR 582

Bolton v Stone [1951] AC 850

Bourhill v Young [1943] AC 92 HL

Byrne v Van Tienhoven [1880] 5 CPD 344

Cable & Wireless PLC v IBM United Kingdom Ltd [2002] EWHC 2059 (Comm)

Caparo Industries v Dickman [1990] 1 All ER 568 HL

Carlill v Carbolic Smoke Ball Co. [1893] 1 QB 256 CA

Channel Tunnel Group Ltd & Another v Balfour Beatty Construction Ltd & Others [1992] QB 656 CA

Chaplin v Hicks [1911] 2 KB 786

Chappell & Co. v Nestle Co. Ltd [1960] HL

Chaudry v Prabhakar [1989] 1 WLR 29

Corenso (UK) Ltd v Burnden Group PLC [2003] EWHC 1805 (QB)

Courtney & Fairbairn Ltd v Tolaini Bros (Hotels) Ltd [1975] 1 WLR 297 CA

Cowl v Plymouth City Council [2001] EWCA Civ 1935

Dickinson v Dodds [1876] 2 CPD 463 CA

Donoghue v Stevenson [1932] AC 562

Dunnett v Railtrack PLC [2002] EWCA Civ 302

Entores v Miles Far East Corporation [1955] 2 QB 327 CA

Fairchild v Glenhaven [2002] UKHL 22

Farley v Skinner [2001] 4 All ER 801 HL

Felthouse v Bindley [1862] 11 CBNS 86

Fisher v Bell [1961] 1 QB 394

Froom v Butcher [1976] QB 286

Glasbrook Bros. v Glamorgan County Council [1925] AC270 HL

Glasgow Corporation v Muir [1943] AC 448

Hadley v Baxendale [1884] Exch 341

Hadley v London Electricity Board [1965] AC 778 HL

Hartley v Ponsonby [1857] 7 E&B 872

Hedley Byrne & Co v Heller & Partners Ltd [1964] AC 465

Hilder v Associated Portland Cement Manufacturers [1961] 1 WLR 1434

Holwell Securities v Hughes [1974] 1 WLR 155 CA

Hughes v Lord Advocate [1963] AC 837

Hurst v Leeming [2002] EWCA Civ 1173

Hyde v Wrench [1840] 3 Beav 334

Jarvis v Swan Tours [1972] 3 WLR 954

Jones v Livox Quarries Ltd [1952] 2 QB 608

Marc Rich & Co v Bishop Rock Marine Co Ltd [1996] AC 211

McCook v Lobo [2002] EWCA Civ 1760

McKew v Holland [1969] 3 All ER 1621 HL

Mullin v Richards [1998] 1 All ER 920

Murphy v Brentwood District Council [1990] 2 All ER 908

Owens v Liverpool Corporation [1939] 1KB 394

Parsons v Uttley Ingham [1978] QB 791 CA

Partridge v Crittenden [1968] 2 All ER 421

Pinnel's Case [1602] 5 Co Rep 117

Powell v Lee [1908] 99 LT 284

R v Clarke [1927] 40 CLR 227

Rhone v Stephens [1994] 2 AC 310

Roe v Minister of Health [1954] 2 QB 66

Roscorla v Thomas [1842] 3 QB 234

Routledge v Grant [1828] 4 Bing 653

Royal Bank of Canada v Secretary of State for Defence [2003] EWHC 1841

Ruxley Electronics & Construction Ltd v Forsyth [1996] 1 AC 344 HL

Scammell v Ouston [1941] AC 251 HL

Shirlaw v Southern Foundries [1939] 2 KB 206

Smith v Eric S. Bush; Harris v Wyre Forest District Council [1989] 2 WLR 790 HL

Smith v Leech Brain & Co. Ltd [1962] 2 QB 405

Socit Internationale de Telecommunications Aeronautiques SC v Wyatt Co (UK) Ltd (Costs) [2002] EWHC 2401 (Ch)

Spartan Steel & Alloys Ltd v Martin & Co [1973] QBD 27

Stevenson v McLean [1880] 5 QBD 346

Stilk v Myrick [1809] 2 Camp 317

The Wagon Mound (No.1) [1961] AC 388

Tulk v Moxhay [1848] 2 Ph 774

Valentine v Allen [2003] EWCA Civ 1274

Wieland v Cyril Lord [1969] 3 All ER 1006

Williams v Cowardine [1833] 4 B&Ad 621

Williams v Roffey Bros & Nicholls (Contractors) Ltd [1990] 1 All ER 512

Yates v Pulleyn [1975] 119 SJ 370 CA

Biographical Note

One of fewer than 700 people worldwide to have graduated from The Royal Botanic Gardens Kew; a Chartered Member of the Landscape Institute; Master of Business Administration; and Barrister, the author draws upon 30 years' experience of project management and professional practice; his specialism in specifying projects, setting-up and administering contracts and conflict resolution; and his well-received lecture series delivered in some of the country's leading design schools. A former member of the Chartered Institute of Arbitrators trained in mediation techniques by The Inns of Court, the author has employed his unique skill set in the cost-effective resolution of multi-million pound construction and housing disputes, using a range of alternative dispute resolution procedures while simultaneously preserving ongoing contractual relationships between parties.

Foreword

Since the first publication of the book of the same title by Hugh Clamp in 1988, the profession of landscape architecture has 'grown-up' significantly. For many years, and most certainly since the Landscape Institute (LI) obtained its Royal Chartered status in 1997, practitioners, potential LI members, and students alike have been underpinning their baseline knowledge on the information presented in Hugh Clamp's original book for want of any comparable alternative – a fact that Gordon Fraser highlights quite pertinently in his introduction. Just a brief dip into the contents of that original publication indicates what might now be considered a degree of naivety and a lack of the professionalism that is necessary to compete in the highly professional world of landscape architecture and the built environment today. This is not, in any way, to denigrate or dismiss the importance of Hugh Clamp's original book to the development of our profession, merely to highlight the need for someone to review the material and bring it, necessarily, into the twenty-first century.

Many of us may have been tempted to take on that considerable challenge but until now we have all failed to do so. Gordon Fraser has brought his wealth of knowledge, understanding, experience and perhaps quite unique skillset to bear in a manner that, as he suggests, 'is considered relevant to all landscape professionals'. He should be highly applauded for having done so.

Each chapter begins by clearly identifying the aims of the topic about to be discussed – these are presented in a series of concise, precise and comprehensive bullet points. The chapters are equally summarised in a series of short, similarly constructed, conclusive sentences leaving the reader in no doubt as to what has just been interrogated. In taking great pains to present a highly detailed 'Contents' page, the author presents the reader with an exceptionally accessible reference book that offers equally accessible information across the widest range of professional landscape architectural needs.

The range of information presented has also increased and improved considerably since Hugh Clamp's original publication adorned our office shelves. The author has not only brought the standard information up to date but has used his extensive knowledge of the law to introduce a wide range of baseline legal cases that help to explain and identify the various legal precedents against which we as professionals might be judged in this increasingly litigious world. Once again an invaluable reference resource, set within the general narrative of each chapter that is easily understood and highly accessible for everyone, irrespective of whether they are established practitioners, students or someone with just a passing interest.

It is rare in today's demanding professional world that a landscape architect can define her or himself as purely a 'designer' – with that role comes many more professional responsibilities and demands than many may imagine and thus, this book will be of benefit to every established and budding professional in the landscape architectural industry. Just as Hugh Clamp's *Landscape Professional Practice* was a 'must have', 'must study', 'must refer to' professional reference of the late twentieth century, so Gordon Fraser's new reference will be the favoured reference of the early twenty-first century.

This book will be an important reference guide for many years to come, helping to identify, clarify and elucidate many of the fundamental elements of professional practice for landscape architects not only in the UK but around the world.

Nigel Thorne MSc FRSA FIHort FLI PPLI
Consultant Landscape Architect / Specialist Landscape Manager

Acknowledgements

Without the tremendous support, encouragement and practical assistance of Carol and Niall Watkins and Frank Afful this book might never have completed its long gestation. For their patience and understanding and the guidance and enthusiasm of my publisher, Valerie Rose, I really am most grateful.

Gordon Rowland Fraser Dip Hort Kew LLDip MBA BVC CMLI

Introduction

In broader usage, what Koimn (2011) refers to as the 'politically correct professional' has come to mean anyone paid for doing a specific type of job, for example a skilled construction worker who possesses a 'trade' or a 'craft' learnt through mentored training, practical experience and job-specific education undertaken at some form of technical college.

In the narrower, more traditional, sense a professional will generally have completed university level education; an internship, pupillage or some other form of mentored training; will have passed a professional examination by which they have been certificated or accredited by an association that will regulate the profession through strict codes of conduct, ethics, standards of practice, and by requiring its members to regularly update their education and practice skills in order to maintain their professional standing and continue to perform the role of that profession.

The distinction might more simply be made between the craftsperson, who is trained for and engages in some form of manual labour, and the professional, who is specifically trained to do mental, administrative and/or advisory work. It is with this latter category, specifically with the professional practice of landscape architecture, which this book is concerned.

> ACCORDING TO KOIMN (2011):
>
> *The traditional professionals obtain input through communicating with a client or patient to obtain critical information on the circumstances, needs, conditions of the client in matters of the field of expertise of a specific profession. This provider listens, observes, records, interprets, investigates, and in other ways makes determinations and offers advice on the solutions or remediation of the problematic issue presented ... There is a bond of trust between the client and the professional ... You do not tell the doctor how to treat your health issue(s). You tell him your symptoms, how you feel, where you hurt, etc. The doctor makes physical examinations and observations. Then, based upon that critical client/professional exchange of information, the doctor advises the patient on a course of action to treat the condition(s).*

As described by Koimn (2011), after gathering information from the client, the professional practitioner makes recommendations or offers advice as to how the client should proceed. Clients should look to obtain advice from an appropriate professional, for example a member of the General Medical Council for medical professionals; of the Royal Institute of Building Architects for building professionals; the Royal Institute of Chartered Surveyors for surveying professionals; and the Landscape Institute for landscape professionals. That is to say the client should commission the advice it requires from someone who is educated, trained and experienced sufficiently in the particular professional expertise they require; someone who is accredited, regulated and constrained by the moral and ethical codes imposed by the professional association responsible for regulating that particular profession.

According to Bennett (1997) professional associations should be seen as intermediary bodies between business and government, or market and state; professional associations should communicate with government on behalf of their industries; enhance the performance of individual practices; and thereby increase the overall competitiveness of their particular profession in the wider context of the competitiveness of a nation.

> **ACCORDING TO BENNETT (1997, p. 71):**
>
> *The potential benefits of associations to government are contributions to improved business competitiveness, enhanced levels of compliance…, lower administration costs of regulation and better designed regulations to take account of technical and market developments.*

According to Walker (1995, p. 288), the pre-requisites of effective performance on the part of business associations are formal organisation, internal allegiances and a group consciousness. The group remains 'passive until it becomes organised; thereafter its energy potential is transformed from latent and static to active and kinetic.' Group cohesiveness is significantly enhanced by the presence of articulate and charismatic spokespersons, effective leadership and normative bonds, and by the identification of a common opponent, the latter often precipitating co-operation between individual organisations in support of a common cause.

Streeck and Schmitter (1985) concluded that associations based solely on forms of collective influence tend to be small and fragmented. To appeal more widely, Bennett (1997) suggested business associations should concentrate upon the provision of individual, income-generating services that will, in turn, facilitate collective activities intended to exert influence. Bennett's view ran counter to that of Olson (1971), who argued that business associations tend towards sub-optimal provision when collective activities become by-products of service activities.

> **ACCORDING TO COMPETITIVENESS WHITE PAPER**
>
> (HM Government, 1995, p. 52):
>
> *The more effective trade associations and professional bodies become, the more influence they exert on government and the greater the service they will render to their industries.*

Research in the area of business associations, critical of the 'intrinsic functionality of professional groups' (Chua and Poullaos, 1998, p. 156) and sceptical of the relationships between professional associations and government bodies, concentrates on the social processes which enable the establishment of 'professional privilege'. The notion of 'market closure' (Weber, 1968; Parkin, 1979; Murphy, 1988) suggests members of associations seek market dominance through 'monopolising social and economic opportunities and closing off opportunities to outsiders' (Chua and Poullaos, 1998, p. 156). Professional associations are seen not as functional occupational groups but as collectives pursuing 'professionalisation' in order to 'translate one order of scarce resources – specialist knowledge and skills – into another – social and economic rewards' (Larson, 1977, pp. 16). According to Wilmott (1986), the state franchises elements of its power to the professions by providing them with legal monopolies or near monopolies and in return, according to McKinstry (1997, p. 797), 'the professions enforce and reinforce the powers of the state'.

According to Bennett (1997), the major tension for professional associations in Britain arises from their position as voluntary organisations. Voluntary status means business associations in Britain lack any form of legal protection or privileged status, they receive no significant financial support, and there is often no coherent policy among government departments concerning their dealings with such bodies. This makes the role of business associations in the UK quite different from that in France, Germany or Japan where they have a more formalised position.

Successive UK governments have wrestled with the effectiveness of business associations over a considerable period of time, generally tending towards government that does not favour 'a rigid structure of representation ... with the CBI as some kind of national federation heading a series of lesser federations below it' (Heseltine, 1993, p. 9). What governments *have* encouraged is a situation where business associations represent their members more effectively and do more to increase the competitiveness of their industries. Bennett (1997) identified the four key features of government policies toward business associations as follows:

- Preference towards a smaller number of associations or federations representing industry to government, each body being recognised as the lead association for its industry.

- Lead associations improving the performance of business associations primarily through the more efficient use of association resources.
- Lead associations contributing directly to the business practice of their members and satisfying the needs of government in terms of representation and communication.
- Increased competitiveness of industry sectors through association membership.

Against this background the Landscape Institute, founded in 1929 as the Institute of Landscape Architects and a member of the International Federation of Landscape Architects, was granted a Royal Charter in 1997. According to clause 5(1) of its Royal Charter, the objects and purposes of the Landscape Institute are 'to protect, conserve and enhance the natural and built environment for the benefit of the public by promoting the arts and sciences of Landscape Architecture'. Section one of this volume therefore concerns professional judgment ethics and values and, in particular, the standards of conduct and practice imposed upon its members by the Landscape Institute as the professional association for landscape architects in Britain, together with the Landscape Institute's continuing professional development (CPD) requirements and how these impact upon Landscape Institute members in practice.

Although not all aspects of the 6th Edition of the Landscape Institute's Pathway to Chartership Syllabus (July 2013) are included, this volume follows the structure of the syllabus, while taking care to ensure the sequence of chapters remains intuitive to seasoned practitioners, the latter expected to be the main audience for the book. Section two therefore concerns the organisation and management of professional practice, explaining the fundamental principles of legally binding contractual agreements by the use of case histories; professional negligence and misrepresentation whether negligent or otherwise; health and safety requirements and guidelines; business performance development and management, including a comparison of trading formats and a guide to understanding information contained within financial statements; the scope of services and forms of agreement recommended for use when engaging the services of a Chartered Member of the Landscape Institute; the method of calculating hourly fee rates; and the relative merits of different methods of presenting fee bids for professional services to clients.

The chapters concerned with business performance, development and management, which could themselves be stand-alone volumes, are intended to provide the professional practitioner with the essential elements of understanding how businesses function, develop and hopefully succeed within their marketplace. The chapters do not seek to make creative professionals into world-class business leaders, but aim to impart sufficient knowledge to landscape professional practitioners that they might understand and appreciate commercial realities; those of their clients and also those of their own practice, never more so than if the landscape professional practitioner is personally responsible for the administration or management of their particular practice.

Section three of the volume concerns the legislative bases of assessment and analysis, that is to say, the plethora of legislation in relation to development control and environmental management with which the landscape professional practitioner must be familiar. Development control and environmental legislation are very large and complex subjects, aspects of which have been and will continue to be covered in a great many authoritative texts. This book is not intended to provide a practical guide to the details of planning applications, appeals, environmental impact assessments or environmental protection measures. Instead, it provides an overview of the major pieces of legislation upon which development control and environmental management are based. The intention being that the professional practitioner might understand at what point practical interventions are required and ensure they have the necessary expertise at their disposal to comply with the legislative requirements and those of their professional code of conduct.

Section four concerns contract documentation, project implementation, administration and alternative methods for resolving contractual disputes should they arise. From a thorough consideration of contractual relationships and alternative procurement strategies in Chapter 9, this second half of the book focusses upon the 'traditional' form of procurement, by far the most common within the landscape industry, and retains this position throughout the remainder of the book, only briefly touching upon the alternatives by way of explanation.

There is a thorough exposition of what it is the professional practitioner needs to know about the Construction Design and Management Regulations in their most recent iteration, contained within Chapter 10, not least the specific responsibilities placed upon the professional practitioner whether or not the project must be notified to the Health and Safety Executive.

Chapter 11 provides a step-by-step guide to preparing accurate, well-structured and reliable estimates of project budgets; explains why these are essential and how they are to be used; provides useful suggestions as to where the inexperienced practitioner might source the information they will need in order to prepare accurate and reliable estimates of project implementation costs; and introduces industry standard sources the practitioner may find useful.

Introducing the suite of contract documents necessary to obtain competitive quotations from contractors; to administer the resultant contracts; and touching briefly on the digital alternatives provided in the form of Computer Aided Design packages linked to the recent innovation of Building Information Modelling, Chapter 12 explains how project specifications should be structured and presented using the Common Arrangement of Works Sections. The chapter includes very practical advice on the drafting of project specifications and, for the benefit of inexperienced practitioners, from where information essential to the project specification may be obtained along with the use of industry standard sources.

Chapter 13 explains the importance of conditions of contract; the significance of and how the conditions apply to sub-contracts; and advises on the use of standard forms of agreement. The chapter provides a step-by-step guide to setting-up an agreement between client and contractor using the JCLI Landscape Works Contract

2012 and points to sources of alternative forms of contract used throughout the landscape and construction industries.

Formulating a select list of contractors from whom to obtain quotations and the processes of single stage selective tendering are explained in Chapter 14, before Chapter 15 again provides an entirely practical explanation of the use of standard forms, provided by the Landscape Institute to its members, for administering an implementation contract using the JCLI Landscape Works Contract 2012.

Chapter 15 also emphasises the importance of methodical and consistent record keeping to a successful landscape professional practitioner before, finally, Chapter 16 examines the different forms of alternative dispute resolution procedures the professional practitioner might encounter, upon which they may wish to advise their client in the event of a contractual dispute, and how these compare each with the other.

Whether a knowledge of professional ethics, contract administration, business management and law is acquired at university or in the process of professional life, it is accepted that very few books are currently on the market, aimed specifically at the landscape professional practitioner, from which to acquire such knowledge, to ensure the individual practitioner's knowledge base is kept up to date, or to use as an occasional reference point by which to address specific areas of weakness in a particular individual's knowledge of a given area.

Written from the standpoint of an experienced practitioner with a unique skillset within the landscape profession, complex relationships are explained, roles thoroughly explored, and the author's considerable knowledge and experience, gleaned from an entirely practical and applied perspective, made available to students and practitioners alike.

In short, the present volume has been written with the intention that it should offer a genuinely clear, concise, yet comprehensive, professional handbook which the landscape professional, whether student, novice or seasoned practitioner, currently lacks. In essence, a step-by-step guide which the reader may read from end to end or dip into as necessary.

There is no distinction made between sections of the book that may be more relevant to students and those of relevance to seasoned professionals in need of guidance; the information contained herein is considered relevant to all landscape professionals. However, each chapter begins with an overview of its aims and concludes with a summary of key points. This enables readers to determine for themselves what is most relevant and helpful to their particular need, question or problem as it arises and when it arises.

The table of contents is so extensive that, together with copious use of clear and succinct sub-headings to aid accessibility, it functions almost as an index in itself. This makes for convenient and very quick reference to a particular subject or term as the need arises.

Rather than collect all the information pertaining to the legal aspects of landscape professional practice together into what would be one very large and rather intimidating chapter, such legal information is sub-divided into self-contained chapters, making it easier to find what is needed at any given moment, and the sequence of chapters throughout the book replicates that which the professional practitioner is likely to encounter in practice.

It is intended that the contextual advice given around legal or formal requirements will be not only useful to the landscape professional practitioner, but it is written in a friendly and agreeable tone, in the hope that what might otherwise be very daunting subject matter is made a little less intimidating and a little more accessible to the reader.

Recognising there are landscape professional practitioners who, reasonably and legitimately, prefer to focus solely upon the design aspects of the profession and that there are, similarly, professional practitioners majoring on specifying projects, setting up and administering contracts and resolving contractual disputes, throughout the present volume there are suggestions as to those areas in which suitably skilled and qualified professionals might broaden the scope of their practice, if they so desire, and where those with a purely design bent might defer to a fellow professional practising a very different skill set.

SECTION I
Professional Judgment Ethics and Values

1

Professional Association

THE AIMS OF THIS CHAPTER ARE TO:

- Introduce the concept of professional association
- Describe the Landscape Institute's role in promoting the arts and sciences of landscape architecture
- Consider what constitutes professional behaviour and how the ideal of professionalism differs from a purely commercial position by reference to the Landscape Institute's code of conduct
- Describe the Landscape Institute's continuing professional development requirements and how they apply in practice

Professional associations accredit, regulate, educate and impose ethical and moral constraints upon professional practitioners in their particular area of expertise, for example the General Medical Council for medical professionals; the Royal Institute of Building Architects for building professionals; the Royal Institute of Chartered Surveyors for surveying professionals; and the Landscape Institute for landscape professionals.

1.1 THE LANDSCAPE INSTITUTE

Founded in 1929 as the Institute of Landscape Architects, the Landscape Institute is a member of the International Federation of Landscape Architects and aims to regulate the profession in the UK via a code of conduct that members must abide by. Granted a Royal Charter in 1997, the Landscape Institute in 2013 had 6,000 members divided between three divisions: Landscape Design; Landscape Science;

and Landscape Management.[1] Of this number, 3,300 were chartered members. The Landscape Institute publishes the professional journal *Landscape*, formerly known as *Landscape Design*, on a quarterly basis.

> THE OBJECTS AND PURPOSES OF THE LANDSCAPE INSTITUTE
>
> (Clause 5(1) of the Landscape Institute's Royal Charter revised in 2008):
>
> *To protect, conserve and enhance the natural and built environment for the benefit of the public by promoting the arts and sciences of Landscape Architecture.*

The Landscape Institute aims to disseminate knowledge, promote research and advance standards of education, qualification, competence and conduct in the practice of landscape architecture. To gain membership applicants must firstly demonstrate their suitability by successfully completing an accredited university degree course or by satisfying the requirements of the member panel (formerly known as the admissions assessment panel). Having satisfied either one of the foregoing criteria, a 'licentiate' (formerly known as an associate) who wishes to progress to chartered status and become a full member of the Institute must join the 'Pathway to Chartership'.

The Pathway to Chartership focusses on active learning based on a system of continual assessment. With the help of a professionally qualified mentor candidates plan, review and reflect on their learning and receive regular feedback from a Landscape Institute appointed supervisor via the pathway online system. When candidates can demonstrate they have developed sufficient knowledge and understanding to progress, and have met the requirements of the pathway (normally a minimum of two years post qualification experience) they may register for the final stage, the oral examination.

Only after successfully completing the oral examination will an applicant be admitted to the Landscape Institute as a full member, at which point they are permitted to use the protected title 'Chartered Member of the Landscape Institute' or the alternative title 'Chartered Landscape Architect' and the letters designate 'CMLI'. Letters designate of 'MLI' or 'ALI' formerly used may still be seen but are no longer recognised by the Institute.

---

[1] On 25 November 2014 the Landscape Institute's Board of Trustees are to vote upon whether to immediately adopt the 'Elements and Areas of Practice' document, introduced in 2012, thereby removing the three historical divisions of membership, recognising instead that the multi-disciplinary requirements of landscape professional practice encompass landscape design; landscape planning; landscape management; landscape science; and urban design, without any division in the categories of membership.

1.2 STANDARDS OF CONDUCT AND PRACTICE FOR LANDSCAPE PROFESSIONALS

Central to the professional life of a landscape architect, *The Landscape Institute Code of Standards of Conduct and Practice for Landscape Professionals* (The Landscape Institute, May 2012) places considerable emphasis on integrity, competence and professionalism. According to the code of conduct: 'It is only through the maintenance of high standards by individuals that landscape architecture as a whole will be served, the public will be protected and the profession as a whole will thrive.' The code of conduct lays down the standards of professional conduct and practice expected of all Landscape Institute members, as follows:

1.2.1 To preserve the character and quality of the environment

> **STANDARD 1**
>
> The Landscape Institute Code of Standards of Conduct and Practice for Landscape Professionals (May 2012):
>
> *The Landscape Institute expects members who are carrying out professional work to have regard to the interests of those who may be reasonably expected to use or enjoy the products of their work.*

To creative professionals, the requirements of Standard 1 of the Landscape Institute's code of conduct should require little explanation. Landscape Institute members have responsibilities to the character and quality of the environment and should seek to manage change in the landscape for the benefit of this and future generations.

In terms of professional judgment, ethics and values, Standard 1 is perhaps as much about what members of the Landscape Institute are expected *not* to do as it is about the positive interventions they should seek to make. That is to say, the Landscape Institute's code of conduct expects its members not to involve themselves in professional undertakings that are non-sustainable, likely to diminish the diversity of the natural environment or denude the human environment.

As a result, Standard 1 is perhaps not quite as straightforward as it might at first appear. For example, whilst one professional practitioner might consider refusing a commission involved with expansion of the road infrastructure because of its perceived negative impact upon the environment, another practitioner might consider the involvement of a landscape professional essential to ameliorate the environmental impact of a project likely to go ahead in any event.

From the above example it can be seen that professional practice often requires judgments that are very far removed from clear-cut decisions and frequently driven by individual practitioners' ethical and moral views.

1.2.2 To uphold the reputation and dignity of the profession

> **STANDARD 2**
>
> The Landscape Institute Code of Standards of Conduct and Practice for Landscape Professionals (May 2012):
>
> *The Landscape Institute expects members to uphold the reputation and dignity of their profession and their professional organisation.*

Standard 2 of the Landscape Institute's code of conduct is again not quite as straightforward as it might at first appear, since it too requires a degree of professional judgment as to what might be considered 'dignified' where professional practice is concerned. It is, of course, indefensible that any Landscape Institute member should be party to any action likely to bring the profession into disrepute; to any statement contrary to their professional opinion, or which they know to be misleading, unfair to others or otherwise discreditable to the profession; or to any communication likely to be construed as defamatory or discriminatory in any way or contrary to legislation. But since the practice of landscape architecture is based upon 'arts' and 'sciences', should not part of its purpose be to challenge and expand the boundaries of current thinking and received wisdom?

Might it be that a Landscape Institute member, with what to some might be an outlandish opinion of what ought to be acceptable in a managed landscape, could be considered to be bringing the profession into disrepute by promoting those ideas? For example, would it be discreditable to the profession if a member of the Landscape Institute promoted the idea of siting landfill and waste management facilities within the boundaries of national parks and forests where they would be well away from population centres and their impact upon the natural environment could be readily mitigated and managed? Although many might disagree with such an idea, would it discredit the profession for an individual member or members to hold and champion such an idea? Is it a pre-requisite of professional association that all must hold the same opinion?

1.2.3 To actively promote the code of conduct

> **STANDARD 3**
>
> The Landscape Institute Code of Standards of Conduct and Practice for Landscape Professionals (May 2012):
>
> *The Landscape Institute expects members to actively and positively promote the standards set out in this code of conduct.*

Standard 3 of the Landscape Institute's code of conduct expects members to order their professional lives in accordance with the code of conduct if they wish to remain members. As seen from the above consideration of Standard 1 and Standard 2, there is room for debate as to when a professional practitioner may or may not be observing the code of conduct. This debate is heightened when Landscape Institute members are expected (by Standard 3) to do whatever they reasonably can to ensure observance of the code of conduct by other members.

Standard 3 requires Landscape Institute members not take as business partners or co-directors any unsuitable person, such as a person who has been expelled from membership of the Landscape Institute (or any other recognised professional organisation) for disciplinary reasons and to report without delay if they are themselves convicted of an indictable offence, imprisoned in respect of any offence or disqualified from acting as a company director by any court. Such legal matters are, of course, generally quite easily defined and therefore unimpeachable.

However, Standard 3 of the Landscape Institute's code of conduct also requires members to report to the Chief Executive Officer any serious failing on the part of any other member of which they are aware. This begs the question, what does or does not constitute a 'serious failing on the part of any other member' and at what point it may be necessary to report the activities of other members? Something that clearly calls for careful and reasoned professional judgment.

1.2.4 To actively promote and further the Landscape Institute objectives

> **STANDARD 4**
>
> The Landscape Institute Code of Standards of Conduct and Practice for Landscape Professionals (May 2012):
>
> *The Landscape Institute also expects members to actively and positively promote and further the aims and objectives of The Landscape Institute, as set down in its Charter, and to contribute to the work and activities of the Institute.*

Standard 4 of the Landscape Institute's code of conduct requires members to conduct themselves in an appropriate professional manner with all persons they come into contact with; to accurately represent their professional status and qualifications and that of anyone who works for them; and to conduct their professional affairs in accordance with the law.

1.2.5 To act with integrity consistent with professional obligations

> **STANDARD 5**
>
> The Landscape Institute Code of Standards of Conduct and Practice for Landscape Professionals (May 2012):
>
> *The Landscape Institute expects members to act at all times with integrity and avoid any action or situations which are inconsistent with their professional obligations.*

Standard 5 of the Landscape Institute's code of conduct is arguably one of the most important, since it requires Landscape Institute members' professional obligations to take precedence over their personal interests. This is particularly important with respect to members' financial affairs. For example, Landscape Institute members are generally discouraged from having a controlling or financial interest in a contracting organisation. That would potentially be a source of conflict between the financial interests of the contracting organisation and those of the client.

When finding personal or professional interests in conflict with those of the client or of other relevant parties, Landscape Institute members should inform all parties and either withdraw from the situation, remove the source of conflict or obtain the agreement of the parties concerned to the continuance of the engagement. In the example quoted above, the Landscape Institute member would therefore be required to inform the client and other relevant parties of their interest in the contracting organisation; to ensure the contracting organisation was not employed on a project on which the Landscape Institute member has been engaged to provide professional services; or must leave it to the client and other relevant parties to decide what is appropriate. Most commonly it is preferable for the professional practitioner to keep potentially conflicted interests completely separate and to ensure such interests are declared from the outset.

When two or more clients whose interests may be in conflict both require services, Landscape Institute members must ensure the interests of one client do not adversely affect the other. For example, it would not normally be appropriate for a Landscape Institute member to be engaged on the submission of a planning application and also be engaged by those in opposition to the application. That said, when acting as an expert witness it is frequently the case that Landscape Institute members are instructed as single joint experts in order to reduce costs. When acting between parties, or giving advice in this way, Landscape Institute members must exercise impartial and independent professional judgment to the best of their ability and, when doing so in connection with court or tribunal proceedings, must remember that their first and overriding duty is to the court or tribunal, irrespective of who is paying their fees.

It should go without saying that Landscape Institute members must not offer or accept bribes, that is to say financial inducements, and should maintain a record of any hospitality provided or received. If any introductory or referral fees are to change hands these should be disclosed to any prospective client. For example, a Landscape Institute member may sometimes be paid a commission by the suppliers of nursery stock for recommending the use of their stock on a project as opposed to that of their competitors. As long as the Landscape Institute member has ensured the stock to be provided is at least as good, if not better, than that of the competitors the payment of a commission is not contrary to the code of conduct, but the Landscape Institute member must make clear to the client that such a commission is being charged or paid.

It should equally go without saying that Landscape Institute members must respect the beliefs and opinions of other people, recognise social diversity and treat everyone fairly, taking care not to discriminate because of disability, age, gender, sexual orientation, ethnicity or any other inappropriate consideration.

Landscape Institute members must also observe the confidentiality of clients' affairs and the privacy of others (except where there is conflict with the Landscape Institute member's professional or legal obligations) and only disclose confidential information with prior consent or other lawful authority.

1.2.6 To only undertake professional work for which competent

> **STANDARD 6**
>
> The Landscape Institute Code of Standards of Conduct and Practice for Landscape Professionals (May 2012):
>
> *Landscape Professionals should only undertake professional work for which they are able to provide proper professional and technical competence, and resources.*

Standard 6 of the Landscape Institute's code of conduct requires Landscape Institute members to be competent to carry out work for which they have been engaged. Since Landscape Institute members are allocated to one or more divisions of membership according to their particular expertise – that is to say Landscape Design, Landscape Science or Landscape Management – they should only undertake work in the division or divisions of membership in which their skills have been recognised and accredited by the Landscape Institute.

As is frequently the case in larger practices where Landscape Institute members may engage others to provide services they are not themselves qualified to provide (for example, a Landscape Manager may employ a Landscape Designer for the drafting of design proposals and contract drawings), employer members will be responsible for ensuring those employed are competent to perform the task they have been allotted and that the employee is adequately supervised in their efforts.

1.2.7 To maintain and promote professional competence

> **STANDARD 7**
>
> The Landscape Institute Code of Standards of Conduct and Practice for Landscape Professionals (May 2012):
>
> *The Landscape Institute expects members to maintain their professional competence in areas relevant to their professional work and to provide educational and training support to less experienced members or students of the profession over whom they have a professional or employment responsibility.*

Because competence is at the heart of professional life, Standard 7 of the Landscape Institute's code of conduct requires Landscape Institute members to keep themselves informed of changes affecting the profession and broader developments relevant to their work; to ensure their practice, knowledge, skills and techniques are up to date; and to maintain, record and provide evidence of continuing professional development in compliance with the Landscape Institute's continuing professional development requirements (discussed later in this chapter).

Landscape Institute members are also expected to actively promote continuing professional development for any staff they employ and to ensure an appropriate amount of time is devoted to such activities. Because the Landscape Institute places such emphasis on professional training and development, Landscape Institute members are expected to mentor junior staff employed, or ensure others are available to do so, and more experienced Landscape Institute members are encouraged to become formal mentors within the Pathway to Chartership, assisting licentiates outside their place of work who may not be employed by a fully chartered member.

1.2.8 To organise professional work responsibly with regard to clients

> **STANDARD 8**
>
> The Landscape Institute Code of Standards of Conduct and Practice for Landscape Professionals (May 2012):
>
> *The Landscape Institute expects members to organise and manage their professional work responsibly and with integrity and with regard to the interests of their clients.*

Landscape Institute members should not undertake professional work unless the terms of their engagement have been agreed in writing (as discussed in Chapter 7). Once an agreement is in place, the Landscape Institute member must ensure changes to the fee arrangements are similarly agreed in writing; that appropriate and effective procedures are in place for monitoring and control of the undertaking; and sufficient suitably qualified and supervised staff are available.

Standard 8 of the Landscape Institute's code of conduct also expects that papers, plans or other property to which the client is legally entitled will be returned if the Landscape Institute member is reasonably requested to do so and that, in the unfortunate circumstances of the Landscape Institute member's death, incapacity or absence from work, arrangements are in place to ensure any remaining work is completed to the client's satisfaction.

1.2.9 To carry out professional work with care and to relevant standards

> **STANDARD 9**
>
> The Landscape Institute Code of Standards of Conduct and Practice for Landscape Professionals (May 2012):
>
> *The Landscape Institute expects members to carry out their professional work with care, conscientiously and with proper regard to relevant technical and professional standards.*

Standard 9 of the Landscape Institute's code of conduct requires that Landscape Institute members perform their work with due skill, care, diligence and as might reasonably be expected by relevant technical and professional standards. There could rarely be a clearer expectation from any code of professional conduct. To ensure this requirement is achieved, Standard 9 of the code of conduct expects Landscape Institute members to keep their clients informed of progress; of any key decisions made; of any issue which may affect the quality of the work or its cost; and have effective systems in place for regular monitoring and review to ensure projects are completed within the timescales and cost limits agreed with the client. Landscape Institute members are also expected to ensure they have security for electronic and paper-based records and that all data protection legislation is complied with.

1.2.10 To promote professional services in a truthful and responsible manner

> **STANDARD 10**
>
> The Landscape Institute Code of Standards of Conduct and Practice for Landscape Professionals (May 2012):
>
> *Members of the Landscape Institute should only promote their professional services in a truthful and responsible manner and such promotion shall not be an attempt to subvert professional work from another member.*

Standard 10 of the Landscape Institute's code of conduct is perhaps that which is the least straightforward of all, as it requires that Landscape Institute members must not make untruthful or misleading statements in the promotion of their services. Whilst advertisements must be in accordance with requirements of the Advertising Standards Authority or any other body having oversight of advertising standards, anyone with any knowledge of commercial marketing and promotion will know that a competitive market for professional services demands that the most positive 'spin' must be put upon a practitioner's skills and experience. For example, at what point might legitimately and properly referring to specialist expertise and experience cross over into claiming to be better than other professional members, which Landscape Institute members are not permitted to do? It would surely be remiss of any commercial undertaking not to seek to differentiate itself from its competitors?

What is clear is that Standard 10 of the Landscape Institute's code of conduct requires that the business style of a practice should not be misleading; should not be capable of being confused with another practice or service; and that Landscape Institute members should not attempt to subvert business from another practitioner, that is to say they must not attempt to gain work for which they are aware a client already has a contract with another Landscape Institute member.

1.2.11 To ensure personal and professional finances are managed prudently

> **STANDARD 11**
>
> The Landscape Institute Code of Standards of Conduct and Practice for Landscape Professionals (May 2012):
>
> *The Landscape Institute requires members to ensure that their personal and professional finances are managed prudently and to preserve the security of monies entrusted to their care in the course of practice or business.*

Standard 11 of the Landscape Institute's code of conduct requires Landscape Institute members to deal with creditors and debtors in accordance with best practice and to maintain adequate business records of all costs and expenses in accordance with legal requirements. Should the business finances of a Landscape Institute member fail, this may bring the individual member or the profession into disrepute. Members should therefore inform the Landscape Institute's Chief Executive Officer within 28 days of being made the subject of a bankruptcy order; if they are the director of a company that has been wound up (other than for amalgamation or reconstruction purposes); if they make an accommodation with creditors (including a voluntary arrangement); or in the event they fail to pay a judgment debt. These are clear-cut and immutable requirements with which Landscape Institute members must comply.

In addition, when Landscape Institute members hold monies belonging to a client or third party, Standard 11 of the Landscape Institute's code of conduct requires that they must arrange for its receipt to be recorded and for the money to be kept (where possible) in an interest-bearing client account, with a bank or similar institution, separate from any personal or business account belonging to the Landscape Institute member or their practice. The deposit taker is to be given written instructions that all money held in the client account is held to the client's order; that the money held must not be combined with any other account; nor used as counterclaim or set-off against any other debt, for example if the Landscape Institute member's own account should become overdrawn beyond its agreed limit. A Landscape Institute member may only withdraw money from a client account to make a payment to or on behalf of a client, or on the client's written instructions. Unless otherwise agreed by the client, any interest (or other benefit) accruing to a client account must be paid to the client.

1.2.12 To maintain adequate and appropriate professional indemnity insurance

> **STANDARD 12**
>
> The Landscape Institute Code of Standards of Conduct and Practice for Landscape Professionals (May 2012):
>
> *The Landscape Institute expects members to have adequate and appropriate Professional Indemnity Insurance.*

In accordance with Standard 12 of the Landscape Institute's code of conduct, members are expected to maintain adequate and appropriate Professional Indemnity Insurance (discussed in Chapter 3) which must extend cover beyond the professional work undertaken by an individual Landscape Institute member to work undertaken by the member's employees, sub-contractors or consultants. Standard 12 of the Landscape Institute's code of conduct requires that members and third parties have a level of Professional Indemnity Insurance cover commensurate with the level of risk inherent in the work undertaken. The Landscape Institute does not prescribe what amount this should be but leaves the decision to the professional judgment of individual members and their advisers. Where Landscape Institute members are employees it is their duty to ensure, as far as they are able, that Professional Indemnity Insurance cover is provided by their employer for the work they undertake.

1.2.13 To deal with professional complaints promptly and appropriately

> **STANDARD 13**
>
> The Landscape Institute Code of Standards of Conduct and Practice for Landscape Professionals (May 2012):
>
> *The Landscape Institute expects that any complaints concerning the professional work of individual members or their practice should be dealt with promptly and appropriately.*

Standard 13 of the Landscape Institute's code of conduct expects members to adhere to written procedures for the prompt and courteous handling of complaints including the requirement that a named individual should respond to such complaints. In the case of a firm or company, the named individual should be a director or partner in the firm. If the named person is unable to resolve a complaint to the satisfaction of the complainant, the expectation of Standard 13 of the Landscape Institute's code of conduct is the complaint will promptly be referred to the senior partner or managing director of the practice. If, after reviewing the complaint, the senior partner or managing director of the practice is unable to resolve the complaint the complainant must be informed, if they can demonstrate a Landscape Institute member has been guilty of unacceptable professional conduct or serious professional incompetence, they may take their complaint to the Landscape Institute and the individual member may be subject to disciplinary proceedings.

The Landscape Institute expects its members to be guided as much by the spirit of its code of conduct as by the express terms therein. In addition to the requirements of the code of conduct, the Landscape Institute has a formal procedure for making complaints and a formal disciplinary procedure as mentioned above.

1.3 CONTINUING PROFESSIONAL DEVELOPMENT

The Landscape Institute's Royal Charter requires that it 'establish, uphold and advance the standards of education, qualification, competence and conduct of the profession'. The strength and reputation of the landscape profession is dependent upon the competence of its members whose knowledge, skills and expertise are their key assets and must be actively developed.

> CONTINUING PROFESSIONAL DEVELOPMENT (CPD)
>
> The Landscape Institute (June 2012):
>
> *The systematic maintenance, improvement and broadening of knowledge and skill, and the development of personal qualities necessary for the execution of professional and technical duties throughout working life.*

Standard 7 of the Landscape Institute's code of conduct requires members to maintain their professional competence in areas relevant to their professional work, as well as supporting the development of other less experienced members. All chartered members of the Landscape Institute are required to undertake a minimum of 25 hours continuing professional development each year. There is no set syllabus; members being required to take responsibility for identifying their own development needs and planning their learning to ensure their knowledge and skills are kept up to date.

Continuing professional development can include formal activities, for example seminars and courses, but may also include study, education, research, practical training, experience, and the mentoring of others, as may be appropriate or desirable to maintain and enhance individual members' professional knowledge, competence and understanding.

The Landscape Institute periodically selects a random sample of chartered members to monitor in respect of continuing professional development. The members selected will be required to submit records of activities undertaken in at least 12 of the last 18 months. Records submitted by members will be reviewed by a panel appointed by the education and membership committee.

> REQUIREMENTS OF THE EDUCATION AND MEMBERSHIP COMMITTEE
>
> The Landscape Institute (June 2012):
>
> *Members must have submitted comprehensive and relevant and legible records covering the stipulated period ... engaged in a range of continuing professional development activities, and a balance of continuing professional development topics; actively engaged in the continuing professional development process in accordance with the spirit and requirements of the Landscape Institute's continuing professional development policy.*

A reviewing panel appointed by the education and membership committee of the Landscape Institute will provide feedback to members included in the monitoring exercise. The panel will indicate whether records are satisfactory, offer more detailed feedback or recommendations, and in some cases may require a member to make a further submission of their records as part of a future period of monitoring.

In exceptional circumstances, Landscape Institute members may ask the reviewing panel to defer the monitoring exercise. Members may only defer on one occasion. Members failing to provide records of their continuing professional development within a reasonable time period may be considered in breach of the Landscape Institute's code of conduct and be subject to further investigation under the Institute's disciplinary procedures.

The Landscape Institute may include in its monitoring of continuing professional development members who have re-joined the Institute after a gap of more than 12 months. In this case the reviewing panel appointed by the education and membership committee will be looking for evidence that individuals have maintained their competence and have continued to actively engage in continuing professional development since re-joining the Landscape Institute.

The Landscape Institute encourages members to maintain records of continuing professional development using the forms it provides. Alternative formats, for example those used by individual employers, will normally be acceptable as long as they provide adequate evidence of continuing professional development as described above.

CHAPTER SUMMARY

- Professional associations regulate, educate and impose ethical and moral constraints on professional practitioners in their particular area of expertise
- A professional has generally completed university level education; some form of mentored training; has passed a professional examination; and has been accredited by a professional association
- The Landscape Institute requires its members to conduct their professional and business lives in accordance with its code of conduct
- If a member of the public or another profession, or another member of the Landscape Institute, is dissatisfied with the conduct of a Landscape Institute member they may consider making a formal complaint
- Landscape Institute members are required to regularly update their education in order to maintain their professional standing and to continue providing professional services to the public

SECTION II
Organisation and Management

2

The Law of Contract

> THE AIMS OF THIS CHAPTER ARE TO:
>
> - Explain the fundamental principles of legally binding contractual agreements by reference to case law
> - Explain the doctrine of 'privity of contract' and its implications for professional practitioners working as 'agents' for clients
> - Explain how and when a contract may be 'discharged' at what point either party may be in 'breach' of contract and the implications of such breach
> - Consider the significance of 'statements', 'terms' and 'representations'
> - Explain the importance of misrepresentation in relationships of utmost good faith such as those for the provision of professional services

Common to all legally binding agreements is that an 'offer' made by one party must be on specified terms, for example a contractor might offer to carry out a defined parcel of work by the submission of a quotation or tender (discussed in Chapter 14) and the offer must be met by an 'acceptance' from the other party, communicated in the form of a final and unconditional consent on exactly the same terms as those made in the original offer.

For an agreement to be given legal validity there must also be a 'consideration' or exchange. Most frequently a consideration takes the form of an agreement to pay a specified sum of money, but a consideration may also take the form of a benefit in kind, for example an exchange of goods or services, or the payment of just a nominal sum.

Whatever form the consideration takes, a legally binding contract comes into being when an agreement is reached, that is to say, when the parties indicate an intention to be legally bound; the actual exchange of goods or services, or the payment of an agreed sum, constituting performance of the contract within a (normally) specified timescale after the agreement has been reached.

2.1 INVITATION TO TREAT

An 'invitation to treat' is a preliminary statement in contractual negotiations merely intended to supply information and therefore not capable of acceptance. For example, the leading case of *Fisher v Bell* [1961] held that a shop window display, though indicating a specific price, was merely an invitation to treat because the retailer could refuse to sell the goods displayed or may not even have the goods to sell.

The general rule is that display or advertisement is merely an invitation to treat unless it makes a specific offer capable of acceptance. For example, in the leading case of *Partridge v Crittenden* [1968] an advertisement was held to be an invitation to treat because, although the advertisement specified the goods on offer and the price, it gave no indication of how many items there were to sell and was therefore not sufficiently specific to be an offer.

For further reading on invitations to treat see Stone (2003) para. 2.6.4.

2.2 OFFER

An offer is a statement made by one party with the intention it shall become binding when the offer is accepted by the party to whom it is addressed. The submission of a quotation or tender (discussed in Chapter 14) by a contractor would most commonly be regarded as an offer.

The proposition made in the offer must be sufficiently specific and comprehensive to be capable of immediate acceptance. For example, in the leading case of *Scammell v Ouston* [1941] the House of Lords held a hire purchase agreement that failed to state the value of the goods or the terms of the agreement was not enforceable; that there is no such thing as standard hire purchase terms; that the meaning has to be determinable with a reasonable degree of certainty. A quotation or tender by a contractor therefore has to be for a clearly defined piece of work at a specified price.

An offer may be made orally, in writing or by conduct. The offer can be made to an individual, a group or to 'the world at large' as in the leading case of *Carlill v Carbolic Smoke Ball Co.* [1893] in which the offer of '£100 to anyone who caught flu after using the smoke ball correctly' was held by the court to be capable of acceptance by anyone who came forward.

An offer may be revoked at any time before it is accepted. In the leading case of *Routledge v Grant* [1828] the court held that a promise to keep an offer open for acceptance for a defined period of time constitutes a separate offer, acceptance of which must itself be supported by a consideration even if the amount is only a nominal £1. This is termed an 'option' to purchase and can only become legally binding on acceptance and an agreement to pay the specified amount.

Revocation of an offer is only effective when notification is received, that is to say if acceptance of the offer is communicated before revocation is received, then the agreement must be honoured, as in the leading case of *Byrne v Van Tienhoven*

[1880]. However, revocation of an offer does not need to be communicated if the other party reasonably knows the offer has been revoked. For example, in the case of *Dickinson v Dodds* [1876] an offer was held to have been revoked when a potential buyer was informed by a third party that the seller had agreed to sell to someone else.

2.3 ACCEPTANCE

Acceptance of an offer can only be made by a final and unconditional expression of consent on exactly the same terms as those offered. Attempts to introduce different terms are counter offers that cause the original offer to lapse. For example, the leading case of *Hyde v Wrench* [1840] held that an offer to buy at a lower price varied the terms, making the original offer to sell at a specified price incapable of acceptance, such that a subsequent offer, even though at the original asking price, constituted a new offer which the seller was not bound to accept.

A counter offer must be distinguished from a request for information. For example, in the leading case of *Stevenson v McLean* [1880] the buyer was prepared to pay the full asking price for the goods and only wished to know over what period of time the goods could be delivered. The offer was still capable of acceptance because the communication was a request for information – for clarity of terms – and not a counter offer.

Acceptance may be oral, in writing or by conduct. For example, picking up goods in a shop and taking them to the checkout would be considered acceptance by conduct and similarly so in the case of *Carlill v Carbolic Smoke Ball Co* [1893], where acceptance was held to be by use of the smoke ball.

A form of acceptance specified in the offer will only be binding if the requirements are clear and unequivocal. For example, in the leading case of *Yates v Pulleyn* [1975] the court held the defendant was simply trying to find an excuse not to fulfil the contract when it argued the claimant's acceptance of its offer by ordinary post, within the specified time scale, was not binding because the terms of the offer required acceptance to be communicated by registered post or recorded delivery.

A party purporting to accept an offer must know of the offer at the time of acceptance. For example, in the Australian case of *R v Clarke* [1927] the court held that an accomplice to murder who gave information leading to conviction of the murderer was not entitled to the reward offered because he admitted that, at the time he gave the information, he had forgotten about the reward and was intent only on avoiding being prosecuted himself.

Contrast *R v Clarke* (above) with the case of *Williams v Cowardine* [1833] where the claimant, in similar circumstances, knew of the reward, was dying and gave information to ease her conscience. On the particular facts of the case the court held there was an enforceable contract because the claimant *was* aware of the reward when she gave the information; that her motive for giving the information was irrelevant.

The general rule from the leading case of *Entores v Miles Far East Corporation* [1955] is that acceptance must be communicated and is only effective when communication of acceptance is received. Exceptions to the rule in *Entores v Miles Far East Corporation* are:

1. Where an offer is accepted by conduct, for example in the case of *Carlill v Carbolic Smoke Ball Co* [1893]. However, acceptance by conduct must be distinguished from consent by silence. For example, in the leading case of *Felthouse v Bindley* [1862] the court held there was no contract where the party purporting to accept the offer stated he would consider the goods to be his if he heard no more from the seller. Had the seller indicated he intended to be bound by his silence the court may have taken a different view.

2. If the postal rule applies, acceptance takes effect as soon as the letter is posted. In the leading case of Adams v Lindsell [1818] the defendant posted an offer to sell in which he requested an answer 'in the course of the post'. The claimant received the offer and posted a letter of acceptance. The defendant sold the goods to someone else before receiving the claimant's letter of acceptance. The court held that, because a postal response was specifically requested, the offer was deemed to have been accepted by the claimant at the time of posting.

   The postal rule will not apply if it is clearly absurd. For example, in the leading case of *Holwell Securities v Hughes* [1974] the defendant made an offer and stated acceptance was to be 'by notice in writing at any time within six months'; acceptance was posted within six months but did not arrive. The court held that the offer had excluded the postal rule by implication because it stated acceptance was to be 'by notice in writing' and thereby implied written notice had to be actually received.

> FOR THE POSTAL RULE TO APPLY:
>
> - Post must be a reasonable method of communication
> - Acceptance must have been properly posted to the correct address
> - It must not have been excluded expressly or by implication in the offer

Acceptance can only be communicated by the party accepting or their duly authorised agent. For example, in the leading case of *Powell v Lee* [1908] the court held there was no enforceable contract when acceptance of a candidate, following interview, was communicated by a secretary who the court determined did not have authority to communicate the acceptance.

For further reading on acceptance see Stone (2003) para. 2.11.12

2.4 CONSIDERATION

A consideration must generally be 'sufficient' but it need not be 'adequate'. It is immaterial whether the value of that on offer exceeds the price asked for it.

> ACCORDING TO LORD JUSTICE SOMERVELL
>
> (*Chappell & Co. v Nestle Co. Ltd.* [1960]):
>
> *A contracting party can stipulate what consideration he chooses. A peppercorn does not cease to be good consideration if it is established that the promisee does not like pepper and will throw away the corn.*

A consideration has only to be something of value in the eyes of the law in exchange for the other's promise. It may be some detriment to one party or some benefit to the other.

A past consideration is not a lawful consideration. In the leading case of *Roscorla v Thomas* [1842] the court held no consideration had been given for an assurance as to the condition of the goods, made after the goods had been bought, because the consideration was for the purchase of the goods. As no consideration had been given for the *subsequent* assurance as to the condition of the goods the seller was not bound by the assurance made.

If something extra is given this *will* be sufficient consideration. For example, in the leading case of *Glasbrook Bros. v Glamorgan County Council* [1925] the court held the police had provided extra cover during a miners' strike at the request of the mine owners. Although it was argued the police were under a duty to maintain public order, the promise to pay was supported by a consideration on the part of the police in providing the extra cover and the mine owners were therefore bound to pay as they had promised to do.

Where there are existing contractual duties owed, the basic rule is that performance of, or a promise to perform, an existing duty is *not* generally sufficient consideration. In the leading case of *Stilk v Myrick* [1809] the court determined that sailors, offered a bonus to sail a ship after two crew members deserted, were not entitled to the bonus offered because they did no more than their existing duty and gave no consideration for the promise of a bonus.

Contrast the case of *Stilk v Myrick* [1809] (above) with that of *Hartley v Ponsonby* [1857] in which 17 members of a 36-member crew abandoned ship, making further progress hazardous as only five able seamen remained. On the facts of the case, the court held the desertions made the voyage much more hazardous; the remaining sailors were promising to do something more than they were originally contracted to do; and the promise to pay the bonus *was* legally enforceable because the remaining sailors had provided consideration over and above their contractual duties.

The general rule that if something extra is given or promised this will be sufficient consideration remained until 1990 and the leading case of *Williams v Roffey Bros & Nicholls (Contractors) Ltd* [1990]. Roffey Bros were contracted to build a block of flats within a specified period of time and were subject to a large penalty clause if they failed to do so. Roffey Bros subcontracted the carpentry to Williams and specified the date by which the work should be finished. Partway through the carpentry contract Williams got in financial difficulty. Roffey Bros were afraid the carpentry would not be finished on time; that they in turn would be unable to complete the block of flats; they knew they would be subject to the large penalty clause in these circumstances; and voluntarily offered to pay Williams an extra amount per flat as each flat was completed.

Under the general rule in *Stilk v Myrick* [1809] (above) Williams would not be entitled to the bonus because he was doing nothing more than he had originally contracted to do. Finding in favour of Williams, the Court of Appeal refined the rule in *Stilk v Myrick* [1809] stating that, by avoiding the large penalty clause, Roffey Bros derived benefit that amounted to a consideration sufficient to make the offer of the bonus legally enforceable; a judgment regarded as a narrow interpretation of the general rule of *Stilk v Myrick* [1809], driven by the specific circumstances of the substantial penalty clause, and little followed by courts thereafter.

In relation to the settling of undisputed contractual debts, *Pinnel's Case* [1602] established the general rule that payment of, or a promise to pay, a smaller amount than that agreed to be owed, is *not* sufficient consideration for a promise by a creditor to release the debtor from the balance of the debt. Although on the particular facts of *Pinnel's Case* [1602] the court found there *was* sufficient consideration (because a lesser amount had been paid at the creditors request before the debt was due), generally speaking, in circumstances where the debtor pays or offers to pay a smaller amount the creditor will still be able to sue for the balance of the debt.

In circumstances where partial payment of a debt is made by a third party and accepted by the creditor 'in full settlement', the creditor can no longer sue for the balance of the debt. Similarly, if creditor(s) accept a 'composition' agreement, that is an agreement whereby a debtor pays only a proportion of every pound owed, for example in a bankruptcy situation, acceptance of such an arrangement is legally binding on the creditor.

In situations where a contractual debt is disputed, then any promise to settle is binding – the promise to pay being consideration for the creditor agreeing not to sue for the claim either in relation to quantum or liability.

2.5   CONTRACT TERMS

The terms of a contract may be specifically expressed by the parties to a contract, whether orally or in writing, for example what is to be done; within what time limits; and for how much. Terms may also be 'implied' into a contract by custom or trade usage. For example, a 'baker's dozen' always means 13. Terms can only be so implied if they are consistent with the express terms of the contract, that is to say express terms will always prevail if they contradict custom.

Terms may also be implied into a contract by a previous course of dealings between the parties. For example, where a public house buys regularly from a brewery there is no need to expressly repeat the terms on each occasion.

Courts may imply terms into a contract in order to reflect the presumed common intention of the parties but will only imply that which is reasonably necessary to make the contract work.

> ACCORDING TO LORD JUSTICE MACKINNON
>
> (*Shirlaw v Southern Foundries* [1939]):
>
> Prima facie *that which in any contract is left to be implied and need not be expressed is something so obvious it goes without saying. Thus, if, while the parties were making their bargain an officious bystander were to suggest some express provision for it in their agreement, they should testily suppress him with a comment "Oh, of course".*

Courts may imply terms into a contract because of the nature or type of the contract or on public policy grounds. For example, in employment contracts it is implied the employee will exercise reasonable care and skill and the employer will provide a reasonably safe place in which to work.

Terms may also be implied into a contract by parliamentary statute, such as section 13 of the Sale of Goods Act 1979, which implies that goods sold will correspond with the description given to them where that description is a substantial part of their identity. For example, it would be implied that a bottle of Coke contains Coke and not Pepsi.

2.6 PRIVITY OF CONTRACT

The doctrine of privity means that a contract cannot confer rights or impose obligations on any person other than a party to the contract. It is an extremely important concept in 'traditional' contractual relationships (discussed in Chapter 9) where the professional practitioner acts only as the client's agent (discussed below) in the setting-up and administration of contracts for the implementation of project proposals.

There is an exception to the doctrine of privity provided by Section 1 of the Contracts (Right of Third Parties) Act 1999. This allows a third party to enforce, that is to say, to benefit from a contract term if the contract expressly provides that s/he may do so or clearly purports to do so. In either case the third party must be identified by name; as a member of a class of persons; or answering to a particular description of such persons, for example 'the client's authorised agent'.

A third party cannot, in any eventuality, be burdened by a contract to which s/he is not a party. The professional practitioner in a 'traditional' procurement strategy therefore cannot be sued for any failure by a contractor to fulfil the terms of an agreement between a contractor and the client.

2.7   AGENCY

Provided s/he is an authorised agent of the client, the professional practitioner is permitted to create a contract between the client and a contractor. All rights and obligations under the contract bind the client and the contractor, each of whom may sue the other and be sued. The agent stands outside the contractual relationship unless joined as a third party (as discussed above).

To act as the client's agent the professional practitioner must be expressly authorised to do so under the terms of their own agreement with the client (discussed in Chapter 7). Alternatively, the agent may have apparent authority to act on the client's behalf where there is an express or implied representation by the client as to the powers of the agent; the contractor relies upon the client's representation; and the contractor alters its position, that is to say the contractor acts in reliance upon the client's representation. In such circumstances the contractor's remedies remain against the client, although the client may in turn have cause to sue the agent.

According to the doctrine of the undisclosed principal, if the agent does not tell the contractor s/he was acting as such then the contract is taken to be between the contractor and the agent, as opposed to between the contractor and the client. It is therefore vital the professional practitioner makes clear that s/he is working as the client's agent only.

If the professional practitioner tells the contractor s/he is authorised to act on the client's behalf and is not, the client cannot sue the contractor or be sued by them. The contractor may sue the agent for deceit or breach of implied warranty, in giving the false impression of having authority, but the agent still cannot be sued on the contract itself.

2.8   DISCHARGE OF CONTRACTS

A contract may be discharged, that is to say terminated or brought to an end, by performance; breach; agreement; or by frustration. It should most commonly be the case that both parties will fully perform their respective obligations and the contract is discharged by performance.

The basic rule is that performance of contractual obligations must be precise and exact. If one party has to perform their obligations first and does not carry out those obligations precisely they are in 'breach' of the contract and the other party may refuse to perform their obligations. For example, if the contractor fails to perform, the client might refuse to pay.

The breach may be 'repudiatory', that is to say, a significant failure to fulfil a condition of the contract, for example an implied term of exercising reasonable skill and care. In this case the other party has the choice of whether to treat itself as discharged from the performance of their future obligations (such as to pay) and to claim damages or to continue with the contract in addition to claiming damages.

There may also be a 'non-repudiatory' breach of contract, that is to say a minor breach with the contract being otherwise substantially performed. In this case the other party may only seek damages for loss and cannot treat itself as discharged from the contract.

In either case and provided they have a choice, if the aggrieved party freely accepts only partial performance of a contract, the party who has partially performed is entitled to claim a reasonable sum for that part of the contract correctly undertaken. This is known as a *quantum meruit*.

It is sometimes the case that, after a contract has been formed, the parties reach an 'agreement' to vary or discharge the contract. In order for such an agreement to be legally binding it must itself consist of an offer, an acceptance, an intention to be bound and a consideration of some form. If performance of the contract has already begun and given what has been said above about partial payment of a debt, very careful consideration must be given to what might constitute sufficient consideration for the other party's agreement not to sue for any amounts owed.

The doctrine of 'frustration' recognises that events occurring subsequent to the contract coming into effect and not the fault of either party can have a significant impact on the parties' abilities to perform their contractual obligations. In such circumstances the parties may be wholly or partially relieved from further obligations. Unlike discharge by breach, no damages are recoverable by either party and the contract simply comes to an end.

For further reading on the doctrine of frustration see Stone (2003) Chapter 17.

2.9   REMEDIES FOR BREACH OF CONTRACT

The claimant must show that s/he has suffered loss or damage as a result of the defendant's breach of contract and that the loss or damage is not too remote a consequence. That is to say the loss or damage must have been a foreseeable outcome of the breach.

The object of remedies in contract law is to put the aggrieved party in the position it would have been in had the contract been properly performed. That is to say to compensate for the loss to the claimant as opposed to punishing the defendant.

Loss may include loss of profit as well as damage to goods or property and physical injury. If goods are defective, the *prima facie* rule is that damages are the difference between the value of the actual goods and what the value of the goods would have been had they not been defective.

With contracts for services the *prima facie* rule is that damages are the cost of putting the works right. However, the leading case of *Ruxley Electronics & Construction Ltd v Forsyth* [1996] introduced a third possibility, that being loss of amenity value.

In the particular circumstances of *Ruxley Electronics & Construction Ltd v Forsyth* [1996] the House of Lords determined the value of a swimming pool, incorrectly constructed to six feet deep, was no less than the value of a pool constructed to the specified depth of seven feet six inches. Because the extra depth could not be added without completely reconstructing the pool, their Lordships held that the cost of putting right the failure to construct the swimming pool to the specified depth was disproportionate to the benefit of so doing. Their Lordships therefore awarded just a small amount of financial damages for 'loss of amenity value'.

The general parameters of contractual damages were also altered by the courts in the case of *Chaplin v Hicks* [1911] in which a newspaper ran a beauty contest; selected the top 50 applicants from photographs submitted, of which the claimant was one, and required those 50 to attend an audition where 12 winners would be selected. The organisers failed to tell the claimant the time and place of the audition and the court awarded damages for what it considered to be a genuine, though imprecise, 'loss of opportunity'.

Damages for distress or disappointment will not normally be permitted under contract law, so, in the case of *Addis v Gramophone Ltd* [1909], a managing director dismissed for breach of contract was awarded damages for his pecuniary loss only and not for the distress it was claimed he had suffered as a result of his dismissal.

There are exceptions to the rule in *Addis v Gramophone Ltd* [1919] (above). For example, in the leading case of *Jarvis v Swan Tours* [1973] the claimant sued for damages arising from 'disappointment' after the holiday he had booked turned out to be a disaster and promised attractions were not provided. The court held the defendant had contracted to provide a pleasurable holiday; the holiday was inferior; the claimant's legitimate expectations were not fulfilled; and so damages should be awarded.

In the leading case of *Farley v Skinner* [2001] the House of Lords overruled the Court of Appeal and awarded damages after the house the claimant bought near Gatwick Airport suffered badly with aircraft noise; the surveyor having negligently provided a favourable report in this respect. Their Lordships held that the provision of 'pleasurable amenity' and 'freedom from distress' were major components of the contract because the claimant had specifically asked the surveyor to consider the issue of aircraft noise. Whilst creating a further exception to the general rule in *Addis v Gramophone Ltd* [1919] (above) in principle, on the specific circumstances of the case the claimant was awarded only nominal damages of £10.

Although the object of remedies in contract law is normally to put the aggrieved party in the position it would have been in had the contract been properly performed, a much less common form of remedy is to put the aggrieved party in the position it would have been in had the contract never been made. For example, in the case of *Anglia Television Ltd. v Reed* [1972] an actor was successfully sued for the expenses incurred by a television company after the actor contracted to take part in a television production and subsequently refused to perform.

As for remoteness of loss, that is to say the foreseeability that the particular loss or damage might be an outcome of the breach of contract, the general rule from the leading case of *Hadley v Baxendale* [1884] is the loss must be that which flows naturally from the particular breach, or that it was 'within the reasonable contemplation' of the parties as a probable outcome of breach at the time the contract was made.

On the particular facts of *Hadley v Baxendale* [1884] a mill owner was refused damages by the court after the defendant's delay in providing a piece of mill equipment caused the mill to be idle and lose money. The court held the mill closure was not obvious, as the defendant would assume there was a spare piece of equipment and did not know this to be an incorrect assumption. The losses caused by the mill closure were held neither to have arisen naturally from the defendant's breach in providing the piece of equipment late, nor were they within the reasonable contemplation of the parties at the time the contract was agreed.

The leading case of *Parsons v Uttley Ingham* [1978] is important in relation to the foreseeability of loss because the Court of Appeal emphasised that if a particular type of loss is within the parties' contemplation as a serious possibility then all loss of that type is recoverable, even if the extent of loss is more serious than could have been contemplated. On the particular facts of *Parsons v Uttley Ingham* [1978] the claimants received damages for the death of their pigs after a storage hopper installed on the claimants' farm was incorrectly sealed and the pig food became contaminated. The court held contamination of the pig food would have been within the parties' contemplation as a result of failing to correctly seal the top of the storage hopper and, even though the death of the pigs might not have been in contemplation, the loss was of the same type and therefore recoverable by the claimants.

A claimant is however always expected to mitigate its loss, that is to say, to take all reasonable steps to keep the losses incurred to a minimum. The onus of proof is on the party in breach to show the claimant could have mitigated its loss but did not do so. If the defendant can show the claimant has failed to mitigate its loss the court will not award damages for that part of the loss that was caused by a failure to mitigate.

2.10 MISREPRESENTATION

A 'statement' made during contractual negotiations may be extravagant in an obvious way, such as an advertising gimmick. There is no right of action in respect of this type of statement.

A 'term' is part of the contract and, if untrue, the aggrieved party will be entitled to sue for breach of contract.

A 'representation' is a statement not forming part of the contract. If the representation is an untrue statement of fact made by one party to a contract before the contract was made and was one of the factors that induced the other party to enter into the contract, it is a misrepresentation, for which the aggrieved party may have a remedy at law.

Silence will not amount to a misrepresentation since there is no general duty to say anything. However, anything that is said must not be misleading. A statement of fact may be true at the time it is made but if circumstances change before the contract is agreed, such that the statement becomes untrue, the party who made the statement has a duty to inform the other party of the change.

Where there is a fiduciary relationship, that is to say, a relationship of trust, or a contract is made in utmost good faith, such as for the provision of professional services, there must be full disclosure of all material facts.

The usual remedy for misrepresentation is to make the contract voidable. That is to say, the aggrieved party may elect to either affirm or rescind the contract. If the decision is to rescind the contract, the other party must normally be informed unless that party cannot be found. When the contract is rescinded neither party need perform any future obligations and each party should return to the other any property that was transferred under the contract.

If it is necessary to apply to the court for an order of rescission (most commonly where the parties do not agree) the court will only make such an order if none of the bars to rescission apply. That is to say the contract has not been affirmed; there has not been unreasonable delay in making the application to the court; where it is impossible to return the parties to substantially the same positions they were in before entering the contract; or where a genuine purchaser who has no knowledge of the misrepresentation has acquired an interest in the subject matter of the contract before the contract was rescinded.

The courts may refuse to grant a rescission order, particularly where the false statement is relatively minor and it would be unjust to rescind the contract. Provided the misrepresentation was not made fraudulently, that is to say the representation was not made knowing it to be untrue; without belief in the truth of the statement; or recklessly as to whether the statement was true or false, the court has discretion under Section 2(2) of the Misrepresentation Act 1967 to award damages in lieu of rescission.

Under Section 2(2) of the Misrepresentation Act 1967, the court will need to consider the seriousness of the false statement, the loss caused by the misrepresentation and the likely impact of rescission on the other party. The court may only award damages where it is just and equitable to do so. Such damages are strictly in lieu of rescission, not as well as, and are intended to place the claimant in the position s/he would have been in if the misrepresentation had not been made.

If the aggrieved party can prove the statement was made fraudulently then s/he can sue for damages in the tort of deceit as well as either affirming or rescinding the contract. Damages for deceit are assessed on tort principles (discussed in Chapter 3) except that the usual requirement for foreseeability of the particular loss or damage does not apply.

If the misrepresentation was made negligently it may be possible for the other party to sue for damages in the tort of negligence. Generally pure economic loss is not recoverable in tort, but in the leading case of *Hedley Byrne & Co v Heller* [1964] the House of Lords recognised an exception in the case of economic loss caused by negligent misrepresentation. This exception is particularly relevant to professional practitioners, where a special relationship exists between the parties.

Negligent misrepresentation is considered in detail in Chapter 3.

CHAPTER SUMMARY

- Common to all legally binding agreements is that the offer made by one party must be on specified terms and the other party must communicate acceptance of the offer unconditionally on exactly the terms offered

- Attempts to introduce different terms are counter offers

- To give legal validity to an agreement there must a consideration and a clear indication of intention to be legally bound

- The doctrine of privity means a contract cannot confer rights or impose obligations on any person other than a party to the contract

- A contract may be brought to an end by performance, breach, or frustration

- Where a contract is made in utmost good faith such as for the provision of professional services, there must be full disclosure of all material facts

3

The Tort of Professional Negligence

THE AIMS OF THIS CHAPTER ARE TO:

- Introduce the concept of tortious liability, in particular the tort of professional negligence and its implications for the work of the professional practitioner
- Explain the meaning and implications of negligent misrepresentation
- Explain the requirement for professional practitioners to hold Professional Indemnity Insurance, what it covers and how to go about obtaining it

Tort law concerns the infringement of a legal right, or the breach of a legal duty, arising independently of contract. Tort law does not provide a remedy for every type of harm. The claimant must persuade the court that s/he has a legal right that has been infringed by the defendant; that the harm is covered by an existing tort; or that the existing law should be extended to cover the particular harm done.

There are a number of established torts that have developed to protect claimants from many types of harm. In each established tort the law has developed a number of elements that the claimant must prove 'on the balance of probabilities' and the defendant must then prove to the same 'better than 50:50' standard that they have an acceptable defence. Some defences are relevant to all torts and some defences are specific to a particular tort. The tort most likely to be of importance to professional practitioners is that of professional negligence with which this chapter is concerned.

3.1   LEGAL DUTY OF CARE

In order for there to be a valid claim in negligence the claimant must first establish as a question of law that the circumstances were such that they were capable of giving rise to a duty of care. If so, then, as a matter of fact, did the particular defendant owe this particular claimant a duty of care in the particular circumstances of the case?

The leading case in the area of establishing a legal duty of care is *Donoghue v Stevenson* [1932], a classic of tort law in which there was no contractual relationship between the manufacturer of a product and the end user of that product who was harmed by it. The court therefore imputed a legal duty of care in order that the end user could sue the manufacturer directly instead of suing the owner of the shop from which the product was bought, with whom there was a contractual relationship but who was not responsible for the fault in the manufactured product.

> **THE NEIGHBOUR PRINCIPLE**
>
> (Per Lord Justice Atkin in *Donoghue v Stevenson* [1932]):
>
> *You must take reasonable care to avoid acts or omissions which you can reasonably foresee would be likely to injure your neighbours ... persons who are so closely connected and directly affected by my act that I ought reasonably to have them in contemplation as being so affected.*

Where professional practice is concerned, it is not difficult to imagine a circumstance in which, for example, the professional practitioner designs a water feature for a retirement home and does not take reasonable care to ensure the choice of adjacent paving is such that it will not become slippery when wet. The professional practitioner might reasonably have foreseen that those in a retirement home are, by definition, elderly and more vulnerable to injury following a slip or a fall and are so closely connected and affected by the choice of paving simply by being residents of the retirement home that they should have been in contemplation when designing the paving.

> **NO DUTY OF CARE TO THE UNFORESEEABLE VICTIM**
>
> (Per Lord Justice Macmillan in *Bourhill v Young* [1943]):
>
> *The duty is owed to those to whom injury may reasonably and probably be anticipated if the duty is not observed. There is no absolute standard of what is reasonable and probable. It must depend on circumstances and must always be a question of degree.*

A victim need not be foreseeable as an individual but may be one of a class of foreseeable victims, as in the leading case of *Hadley v London Electricity Board* [1965], in which a blind person fell into a hole in a pavement that had been dug by the defendants, whom it was held had not done enough to prevent such occurrence. The same might be said for the example of the water feature in the retirement home used above; all residents of the retirement home comprising a class of persons who might reasonably and foreseeably be injured by the professional practitioner's failure to actively consider them in making the choice of paving material.

In some situations, a duty of care may be obvious, as in the leading case of *Marc Rich & Co v Bishop Rock Marine Co Ltd* [1996] in which Lord Justice Steyn stated:

'the relationship between the parties may be such that it is obvious that a lack of care will create a risk of harm and that as a matter of common sense and justice a duty should be imposed'. This is generally the case in all professional practice situations where there is a 'fiduciary' relationship between the parties, that is to say, a relationship of trust. For example, the duty of care owed by a doctor to a patient; a parent to a child; a financial adviser to an investor; and a landscape architect to their client.

In short, according to the House of Lords case of *Caparo Industries v Dickman* [1990] in order for a court to find that a legal duty of care exists, potential harm must be reasonably foreseeable; there must be sufficient proximity of relationship between the parties; and it must be fair, just and reasonable to impose a duty.

3.2 BREACH OF DUTY

Having established that the defendant owes the claimant a legal duty of care, the claimant must then prove the duty of care was breached. That is to say, whether, as a matter of fact, the defendant failed to achieve the standard of care the law determines was required.

> **THE GENERAL STANDARD OF CARE**
>
> (Per Judge Alderson in *Blyth v Birmingham Waterworks* [1856]):
>
> *An omission to do something which a reasonable man guided upon those considerations which ordinarily regulate the conduct of human affairs would do; or something a prudent and reasonable man would not do.*

> **THE 'REASONABLE MAN' TEST**
>
> (Per Lord Justice Macmillan in *Glasgow Corporation v Muir* [1943]):
>
> *Eliminates the personal equation and is independent of the idiosyncrasies of the particular person whose conduct is in question ... the reasonable man is presumed to be free from both over-apprehension and from over-confidence.*

Factors to be taken into consideration by the courts in determining the standard of care required are the likelihood of any harm occurring; the seriousness of the consequence of any injury; the cost and practicality of overcoming the risk; the purpose of the activity creating the risk, for example was it an emergency situation; common practice (which may indicate the defendant acted reasonably but is not conclusive); and whether the activity requires particular knowledge and skill, the latter being particularly relevant to professional practitioners.

> **THE 'ORDINARY SKILLED MAN' TEST**
>
> (Per Judge McNair in *Bolam v Friern Hospital Management Committee* [1957]):
>
> *Where you get a situation which involves the use of some special skill or competence, then the test as to whether there has been negligence ... is the standard of the ordinary skilled man exercising and professing to have that special skill. A man need not possess the highest expert skill; it is well established law that it is sufficient if he exercises the ordinary skill of an ordinary competent man exercising that particular skill.*

The standard of care required is always judged against the standard of knowledge current at the time of the alleged breach as opposed to at the time of any trial, which may be different through the assimilation of new knowledge as in the leading case of *Roe v Minister of Health* [1954].

The duty is to guard against reasonable probabilities, for example the probability of road traffic accidents caused by children playing football on open ground in close proximity to a road, as in the leading case of *Hilder v Associated Portland Cement Manufacturers* [1961], and not fantastic possibilities, as in the leading case of *Bolton v Stone* [1951] in which a passer-by was hit by a cricket ball the batsman hit out of the ground; a distance in excess of 100 metres and clearing a six metre high fence; a feat that had only been achieved six times in 30 years.

The courts will only take a subjective approach to the standard of care required where the claimant(s) undertaking the activity are young, old or physically or mentally impaired. For example, the leading case of *Mullin v Richards* [1998] in which it was held that the likelihood of injury resulting from the game they were playing was not foreseeable by two 15-year-old children. However, if harm occurs because a young person is committing an illegal act, for example a 15-year-old driving a car, no more subjective view would be taken by virtue of the defendant's age.

The party making the allegation must prove the breach of duty and the standard of proof required is the civil standard 'on the balance of probabilities', that is to say 'greater than 50:50', as opposed to the criminal standard of proof, that is to say 'beyond reasonable doubt' or 'sure'.

3.3   CAUSATION

A defendant will not be liable for losses unless caused by his act or omission. This will be a matter of fact to be decided by the courts. Causation in fact is generally determined by the 'but for' test. That is to say would the harm have arisen 'but for' the defendant's act or omission?

The leading case in this area is *Barnett v Chelsea & Kensington Hospital Management Committee* [1969] in which the defendant (the hospital management committee) admitted a duty and a negligent breach of that duty but was not held liable for the loss because the court found the negligence played no part in the cause; that death of the patient was inevitable due to a cause that had nothing to do with the hospital's negligence.

In some circumstances it may be argued there are many causes of the harm suffered, in which case the claimant need not prove a defendant's breach of its duty of care was the only cause of the loss. It is sufficient to establish on the balance of probabilities that the defendant's breach made a 'material contribution' to the loss suffered. In the leading case of *Fairchild v Glenhaven* [2002] the employer accepted it had a duty and its duty had been breached but argued it was impossible to say which of a series of employers triggered the claimant's lung cancer. The House of Lords accepted the strict 'but for' test could not be satisfied but found that justice must be done; that the tort system ought to be just; that sometimes technicalities ought to be varied since, on the particular facts of the case, employers were morally at fault because the problem of asbestos-related cancers had been known about since the 1930s yet employers had been slow to act.

The chain of causation will be broken by a new intervening act. This may be an imprudent act of the claimant, for example in the leading case of *McKew v Holland* [1969], in which a claimant with an already weakened leg fell down a staircase and further injured the leg after descending without holding the handrail. The House of Lords felt the claimant's behaviour was unreasonable in the context of his original injury and therefore broke the chain of causation for the subsequent injury.

Contrast the findings in *McKew v Holland* [1969] (above) with the case of *Wieland v Cyril Lord* [1969], in which a claimant wearing a neck brace following an accident descended stairs without being able to lower her head and fell, causing further injury. On the facts of the case, because there was no assistance available that might have prevented her falling, her actions were not unreasonable and there was no break in the chain of causation.

3.4 REMOTENESS OF DAMAGE

The concept of remoteness of damage may limit a defendant's liability for loss or harm even though the loss or harm was caused by the defendant's act or omission. This will be determined by the court as a matter of law and may overlap with whether a duty of care is owed.

As stated by the Master of the Rolls, Lord Denning, in the case of *Spartan Steel & Alloys Ltd v Martin & Co* [1973]: 'The more I think, the more difficult I find it to put each into its proper pigeon hole. Sometimes I say "There was no duty". In others, I say "The damage was too remote". I think the time has come to discard those tests which have proved elusive'.

The test of remoteness is whether the damage was foreseeable. It matters not if the exact *way* in which the damage occurred, or the *extent* of the damage, were foreseeable; only that the *kind* of damage that occurred could be foreseen.

> **THE 'REASONABLE FORESEEABILITY' TEST**
>
> (Per Viscount Simons in *The Wagon Mound (No.1)* [1961]):
>
> *It does not seem consonant with the current ideas of justice or morality that for an act of negligence ... the actor should be liable for all the consequences however unforeseeable and however grave, so long as they can be said to be 'direct' ... a man must be considered to be responsible for the probable consequences of his act.*

The House of Lords considered and approved *The Wagon Mound (No.1)* [1961] decision when finding, in the case of *Hughes v Lord Advocate* [1963], that the *way* in which the claimant's loss occurred need not have been foreseeable. Provided the *kind* of loss or harm is reasonably foreseeable, a defendant is liable for the full extent of the harm or loss sustained, even though the precise *extent* and/or *manner* of infliction of the harm could not have been foreseen.

> **THE 'EGG-SHELL SKULL' RULE**
>
> (Per Lord Justice Mackinnon *Owens v Liverpool Corporation* [1939]):
>
> *One who is guilty of negligence ... must put up with the idiosyncrasies of his victim that increase the likelihood or extent of damage to him; it is no answer to a claim for a fractured skull that its owner had an unusually fragile one.*

This state of affairs was confirmed in the leading case of *Smith v Leech Brain & Co. Ltd* [1962], in which the defendant's relatively minor negligent act was proved by medical evidence to be the trigger for the claimant's pre-malignant cancer leading to his death.

3.5 DEFENCES

Assuming a claimant has proven on the balance of probabilities that they were owed a legal duty of care; that the duty of care owed to them was breached; that the defendant's breach was the cause of the loss they have suffered; and that the loss suffered was not too remote a consequence of the defendant's act or omission, the burden of proof then shifts to the defendant, on the same 'balance of probabilities' standard, to prove to a 'better than 50:50' standard that they have an adequate defence.

> **THE MOST COMMON DEFENCES TO CLAIMS OF NEGLIGENCE**
>
> - Willing assumption of risk (something almost the same as consent; unpopular with judges; and rarely successful)
> - Exclusion of liability
> - Contributory negligence

3.5.1 Willing assumption of risk

A willing assumption of risk, if proven, is a complete defence. That is to say, it fully bars recovery for the loss or damage incurred. The test is whether a person who knows of a risk and then deliberately incurs it can be said to have implied agreement to take the risk of harm and thereby be prevented from recovering his loss. The courts dislike this form of defence so much that Section 149 of the Road Traffic Act 1988 specifically excludes it, stating:

> Any antecedent agreement or understanding between the user and passenger of a motor vehicle purporting to negative, restrict or impose any conditions on the liability of the user towards the passenger, shall have no effect so far as the user is required to have in force a policy of insurance in respect of his liability for compulsory third party risks and the fact that a passenger has willingly accepted the risk of negligence by the user shall not negative any liability of the user.

3.5.2 Exclusion of liability

All exclusion clauses relating to business or business premises are subject to statute in the form of the Unfair Contract Terms Act 1977. Not surprisingly, the law does not permit clauses that seek to exclude liability for death or personal injury caused as a result of business activities or on business premises. However, any duty of care owed in the course of business extends only to a duty not to damage persons or property. There is no general duty to avoid causing pure economic loss, so businesses may legitimately exclude liability for loss or damage arising in this way.

Exclusion clauses relating to pure economic loss are however subject to a test of reasonableness. For example, that set out in the leading case of *Smith v Eric S. Bush; Harris v Wyre Forest District Council* [1989], in which a claimant relied upon a negligent valuation of a property undertaken on behalf of the building society providing the mortgage. In their defence the firm of surveyors relied upon the disclaimer in their contract saying they were not liable to the householder. The claimant challenged the reasonableness of the exclusion clause and obtained judgment in his favour. On the particular facts of the case, because the claimant was a 'small ordinary house buyer' whom it would be unreasonable to expect would instruct another surveyor independent of the mortgage company and the surveyor knew the report would be shown to the buyer, the House of Lords held the surveyor's duty was to both the mortgage company and to the buyer, rendering the exclusion clause unreasonable and therefore void.

Generally speaking, if a claimant acquires defective goods or services and providing those goods or services have caused no physical harm to the claimant or their property, the claimant may sue for breach of contract but cannot sue in tort for the value of the defective goods or services. However, if and when defective goods or services cause damage to persons or property, the claimant may sue for the loss or damage caused by the defective goods or services.

It should be noted that it is not permitted to exclude one's own negligence, only that of others.

3.5.3 Contributory negligence

> CONTRIBUTORY NEGLIGENCE
>
> (Per Lord Denning *Jones v Livox Quarries Ltd* [1952]):
>
> *A person is guilty of contributory negligence if he ought reasonably to have foreseen that if he did not act as a reasonably prudent man he might hurt himself; and in his reckonings he must take into account the possibility of others being careless.*

> Section 1 of the Law Reform (Contributory Negligence) Act 1945:
>
> *Where a person suffers damage as the result partly of his own fault and partly of the fault of any other person, the claim in respect of that damage is not defeated but the damages recoverable in respect thereof are reduced to such extent as the court thinks just and equitable having regard to the claimant's share in the responsibility for the damage.*

In order for there to be contributory negligence, the defendant must prove there was a causal connection between the claimant's actions and the damage claimed, in which case the damages awarded may be reduced according to the claimant's share in the responsibility for the damage.

In the leading case of *Froom v Butcher* [1976], the claimant's damages were reduced after he suffered head and chest injuries in a motoring accident caused by the defendant's negligence, because the accident occurred at a time before it was compulsory to wear seat belts and the claimant had decided not to wear one. Had the claimant worn a seat belt his injuries would not have been so severe. The claimant was therefore held to have contributed to the severity of his own injuries and his damages were reduced by 15 per cent.

A claimant will not be contributory negligent if he makes an understandable decision in the heat of the moment which turns out to be the wrong decision; a child claimant will be judged by the standard of what an average child of the same age might do; and it is very unusual for rescuers, that is to say fire crew, doctors, police and so on, to be found to have contributed to their own loss or damage except in very extreme cases.

The three defences of willingness to assume the risk, exclusion of liability and contributory negligence are normally used in that order by defendants seeking to defeat a claim in negligence. It is common for the first two of these potential defences to fail but for the claimant's damages to be reduced according to the degree of the claimant's contributory negligence.

In addition, a defendant may escape liability because of time limits that apply; the general rule being that non-personal injury claims must be commenced within six years of the events giving rise to the claim and three years in claims that do involve personal injury allegedly caused by breach of a legal duty. However, time does not run against a person suffering from a disability or a child, unless and until the disability is removed or the child reaches the age of 18.

A defendant may also escape liability for loss or damage arising from his negligent acts or omissions in circumstances where the claimant was committing a criminal offence when s/he was injured and there is a close connection between the offence and the claimant's loss or damage. For example, in the leading case of *Ashton v Turner* [1981] a defendant escaped liability after his negligent driving caused a crash in which the claimant was injured, because at the time of the accident the claimant was the driver of a 'get-away' car following a robbery.

3.6   REMEDIES

The general aim of damages in tort is to put the claimant in the position s/he would have been in if the tort had not been committed, that is to say restitution damages, in contrast to the law of contract which generally aims to put the claimant in the position they would have been in if the contract had been properly performed (discussed in Chapter 2).

As it is often not possible to put the claimant in the position s/he would have been in if the tort had not been committed, particularly where personal injury or death has occurred as a result of the tort, remedies are commonly in the form of monetary damages.

In claims of personal injury arising out of negligence, the claimant may be awarded 'general damages', that is to say non-pecuniary losses including pain and suffering, loss of amenity, loss of enjoyment of life and so on, together with 'special damages' to cover specific pecuniary losses arising from such things as medical expenses, loss of earnings, loss of future earning capacity and interest.

Where the victim of negligence dies as a result of his or her injuries, a claim is usually commenced by the deceased's personal representatives on behalf of certain categories of relatives. Such relatives may be entitled to claim bereavement damages, funeral expenses and major damages in the form of 'loss of dependency'. That is to say, if the deceased was the 'breadwinner' what the deceased would have been awarded had they still been alive. To be awarded such damages the claimant relative must establish some reasonable expectation of dependency and/or benefit. This must be family related and not business related.

As stated above, there is not normally any remedy in tort law for pure economic loss incurred as a result of a defendant breaching its duty of care. This was confirmed in the leading case of *Murphy v Brentwood District Council* [1990] in which a local authority negligently carried out its statutory duty of inspection under building regulations in relation to a house bought by the claimant. The foundations of the building turned out to be defective, resulting in cracks that damaged the whole building. The claimant sold the house for less than the purchase price and sued the local authority for the difference. It was held that the local authority could not be liable to subsequent owners for the cost of remedying dangerous defects because such defects, once known, are purely economic loss rather than property damage.

3.7 NEGLIGENT MISREPRESENTATION

An exception to the general rule that pure economic loss is not recoverable in tort was provided by the leading case of *Hedley Byrne & Co v Heller & Partners Ltd* [1964]. The case established that a duty of care arises in the giving of information or advice where a 'special relationship' exists between the person giving and the person receiving the advice.

As Lord Justice Reid put it, a duty of care will be owed in:

> ... relationships where it is plain that the party seeking information or advice was trusting the other to exercise such a degree of care as the circumstances required, where it was reasonable for him to do that, and where the other gave that information or advice when he knew or ought to have known that the inquirer was relying on him.

Examples of the *Hedley Byrne and Co v Heller* [1964] principle are if someone possessed of a special skill, such as landscape architecture, undertakes to apply that skill for the assistance of another person who relies on that skill, or if a person holds himself out as possessing such skill in circumstances where it is foreseeable that others would rely on it. The *Hedley Byrne & Co v Heller* [1964] principle is therefore directly relevant to the provision of professional services and it is clear from case law that negligent words and negligent deeds are almost indistinguishable even in a non-business context.

In the leading case of *Chaudry v Prabhakar* [1989] the claimant, knowing nothing about cars, asked a friend who had some knowledge of cars to find her a second-hand car, stipulating that it must not have been involved in an accident. The friend found a car and highly recommended it to the claimant who bought it, only to find the car had been involved in a serious accident and was not roadworthy. The court found in favour of the claimant because the defendant voluntarily held himself out as an expert and the claimant reasonably relied upon the advice he provided.

In the leading case of *Caparo Industries v Dickman* [1990] the claimants were shareholders who took over a company relying upon the company accounts stating the company had previously made a large profit. In fact the company had made a large loss. The claimants alleged the company's auditors had been negligent in certifying that the accounts showed a true and fair view of the company's position; that the auditors owed them a duty of care as potential investors and shareholders who, it was clear, were intent on buying the company. The House of Lords decision found that although it was foreseeable the investors would lose money, there was not 'sufficient proximity of relationship' for the duty of care owed by the auditors to extend to anyone beyond those currently controlling the company.

The judgment in *Caparo Industries v Dickman* [1990] set out the requirements in order to establish sufficient proximity of relationship, giving rise to a duty of care in *Hedley Byrne v Heller* [1964] situations. What has become known as the 'Caparo gloss' effectively requires that a defendant must have known his statement would be communicated to the claimant; that the statement would be communicated specifically in connection with a particular, or a particular type, of transaction; and that the claimant would be very likely to rely on the statement in deciding whether to enter the particular transaction. The claimant must still prove that the duty of care was breached causing loss, including financial loss, and the normal rules of remoteness will apply, that is to say the court will award damages in the tort of negligence only if the loss was foreseeable. As a result, takeovers now specifically include 'due diligence' for which auditors are paid and for which they may be sued.

3.8 PROFESSIONAL INDEMNITY INSURANCE

Professional indemnity insurance is a form of liability insurance that focuses on alleged errors or omissions on the part of professional practitioners and financial losses arising from them. These potential causes of legal action are not normally covered by more general liability insurance, for example public liability insurance, which addresses more direct forms of harm.

Professional indemnity insurance can include cover for the cost of defending allegations of professional negligence that turn out to be groundless. Coverage does not however include criminal prosecution.

Many major insurance companies offer professional indemnity insurance and specialist brokers, working with professional associations, often tailor cover to the needs of particular professions. McParland Finn Ltd is one such specialist broker which, endorsed by the Landscape Institute, offers a broad range of insurance broking and risk management services to landscape professionals under the banner of Landscape Institute Insurance Services.

All practices and public sector departments registered with the Landscape Institute are required to carry professional indemnity insurance and to produce evidence that cover is held. In addition, clients, particularly commercial clients, often insist on a certain level of professional indemnity insurance cover before they will consider awarding a commission to a professional practitioner.

Ultimately it is for each practice, public sector department or individual practitioner to determine its own risk and the level of cover required. In an increasingly litigious world, professional practitioners are advised to give careful consideration to ensuring they are adequately protected by professional indemnity insurance before they begin practising.

Professional practitioners should also ensure they maintain professional indemnity insurance for at least six years after they cease practising. As stated above, non-personal injury claims in the tort of negligence must be commenced within six years of the events giving rise to the claim. It is therefore entirely possible that a claim in negligence may be commenced at any time within this period irrespective of whether the professional practitioner alleged to have acted negligently has remained in practice during the intervening period.

> **CHAPTER SUMMARY**
>
> - Tort law concerns the infringement of a legal right, or the breach of a legal duty, arising independently of contract
> - The claimant must first establish they were owed a duty of care
> - The claimant must then prove the duty of care was breached
> - A defendant will only be liable for losses caused by his act or omission
> - The concept of remoteness of damage may limit a defendant's liability for loss or harm even though caused by the defendant's act or omission
> - The three most common defences to claims in negligence are willing assumption of risk; exclusion of liability; and contributory negligence
> - An exception to the general rule that pure economic loss is not recoverable in tort arises if someone possessed of a special skill, such as landscape architecture, undertakes to apply that skill for the assistance of another
> - All practices and public sector departments registered with the Landscape Institute are required to carry professional indemnity insurance to cover alleged errors or omissions in the provision of professional services

4

Health and Safety Legislation

THE AIMS OF THIS CHAPTER ARE TO:

- Outline the health and safety requirements and guidelines as they impact upon organisations and individuals including professional practitioners
- Explain the process of 'designing out' health and safety risks
- Explain the health and safety reporting requirements and how they might impact upon the work of the professional practitioner

Health and safety legislation applies to all businesses environments. The professional practitioner, whether an employer, employee or self-employed, is responsible for the health, safety and welfare of employees and any others who may be affected by what s/he does.

Much of the responsibility for management of health and safety risks on project sites rests with the contractor. The Health and Safety Executive (2006) identifies the main causes of accidents and ill health, explains how to eliminate hazards and to control risks. The guidance is simple but comprehensive and, although aimed at the contractor, applies to everyone involved in projects.

The Health and Safety Executive guide referred to above can be of benefit to the professional practitioner in identifying the most common risks that contractors have to manage on site and what might be done to 'design out' or reduce these risks when designing, specifying and planning projects.

As the focus of the present text is upon professional practice, what follows is a non-exhaustive consideration of the major elements of health and safety legislation with which a professional practitioner in the landscape industry ought to be familiar:

4.1 HEALTH AND SAFETY AT WORK ACT

The Health and Safety at Work Act 1974 applies to all work activities. It requires employers to ensure, so far as is reasonably practicable, the health and safety of their employees, other people at work and members of the public who may be affected by their work.

Employers should have a health and safety policy. If they employ five or more people, the policy should be in writing. The policy should be clear and simple. Everybody in the firm must know about and understand the health and safety systems and how these relate to the operations of the firm. The safety policy should provide:

- A general statement of the firm's health and safety policy including what it intends to do to achieve high standards of health and safety

- How the policy is implemented including who is responsible for what and when and how they will achieve it

- The specific arrangements the firm operates for managing health and safety during its normal work activities including general considerations such as site access and induction; welfare facilities; storage areas; waste materials; emergency procedures; fire; first aid; accident reporting; and arrangements for managing specific risks such as working at height; site traffic and mobile plant; moving goods safely; groundwork; occupational health risks; contact with electricity; protective equipment; work affecting the public; and monitoring/review

Employees have to cooperate with their employer on health and safety matters and not do anything that puts themselves or others at risk. Employees should be trained and clearly instructed in their duties.

The self-employed should ensure, as far as is reasonably practicable, their own health and safety and make sure their work does not put other workers or members of the public at risk.

As stated above, whilst much of the responsibility for managing health and safety risks on site rests with the contractor, the professional practitioner must ensure the contractor complies with its obligations in this regard. The professional practitioner should ordinarily require the contractor to provide a copy of its safety policy, certainly before commencing operations and preferably when submitting its quotation or tender for the works (discussed in Chapter 14).

Professional practitioners should also bear in mind that their own working environment of design studio or office is also a place of work to which the Health and Safety at Work Act 1974 applies. The professional practitioner must similarly appropriately manage risks to the health and safety of their employees; other people at work; and members of the public who may visit them on their premises. The professional practitioner must also have a written health and safety policy if the practice or firm employs five or more people.

Whilst the induction of new personnel to any work environment, whether site, office or design studio, should include familiarisation with the safety policy and procedures, it is generally not possible to treat members of the public and visitors in the same way. Communication of safety procedures to such people doesn't necessarily require an 'airline'-style drill every time there is a visitor to site or office. It does however require the firm's personnel to be sufficiently well informed and capable of implementing procedures such that the safety of members of the public and visitors is appropriately managed in the event of an emergency occurring.

Where it is not reasonably practicable to exercise full control over each and every member of the public or visitor in the event of an emergency, such as where there are large groups of visitors or unrestricted public access, then it is a requirement to communicate emergency procedures to *all* visitors by means of signs to indicate points of exit, location of fire extinguishers and the like. It is also a requirement to bring these notices and procedures to the attention of visitors, as frequently experienced when attending lectures and conferences.

4.2 THE MANAGEMENT OF HEALTH AND SAFETY AT WORK REGULATIONS

The Management of Health and Safety at Work Regulations 1999 apply to everyone at work, regardless of what that work is. The Regulations require employers to plan, control, organise, monitor and assess the risks associated with their operations in order to identify measures that will 'design out' health and safety risks.

Risk assessment requires employers and the self-employed to identify the hazards involved with their work, assess the likelihood of any harm arising and decide on adequate precautions. Those carrying out risk assessments must understand the requirements of the Management of Health and Safety at Work Regulations 1999 and have sufficient knowledge to ensure the most suitable precautionary measures are put in place. Risk assessment can either be carried out on a single task, or the job as a whole, providing the job is not too complex. Risk assessment is generally carried out in five stages:

Stage 1: Consider the hazards

Thought must be given to the job or task being assessed; how it will be done; where will it be done; and what equipment, materials and chemicals might it require? For example, there may be hazards caused by moving vehicles or equipment; the task might involve excavations or lifting equipment; or the professional practitioner might be required to spend long periods in front of a computer screen.

Stage 2: Consider who might be harmed and how

Consideration must be given to employees; the self-employed; personnel of other organisations involved with the task or job; visitors; and members of the public. Safe working practices often require cooperation so it is necessary to identify any problems the task or job might cause for others and jointly agree any necessary precautions.

Stage 3: Evaluate the risks and decide on appropriate action

Where there is a risk that someone could be harmed by the task or job the hazard should preferably be removed completely. For example, by performing the operation in a different way or by using less hazardous materials or equipment.

If the risk cannot be eliminated completely it is necessary to consider how the risk might be managed. For example, the professional practitioner might rearrange the sequence of operations to break up the time spent in front of a computer screen or reallocate the total time in front of the computer so it is shared between several personnel.

Depending on the nature of the risk, it is preferable that safety measures should protect the whole workforce. For example, replacing office flooring that becomes slippery when wet will provide a safer working environment for workers and visitors alike.

Consideration should also be given to reducing the number of people at risk from the task or job. For example, the professional practitioner who has advance ordered semi-mature trees for a project might agree with the supplier that delivery and crane off-loading will take place outside normal site working hours when only essential personnel are present.

Stage 4: Make a written assessment

Producing written risk assessments of their own tasks or jobs and requiring the same of contractors is the most appropriate way the professional practitioner may ensure that suitable and sufficient assessment of risks has taken place. No specific form is required. As long as the information is recoverable the professional practitioner is able to show that risks have been suitably and sufficiently thought through and, in the event of an accident, can demonstrate what measures have been taken to mitigate the risks of the task or job.

Stage 5: Review

Regular reviews are important to take account of particular circumstances or changes in the way the job or task is done; to assimilate learning; and to avoid complacency. A new assessment is not needed every time the job or task is performed, but if there are major changes a new assessment should be conducted.

4.3 METHOD STATEMENTS

Method statements are not required by law but they have proved to be an effective and practical management tool. Method statements take account of risks identified by the risk assessment and communicate the safe system of work to those undertaking the job or task.

A method statement should include any specific training requirements and arrangements for dealing with serious or imminent danger. The method statement should describe in a logical sequence exactly how a job or task can be carried out without risks to health and safety and should describe all necessary control measures.

Method statements permit the task or job to be planned and resourced with the appropriate health and safety resources put in place. They provide information that will allow others affected by the job or task to develop their own health and safety plan as necessary.

Method statements are an effective way of providing information not only to employees but also to the professional practitioner. The most effective health and safety method statements often have a number of diagrams making clear how jobs or tasks are to be carried out. As such they provide an invaluable monitoring tool and the professional practitioner is well advised to require the contractor(s) to seek approval for their method statements before commencing the most complex or high risk operations on site.

4.4 THE CONTROL OF SUBSTANCES HAZARDOUS TO HEALTH REGULATIONS (COSHH)

The Control of Substances Hazardous to Health Regulations 2002 require employers to control exposure to hazardous substances in order to prevent ill health. The Regulations are intended to protect employees and others who may be affected by the hazardous substances, for example adjoining land owners or the general public.

The Control of Substances Hazardous to Health Regulations require a step-by-step approach to the assessment of risks and implementation of any measures needed to control exposure as follows:

Step 1: Assess the risks to health arising from hazardous substances or created by workplace activities;

Step 2: Decide what precautions are needed before carrying out any activities which could result in exposure to hazardous substances;

Step 3: Prepare plans and procedures to deal with accidents, incidents and emergencies involving hazardous substances as necessary;

Step 4: Prevent exposure to hazardous substances or, where preventing exposure is not reasonably practicable, implement measures to adequately control the exposure;

Step 5: Ensure operatives exposed to hazardous substances are properly informed, trained and supervised;

Step 6: Ensure that appropriate control measures are used and safety procedures are followed;

Step 7: Monitor exposure to hazardous substances including the keeping of up-to-date records of substances used; prevailing weather conditions (as appropriate); and the measures taken to prevent exposure; and

Step 8: Carry out appropriate health surveillance/screening where the risk assessment shows this to be necessary or where The Control of Substances Hazardous to Health Regulations specifically requires it.

4.5 THE REPORTING OF INJURIES, DISEASES AND DANGEROUS OCCURRENCES REGULATIONS (RIDDOR)

The Reporting of Injuries, Diseases and Dangerous Occurrences Regulations 1995 came into force on 1 April 1996 and were amended in 2012. Reporting of accidents and ill health at work is a legal requirement whether in respect of on-site operations or any other business environment, including the professional practitioner's office or design studio.

Reporting is not optional. The Regulations apply equally to employers, the self-employed or those in control of work premises. The requirement for reporting occurrences includes those involving members of the general public.

The Reporting of Injuries, Diseases and Dangerous Occurrences Regulations require certain types of accidents, specific cases of occupational ill health and *some* dangerous occurrences to be reported to the Health and Safety Executive. The professional practitioner should know in what circumstances reporting is required so that, as part of the monitoring process on site, s/he is able to check that any such occurrences have been properly recorded and reported. Those occurrences that must be reported are:

4.5.1 Death or major injuries

Death or major injuries, whether to an employee, a self-employed person working on the premises, or involving a member of the public who is killed or admitted to hospital, must be reported without delay to the Incident Contact Centre of the Health and Safety Executive. Reporting is normally by telephone followed up by a completed accident report form (F2508) within ten days. It is also a requirement that death or major injury caused by physical violence must be reported.

4.5.2 Over-three-day injuries

An over-three-day injury is one that is not major but results in the injured person being away from work, or unable to do the full range of their normal duties, for more than three consecutive days. Such injuries must be reported to the Health and Safety Executive by means of a completed accident report form (F2508) within ten days of the continuous absence caused by the accident or dangerous occurrence.

4.5.3 Work-related diseases

Work-related diseases associated with a current job as notified by a doctor must be reported to the Health and Safety Executive by means of a completed disease report form (F2508A). Work-related diseases include certain poisonings; some skin diseases such as dermatitis; lung diseases; infections such as tetanus; and other conditions such as hand-arm vibration syndrome.

4.5.4 Dangerous occurrences

The term 'dangerous occurrence' is applied when something happens that doesn't actually result in a reportable injury but clearly could have done. For example, the failure of a lifting device or contact with overhead electricity cables. Such occurrences must be reported immediately to the nearest Health and Safety Executive office, normally by telephone, and confirmed within ten days by means of a completed accident report form (F2508).

The reporting forms referred to above are available at www.hse.gov.uk or from the local Health and Safety Executive office. A record must be kept of any reportable injury, disease or dangerous occurrence. The record must include the date and method of reporting; date, time and place of the event; personal details of those involved; and a brief description of the nature of the event or disease. The record can be kept in any form, for example copies of the completed Health and Safety Executive reporting forms referred to above.

4.6 ENFORCEMENT

Information reported as a result of the Reporting of Injuries, Diseases and Dangerous Occurrences Regulations enables the Health and Safety Executive or, in relation to offices, shops and small business premises, local authority inspectors, to identify where and how risks arise and to investigate serious accidents or complaints.

Inspectors may visit workplaces without notice but are required to provide identification. The aim of inspections and investigations is to reduce the incidence of injury, disease and dangerous occurrences as a result of work by giving help and advice, particularly to smaller firms that may not have a lot of knowledge.

Inspectors have wide powers that include the right of entry to premises; to talk to and take written statements from employees, safety representatives and anyone who can help with their investigation; to take photographs and samples.

If an inspector encounters a problem s/he is entitled to issue an improvement notice requiring certain actions to be taken or, where a risk of serious personal injury exists, a prohibition notice requiring the cessation of particular activities or stopping the use of particular equipment found to be dangerous. Such notices can and do result in severe business disruption.

If an appeal is lodged against an improvement notice the action required by the notice is suspended until the appeal is determined. If an appeal against a prohibition notice is lodged the cessation required by the notice must continue pending the outcome of the appeal in order to prevent the continuance of what the inspector considers to be a serious risk.

Inspectors have the power to prosecute a business or an individual for non-compliance with health and safety legislation. Monetary fines may also be imposed if a person found to have been responsible for a work-related injury, disease or dangerous occurrence is held to have been negligent or to have failed in their duty of care.

Once found to have been at fault in a work-related injury, disease or dangerous occurrence, an individual or an organisation will be considered a higher risk to an insurer, who is likely to charge a commensurately greater premium for future insurance or decline the cover altogether.

In an increasingly litigious society work-related injuries, diseases or dangerous occurrences also lead to increasing numbers of compensation claims, not just for physical injury but for the stress, anxiety and trauma that may be associated with being involved in or witnessing an incident.

Reporting and investigation is in everyone's interests, although it is rarely seen that way at the time of the occurrence, or in the immediate aftermath, by the person or organisation considered responsible who may very well suffer in a number of ways.

CHAPTER SUMMARY

- Health and safety legislation applies to all businesses environments
- Employers should have a health and safety policy (in writing if they employ five or more people)
- The professional practitioner, whether an employer, employee or self-employed, is responsible for the health, safety and welfare of employees and any others who may be affected by what s/he does
- Professional practitioners are required to 'design out' or reduce the impact of health and safety risks wherever possible
- Much of the responsibility for management of health and safety risks on project sites rests with the contractor who should be required to provide a copy of its safety policy before commencing operations on site
- Method statements are an effective way of providing information not only to employees but also to the professional practitioner
- Reporting of accidents and ill health at work is a legal requirement whether in respect of on-site operations or the professional practitioner's office
- The professional practitioner should know in what circumstances reporting is required and check that legislation is complied with

5

Business Performance and Development

THE AIMS OF THIS CHAPTER ARE TO:

- Explain the 'Transformation Model' of business processes
- Consider comparative methods of analysing business performance
- Introduce general concepts of business promotion and development

Although businesses exist for many reasons, their central objectives fall into two broad categories: commercial organisations trading with the intention of making profits for their owners or shareholders; or not-for-profit organisations reinvesting gains in the pursuit of charitable or public service objectives. What *all* businesses have in common is they produce goods, services or a mixture of the two, by what has been called a 'transformation process'.

5.1 THE TRANSFORMATION PROCESS

The general model of transformation (Slack, Chambers, Harland, Harrison and Johnston, 1995, pp. 11–16) in Figure 5.1 illustrates that businesses input resources used to transform something, or effectively transform the resources themselves, and in so doing produce outputs of goods or services. For example, a landscape contractor inputs resources including craftspeople, labourers, plants, equipment, topsoil and materials, which the organisation transforms to service outputs of constructed landscapes. Similarly, a dumper truck production plant has inputs including sheet metal, equipment, engines, components and skilled labour that it transforms into outputs of finished dumper trucks representing goods for sale or hire.

Input resources may be transformed, as in the case of a professional practitioner who transforms print materials into finished designs or sheet metal that becomes

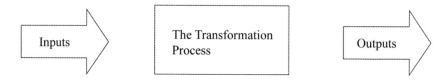

Fig. 5.1   The Transformation Model

dumper trucks, or they may be transforming, as in the case of the craftspeople transforming derelict space into a built landscape.

The central objective of the professional practitioner is error-free and efficient transformation of knowledge and creative energies into fully worked design proposals. The central objective of the landscape contractor is to efficiently transform landscape designs into finished constructions. And the central objective of the dumper truck production plant is to reliably transform raw materials into saleable goods.

Transforming resources vary less from one business to another. All businesses require facilities, whether in the form of buildings, equipment, plant or technology, and all businesses require staff to operate, plan, maintain and manage the transformation process.

A business will frequently transform any or all of its input resources; that is materials, information and customers, at or around the same time. For example, the professional practitioner who transforms print materials into contract documentation often simultaneously oversees the transformation of the printed information into a built landscape, whilst transforming their customer from one with an unsatisfactory derelict space to one with a designed landscape.

From the above, it can be seen that the output of one transformation process frequently inputs to the transformation process of another organisation. For example, the professional practitioner's output of finished design and construction information is essential to the transformation process of the landscape contractor, who is also reliant on the output of the dumper truck manufacturing plant's transformation process to complete its own central objective of transforming derelict open spaces into built landscapes, that is to say the landscape contractor is highly likely to need a dumper truck in order to do so.

As illustrated by Figure 5.2 the context in which business transformation processes take place is extremely complex. Not only will the output of one transformation process provide input to the transformation process of another business, but each business will be reliant upon consumption of their output to replenish the resources required to maintain the process of transformation. For example, unless the dumper truck production plant is able to sell its output of dumper trucks it will be unable to buy the inputs required to continue production; if the landscape contractor and the professional practitioner cannot sell their services they will be unable to maintain facilities and staff essential to the continued provision of those services. In short, the context in which businesses perform their transformation processes is a complex, continuous and interlinked cycle much influenced by a broad range of environmental factors discussed later in this chapter.

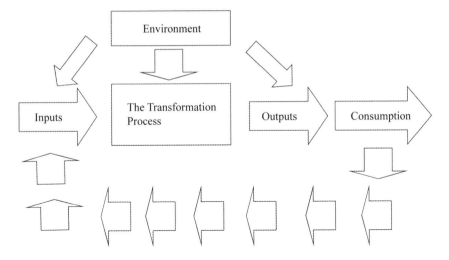

Fig. 5.2 Transformation in Context

5.2 COMPARISON OF GOODS AND SERVICES

Whilst the landscape contractor is largely a business producing services and the dumper truck production plant transforms raw materials into finished goods, the landscape professional practitioner provides a mixture of the two; outputting goods consisting of contract documentation (discussed in Chapter 12) and the service of transforming skills and knowledge into designed landscapes by a process of overseeing contract implementation (discussed in Chapter 15).

Outputs of goods or services vary from one another in their tangibility. Goods such as dumper trucks or paving slabs can be physically touched, whereas the knowledge and skills intrinsic to the services offered by professional practitioners are less tangible but no less valuable.

The tangibility of goods also normally means such outputs can be stored, at least for a short while, and still retain a value to the business through their ability to be sold another day. By contrast, service outputs, for example transforming derelict spaces to designed landscapes, cannot be stored and will represent lost revenue to the business for every day the service is not used.

Because goods can be seen and touched, they are also normally transportable, that is to say, they can be moved to the place they are most likely to be sold, whereas services can be very much more difficult to transport. For example, the service of transforming a derelict space into a built landscape can only be delivered in the location of a particular derelict space. While it may be possible to transport the means of providing the service, that is to say, the craftspeople and materials required, it is not always convenient or financially expedient for a business to do so.

Because dumper trucks and their like are produced in advance of customers taking delivery of them, the consumers of such goods have little or no contact with their producers. By contrast, services such as those output by the landscape contractor transforming derelict spaces into designed landscapes, are normally consumed simultaneously with their production and often involve a considerable degree of contact between producer and consumer.

The lack of contact between consumers and producers of, for example dumper trucks, means that the quality of goods is normally determined by comparison with similar products available from an alternative supplier. In the case of services, the quality of the output can be judged and so too can be the means by which the service was produced and/or delivered according to the quality of the consumer experience.

> BASES OF COMPARISON BETWEEN GOODS AND SERVICES:
>
> - Tangibility
> - Storability
> - Transportability
> - Customer Contact
> - Quality Assurance

5.3   PERFORMANCE ANALYSIS

In order to improve the performance of a business, managers firstly need to know how well the central objective of the business is currently being performed. The transformation process model at Figure 5.1 illustrates the central objective of a business is to transform inputs into marketable outputs, for example that a professional practitioner should transform knowledge of plants, design and landscape materials into finished design proposals, but how can managers effectively analyse how well the business is meeting its objectives in this regard?

Business performance may be analysed by the degree to which a transformation process fulfils five essential performance criteria: quality, speed, dependability, flexibility, and cost, with each of these criteria being an amalgamation of smaller measures of performance (Slack, Chambers, Harland, Harrison and Johnston, 1995, pp. 730–32).

5.3.1   Quality

Some typical measures of quality might be the number of defects, for example what percentage of a landscape contractor's plants die or fail to thrive; level of customer complaints, for example how many complaints might the professional practitioner have received in the last 12 months; the amount of waste, for example how much paper, ink and time does the professional practitioner waste by having to reprint designs because of inaccuracies; the number of warranty claims, for example, how many claims have been made for failure in the dumper trucks manufactured; and frequency of failures, which might be how many times the dumper trucks break down relative to those of alternative suppliers?

5.3.2 Speed

Some typical measures of speed might be enquiry response time, for example how long the professional practitioner takes to respond to a customer's phone call and arrange a meeting; order lead time, for example how long it takes for the landscape contractor to get a new dumper truck; frequency of deliveries, for example how often does the nursery make deliveries to the area in which the supply of plants is required; actual versus theoretical throughput, for example how long does it *actually* take to produce the drawing the professional practitioner promised they could produce in two days; and customer waiting lists, for example how long will the customer have to wait before their preferred landscape contractor is available to commence the project?

5.3.3 Dependability

Some typical measures of dependability might be the percentage of late completions, for example how many times has a landscape contractor failed to finish a project within the time agreed; average length of delay, for example how much longer than intended did it take the professional practitioner to complete their commission; proportion of product in stock, for example can the dumper truck manufacturer supply the particular model of dumper truck when it is required; and schedule adherence, for example can the landscape contractor rely on their place in the queue with the supplier of the built-to-order summer house required by the client?

5.3.4 Flexibility

Some typical measures of flexibility might be the time needed to develop a new product or service, for example how many ash trees might die before an agrochemical company develops a treatment for ash dieback disease; range of products or services, for example the dumper truck production plant might produce extremely reliable dumper trucks but only do so in a two-wheel-drive half tonne capacity; average production run, for example in what numbers can a nursery produce the New Zealand tree ferns *Dicksonia antarctica* in which it specialises; time needed to increase activity rate, for example how quickly can a landscape contractor bring in extra labour if a project is falling behind schedule; average capacity, for example how many projects can the professional practice manage simultaneously; and time to respond to change, for example how quickly can the professional practice increase its capacity to cope with an influx of new projects?

5.3.5 Cost

Some typical measures of cost performance might be variance against budget, for example how much more does a landscape contractor pay to acquire topsoil than the amount expected to be paid at the time of tendering; utilisation of resources, for example what size office is required by a professional practice employing just three practitioners; labour productivity, for example how many projects can one professional practitioner be expected to manage without assistance; efficiency, for example can the professional practice negotiate a better deal by renewing all its Information Technology equipment at one time, overheads, for example how many administrative staff are required to support the office of three professional practitioners; and cost per operational hour, that is the total cost of running the professional practice divided by the number of hours worked?

Analysing performance using the five performance criteria of quality, speed, dependability, flexibility and cost can be of benefit both to commercial and not-for-profit businesses. However, the balance of particular performance criteria may differ between these two.

> FIVE ESSENTIAL PERFORMANCE CRITERIA:
>
> - Quality
> - Speed
> - Dependability
> - Flexibility
> - Cost

After assessing performance against any or all of the five performance criteria, using the measure or measures most appropriate to their particular business, managers need to determine whether current performance is good, bad, or indifferent by making comparison with known performance standards (Slack, Chambers, Harland, Harrison and Johnston, 1995, pp. 730–32).

5.3.6 Historical performance

One such performance standard is likely to be historical performance; the manager comparing current performance in one or other of the five criteria with how the business is known to have performed historically in that particular criteria. For example, if a professional practice historically managed 20 projects simultaneously and currently manages 30 this represents a significant performance improvement. But is this the whole story?

5.3.7 Target performance

An increase in the number of projects managed simultaneously by a professional practice might be a response to a particular performance target. Targets are generally arbitrary standards, so are they appropriate or reasonable? Might the increased number of projects managed simultaneously have been achieved at the cost of an increased number of customer complaints, more defects, or a greater amount of waste caused by insufficient attention being paid to detail? Alternatively, the increase in the number of projects managed simultaneously by a professional practice might be due to current projects being smaller and less complex than those managed historically.

If the target of managing 30 projects simultaneously is what the business manager considers appropriate and this is what the practice actually achieves, then the performance of the practice must surely be appropriate? Not so. As indicated above, setting arbitrary targets in relation to one performance criteria alone, such as the number of projects managed simultaneously, often makes no sense in isolation without reference to other measures of performance and the level of performance *actually* acceptable to the customer.

5.3.8 Competitor benchmarking

If the manager is able to compare performance with one or more of the organisations with which the business competes *then* performance analysis begins to become very useful. For example, by comparing the level of gross profitability of a professional practice with the gross profitability of other practices of similar size and complexity, the manager can actually relate the organisation's performance directly to its competitive ability. This form of 'benchmarking' performance is equally valuable whether the business outputs goods or services and to both commercial and not-for-profit organisations, such as providers of public services.

Whilst public services operate effectively as local monopolies, for example a local parks department generally has no competition for the provision of public parks, such organisations still have to make the most effective use of their resources and benchmarking their performance with other similar organisations is a useful way of measuring how effectively they do so.

While it may be far more important for a charity to fulfil performance criteria in relation to dependability and speed, as lives may depend upon it, and cost may be less important, this does not mean that cost performance is unimportant to a charity. Although donors to a charity are likely to be driven fundamentally by a desire to support the aims of that particular charity, the donors will want to know their donations are being put to the most effective use and not squandered on overly expensive administration. Analysing its performance relative to other similar organisations is therefore just as important whether the transformation process of the business is concerned with making profit or providing outputs on a not-for-profit basis.

PERFORMANCE STANDARDS:

- Historical
- Target
- Competitor Benchmarking

What all successful businesses have in common is that the value of their outputs exceeds the cost of their inputs. The most important measure of performance in business is therefore that the process of transformation adds value. The value of the finished dumper truck must exceed the cost of the inputs and the processes that went into its manufacture so the production plant makes a profit for its shareholders. The value of a designed landscape (even though this may not be a monetary value) is generally considered to exceed the value of the materials and processes that went in to its creation. The value of the personnel and technology employed in a professional practice designing the landscape must also be exceeded by the value placed upon its services by its clients, as the professional practice too generally has to make a profit for its owners.

5.4 THE BUSINESS ENVIRONMENT

As was illustrated by Figure 5.2 inputs to a business transformation process both transformed (materials, information and customers) and transforming (facilities and staff) produce outputs; the output of one transformation process provides input to the transformation process of another business; and each business will be reliant upon consumption of their output in order to replenish the resources required to maintain the process of transformation.

The inter-relationships between business transformation processes form not only a continuous and interlinked cycle but are also just one part of a complex and integrated group of influences known as the business environment. The business environment affects not just the process of transformation but also the acquisition of input resources and the consumption of transformation outputs. In examining the business environment (Worthington and Britton (1994) pp. 6-8) a useful distinction can be made between those factors that have a general influence; factors legal, political, economic, social or technological, arising locally, nationally or internationally and dealt with shortly; and operational influences such as resources, resource markets, customers, and competitors that are factors normally much closer to home and are considered in the next section under the sub-heading 'Market Appraisal'.

5.4.1 Legal

All business activities, from the establishment of a trading organisation to the sale of goods or services, are influenced by law; that is a set of rules designed to regulate and control the activities of individuals or groups, enforcing minimum standards of conduct, for example minimum standards of health and safety in the workplace (discussed in Chapter 4). The legal environment is also enabling, in that it provides a means by which a business can have an independent existence from its members (discussed in Chapter 6) and provides stability for the conduct of business both within and across boundaries.

All businesses enter into legal contracts (discussed in Chapter 2) whether for the supply of goods or services or their sale. When businesses act as intermediaries between parties, for example a professional practitioner overseeing implementation of proposals on behalf of a client, they enter into an agency agreement (discussed in Chapter 3 and Chapter 7). Powerful (and in some cases unscrupulous) suppliers make it necessary for law to provide consumer protection in contracts where the consumer is, or may be, at a disadvantage. For example the Consumer Credit Act and the Sale of Goods Act.

5.4.2 Political

Policies influencing business activity are made by politicians and government employees. They affect businesses directly (by such things as tax levels and importation restrictions) or indirectly, for example by the increased cost of fuel resulting from political instability in oil rich nations; an illustration that political influence is not restricted to state boundaries. Because business activity takes place within and across boundaries the political arrangements, both where the business is located and where it trades, can have a fundamental impact on the operation.

Political systems tend to reflect social values, such that a traditional Labour government might favour public services when making its policies whilst a Conservative government might provide greater impetus to private sector entrepreneurs. Democratic societies have regular elections between competing parties with their alternative policies. Elections create uncertainty which can present opportunities upon which certain businesses might be able to capitalise. Political uncertainty may also create risks that a business will want to control.

The impact of politics upon business will depend to some degree on the nature of the business. For example, multinational corporations operating on a global scale will be more concerned with the stability of political regimes than the owner of a small local shop might be. It is important to note that business are frequently pro-active in the political dimension, not least through trade associations willing and able to represent the interests of their members by political lobbying.

5.4.3 Economic

Macroeconomics is concerned with the wider economic environment in which business must operate. For example, the decision of the UK government in 1992 to remove sterling from the Exchange Rate Mechanism of the European Monetary System. This sent the value of sterling against other world currencies into freefall, making UK exports cheaper (good news for a business selling their output in countries other than the UK, for example the dumper truck manufacturer with a worldwide market for their goods) but imports much more expensive (bad news for a business dependent upon transformation inputs sourced from countries outside the UK, for example a landscape contractor buying plants from Dutch or German nurseries). A 'market-based' economy, where resources and businesses are in private ownership to do with as they wish, arguably addresses the three fundamental questions of what to produce, how to produce it and how to distribute it, by encouraging free market forces. Customers effectively determine what is produced and how much it is sold for as a product of what the consumer is willing to buy and at what price. Business activity is therefore shaped by, but also helps to shape, the economic context in which it exists.

5.4.4 Social

For the majority of businesses labour is a vital input to the transformation process. The quantity and quality of labour available for a workforce is affected by a number of social factors including the size of the population. According to BBC News online (21 October 2007) the UK population of 60 million was forecast to rise to 69 million by 2031 and 75 million by 2051. However, BBC News online (30 June 2011) reported that in 2010 the UK population saw its biggest increase in almost half a century such that it had, in fact, risen to 62.7 million by that point; according to the Office of National Statistics (29 March 2012) 73.2 million being a figure likely to be breached by 2031. Population size depends on birth rate, death rate and net migration (how many people come into the country and how many leave). The age structure or 'demographic' of the population is vital to business. A UK population tending to live longer, with a consistent decline in the birth rate since the 1960s, means increasing numbers of pensioners and fewer people of working age while the impact of population changes on products and services consumers wish to purchase might, for example, mean a less mobile population has less demand for large designed open spaces intended for sport and recreation. Fewer people of working age, a tendency towards a shorter working week and a greater number of holidays, could result in less labour for the transformation process. By contrast 'supply and demand' suggests that increasing wages lead to reduced demand for labour and consequently a greater availability thereof.

5.4.5 Technological

Advanced industrial nations such as the UK require a higher proportion of educated workers who possess specific job-related skills. Over the last 40 years or so business has been disinclined to invest in skills training and government policies have done little to encourage this sort of forward thinking. As a result the UK lags somewhat behind other developed nations in regard to the education and skills of the workforce. On a more positive note the National Insurance Scheme and private healthcare provided by many UK employers provides sickness pay and treatment to maintain a relatively healthy workforce.

Technology is vital to business, both in the organisation of production and in production itself. Technological change leads to the introduction of new products; changes in production methods and in the organisation of production; changes in the quality of resources; and new ways of distributing products and storing information. For example, landscape professional practice underwent nothing short of a revolution when the processes of design moved from the drawing board to the computer screen; altering the physical process of drawing and correction; making the process of visualisation easier; improving communication of ideas to clients; as well as facilitating much easier and quicker exchange of data between participants in the design process.

Technological investment serves to increase the productive potential of a business by investing in the means of production, for example the increase in productivity wrought by Computer Aided Design, but also improved economy by investing in the means of delivering goods and services, for example the economy provided by increased use of email rather than the printing and posting of letters with its use of physical resource and inherent delay.

Technical innovation, whether in respect of product or process, impacts upon the industrial structure of a nation, its workforce and its consumers. Research and development is generally the process by which technical innovation occurs which leads, in turn, to the development of new products and processes to increase productivity and add value to the transformation outputs of business organisations.

ENVIRONMENTAL FACTORS OF GENERAL INFLUENCE:

- Legal
- Political
- Economic
- Social
- Technological

5.5 MARKET APPRAISAL

For any business to remain successful it must continue to satisfy customer demand and market expectations. The ability of a business in these respects will change over time as do market demands. For example, a nursery producing the New Zealand Tree Fern *Dicksonia antarctica* would at one time have sold but a few plants in the UK, to those with large greenhouses or who were prepared to carefully wrap the growing tip to protect it from the winter cold. Since the south of the UK has begun to enjoy milder winters, the growing of these 'exotic' species outdoors has become not only possible but popular. This popularity represents an opportunity for the nursery to exploit; the strength of the business might be that its workforce are experts in cultivating these plants; its weakness might be that it doesn't have sufficient growing area to increase production; and the threat the business might face is that it grows the plants in larger numbers and then finds the increased demand to have been a short-lived phenomenon.

5.5.1 Resources

In approaching the form of 'SWOT' analysis (Worthington and Britton, (1994) pp. 374-375) illustrated above; 'strengths'; 'weaknesses'; 'opportunities'; and 'threats', one of the principal considerations of a business manager will be the availability of input resources for the transformation process at the heart of the particular business operation.

As discussed above, input resources may be transformed (materials, information and customers) or they may be transforming (facilities and staff). Businesses have a considerable dependency on the suppliers of these resources and may need to organise their own operations accordingly. The professional practitioner might very well have a burning desire to live and set up practice on a Scottish island but the relative lack of a local customer base; of a suitably skilled labour force; and the increased cost of delivering a service to the areas in which it is more likely to be required may represent significant weaknesses and threats to this particular business model. Supplier success is often inextricably linked to the decisions and/or fortunes of their customers. For example the supplier of Information Technology, who hitherto supplied our Caledonian-bound professional practitioner, might find sales declining as the new landscape practice has a reduced demand for Information Technology owing to a reduced workload, or simply lacks a broadband connection.

5.5.2 Resource markets

A business might, where practicable, acquire resources overseas and this might, in turn, provide it with a competitive strength. For example, the landscape contractor who sources plants from Dutch or German nurseries might be able to price their services below their competitors paying higher prices to acquire plants from UK nurseries. However, this purchasing strategy brings with it the threat of uncertainty and instability as a result of politics or economics. For example, the landscape contractor might fall foul of fluctuations in the exchange rate as a result of buying plants in Euros and selling in sterling.

> **SWOT ANALYSIS**
>
> (Worthington and Britton, (1994) pp. 374-375):
>
> - Strengths
> - Weaknesses
> - Opportunities
> - Threats

5.5.3 Customers

For a business to be successful and remain so it must create a continuous supply of the goods and services the customer requires. What the customer *actually* wants may be influenced by the business; parts of the business; business networks; or advertising media that may stimulate or create demand for something other than what the consumer currently wants. The role of 'marketing' is to convince the consumer they must have particular goods or services, or the goods and/or services of a particular supplier, as opposed to those of its competitors.

5.5.4 Competitors

Competition is an important part of the business environment. Competition in the supply chain, that is different organisations competing to supply inputs to the transformation process, generally drives down supply costs and improves productivity. The organisation consuming inputs is likely also to be competing for consumers of its outputs. Competition then is equally applicable to the input and output sides of the transformation processes undertaken by any businesses.

It is vital for a business to identify not only who are its most likely customers, that is to say what are the target markets for the business, but also who the business must compete with and what are the strengths and weaknesses of competitor organisations relative to its own. In considering how a business should go about creating a demand for its goods and/or services Preddy (1997, p. 29) asks the question 'If you cannot clearly explain to yourself what you are, what you do, who you do it for and how you do it, how can you hope to explain it to other people?'

5.6 BUSINESS PROMOTION

By utilising the transformation model of business at Figure 5.1 we considered what might be the central objective, or the core activity, of a particular business and, by means of the 'SWOT' analysis above, considered what might be the competitive strengths; weaknesses; opportunities; and threats of such a business. We have therefore gone some way towards addressing the question posed above, of how the manager might position, that is to say promote, the business.

Business positioning is a balance of products, prices, promotional campaigns and places of operation; what Preddy (1997, p. 29) terms 'the traditional "Four Ps" of the marketing mix'. For example, the fully worked design proposals that are the 'product' of the professional practitioner might be 'priced' to appeal to the highly competitive market that is commercial house builders. The 'places of operation' for the practice would therefore be within a reasonable distance of the main centres of housing development; perhaps the south-east of England. We therefore need to consider how our example professional practice might 'promote' its services to its target market, that is to say the variety of 'promotional campaigns' available to the business manager. According to Preddy (1997, p.53) the business manager has two basic 'toolkits' for delivering their sales message to their defined target market. 'Both of the toolkits and the tools they contain are essential parts of any good marketing programme.'

These 'toolkits' comprise indirect marketing, where a focused proposition is put to a group with similar interests but not named individuals, and direct marketing which involves a highly skilled one-to-one approach aimed at carefully selected and named individuals.

Examples of indirect marketing include public relations campaigns via media; advertising in publications; general mailshots; business directories and registers; exhibitions and trade shows; sponsorship; and personal appearances at events and awards.

Examples of direct marketing include public relations through carefully cultivated personal contacts; telephone contact; and personal mail.

According to Preddy (1997, p.54) 'each is valid, but not a straight replacement for another. They work best in combination'.

Where landscape professional services are concerned, which tend by nature to be very personal, it is often found that indirect marketing is a useful way to raise the public profile of the practice and this, in turn, is of value when implementing carefully researched and subtly approached direct marketing. It is, however, often the latter which actually brings in the work or, if not immediately, ensures that the practice is included on a preferred list of suppliers when the need for landscape professional services arises with that particular customer.

For the reader who wishes to explore marketing strategies in greater depth, Rogers (2011, pp.373-409) provides a very helpful appraisal of different marketing techniques from an American perspective.

THE 'FOUR P'S' OF THE MARKETING MIX

(Preddy (1997, p.29)):

- Products
- Prices
- Promotional campaigns
- Places of operation

CHAPTER SUMMARY

- Businesses may be commercial organisations intended to make profits for their shareholders, or they may be not-for-profit organisations intent on reinvesting gains in the pursuit of their charitable or public service aims
- The context in which businesses operate is a complex, continuous and interlinked cycle influenced by a broad range of environmental factors
- Business performance may be analysed by quality; speed; dependability; flexibility; and cost
- For any business to remain successful it must continue to satisfy customer demand and market expectations
- What the customer wants may be influenced by the marketing mix

6

Business Management

THE AIMS OF THIS CHAPTER ARE TO:

- Describe alternative legal formats for business
- Introduce the rudiments of financial accounting
- Explain how to interpret information contained within financial statements

---

Having considered in Chapter 5 the operational, environmental and market factors that affect business performance together with how business performance is analysed, we now consider the various forms that business organisations concerned with the provision of professional services might take in the private, not-for-profit and public sectors, together with the advantages and disadvantages of each trading form.

6.1 PRIVATE SECTOR ORGANISATIONS

Private sector organisations, that is to say, businesses funded by private investments and normally concerned with generating profits to provide a return on the owners' investment, comprise sole trader, partnership, and limited company with subtle variants – particularly of the latter two, from time to time occurring.

6.1.1 Sole trader

A sole trader, that is to say a person commencing business on their own account, is the simplest of trading forms, with the owner/manager being entitled to make sole decisions as to what to produce, where to produce it, where to sell it and whom to employ.

The sole trader contributes the original capital to the business, by personal savings or borrowing, and receives all the gains (if any) that accrue; such profits very often being reinvested to provide working capital with which to fund the continuing operation or to reduce borrowing.

Should losses accrue to a sole trader, these too are the responsibility of the owner/manager who has unlimited personal liability, that is to say in the event of a sole trader accruing debts that the business cannot pay, debtors of the business are entitled to recover what is owed from the sole trader's personal assets. This will often result in the sole trader being declared bankrupt.

A sole trader tends to be the most popular and dominant form of business (based on numbers) because there are few restrictions, other than those relating to trading name (the name of the business cannot be the same as that of a registered company) and Value Added Tax registration (if income exceeds £79,000 per annum as at February 2014). Although a sole trader must keep a record of income and expenditure in order to determine profits on which Income Tax must be paid, there is no requirement to file business records in a public place.

The failure rate of sole traders is high, often due to unpaid debts, increased competition, rising interest rates on debt, falling demand (all of which are common to all businesses), lack of funds for expansion, lack of research, and insufficient management skills (the latter are less common problems in larger businesses).

6.1.2   Partnership

The Partnership Act (1890) defines a 'partnership' as a 'relationship which exists between persons carrying on a business in common with a view to profit'. A partnership can range, for example, from a husband and wife running a nursery business as joint owners to very large firms of professional practitioners, including those in the landscape profession.

There need not be any formality to the partnership, but it is generally held to be preferable that a 'deed of partnership' stating the rights, responsibilities and allocations of each partner, be drawn up before the commencement of business.

Ownership is shared between the partners, of which there is generally to be a maximum of 20. However, in some types of business, particularly professions, a special dispensation allows the business to have many more partners (100+) working in numerous offices. Businesses with more than 20 partners must register as a company unless exempt from the rule.

All partners have joint and several unlimited liability which, as with sole traders, means each partner is liable in full for any debts of the organisation and each may be sued in turn, or their personal assets seized, until the debt is satisfied in full.

A partnership is jointly financed by the partners or their personal borrowings and profits are shared. This will be in accordance with the allocations stated in the partnership agreement and is likely to reflect relative status within the business and the contributions of individuals; a senior partner being likely to receive a greater allocation of profits than does a junior partner.

The advantages of a partnership include shared responsibilities, a broader skills base and increased capital, whether working capital or capital for expansion. The disadvantages of a partnership are potential disagreements and that the actions of one partner are binding on all partners.

Larger partnerships and those involved in providing professional services, where the business has the potential to be sued for very large amounts of money in negligence actions (discussed in Chapter 3) are increasingly adopting the status of Limited Liability Partnership which enjoy most of the benefits of limited companies without being as onerous to administer.

6.1.3   Limited company

A limited company consists of two or more individuals holding shares, though there may be only one active participant. The company may or may not have employees, and the originating capital is provided by the shareholders, who may or may not be actively involved in the operations of the business. Rewards are received in the form of salaries, dividends on share capital or both.

In law a company is an incorporated association with its own legal identity, distinct from those who own it, unlike the sole trader and partnership. This means all business assets belong to the company rather than to the shareholders. Likewise, the shareholders' personal assets do not normally belong to the business, meaning personal liability is limited by the extent to which an individual shareholder has invested in the business unless the individual concerned has provided a personal guarantee, such as for bank loan.

A company is normally formed by registration with Companies House, including the filing of 'Memorandum and Articles of Association' setting out what the company will do; the basis of share ownership; the powers of directors; and the name of the company which, once registered, cannot be used by any other trading organisation. This also means that a company being newly established cannot take the name of an existing limited company, not even if the proposed name is that of the principal shareholder in the new venture.

The general public is normally excluded from purchase of shares in a limited company because the shares are not traded on stock markets, but they may be made available to individuals by private negotiation. The restriction on the sale of shares and therefore on share capital ensures that, although there are many limited companies, the majority are small or medium-sized enterprises and often family businesses.

A limited company must file annual accounts with Companies House, though for smaller companies there is a dispensation as to the level of information required and not until the company turnover exceeds a stated amount (£6.5 million in the 2014/15 tax year) must financial accounts be audited, that is attested to by an independent auditor.

6.1.4   Public limited company

A public limited company or PLC is much like a private limited company but reserved for large organisations where the general public must be permitted to invest in shares through stock market trading.

Public limited companies share all the same characteristics of private limited companies but are much more regulated. They too must have a minimum shareholding of two but it is much more common for them to have many thousands of shareholders, if not millions.

A public limited company must have a minimum share capital of £50,000 which need bear no relationship to the number of shareholders; must have at least two directors though it will often have many more; and must submit fully audited annual accounts which have to be publicly available.

As in the case of design, engineering and project management consultancy W.S. Atkins PLC (extracts of whose financial report are reproduced later in this chapter), public limited companies are normally national or international organisations of considerable size and, as such, are far fewer in number than private limited companies.

Public limited companies are much more influential than private companies in terms of output, investment, employment and consumption of input resources because of their scale of operations.

> PRIVATE SECTOR TRADING FORMS
>
> - Sole Trader
> - Partnership
> - Limited Company
> - Public Limited Company

6.2 NOT-FOR-PROFIT ORGANISATIONS

Not-for-profit organisations, that is, those whose central objective is social or charitable and any trading gains generated are reinvested to further those aims, take a number of different forms. Not-for-profit organisations are increasing in number due to greater interest in social enterprise and the introduction of new trading forms such as the charitable incorporated organisation.

6.2.1 Charitable incorporated organisation

A charitable incorporated organisation, like a trust, must be registered with the Charities' Commission, but thereafter the similarities between the two are fewer. Unlike a charitable trust the charitable incorporated organisation has a separate legal identity and, as such, is entitled to hold business assets, which in the case of a charitable trust could only be held by the trustees thereof. Because the assets of a charitable incorporated organisation are held by the business, its liability is limited to those assets and not to the personal assets of the trustees who administer it, of which there must be at least three.

A charitable incorporated organisation is required to submit business accounts but not until the business is earning more than £250,000 per year is it necessary for those accounts to be audited. Just like a charitable trust there is no requirement to pay tax on any income earned provided the income is used to further the charitable aims of the organisation.

6.2.2 Company limited by guarantee

Common among not-for-profit organisations is a company limited by guarantee, that is to say, a company in which liability is limited to the amount the members have undertaken to contribute, as opposed to the much more common company limited by share capital, that is to say, the form of limited company outlined above.

6.2.3 Consumer co-operative society

Also found in the not-for-profit sector is the consumer co-operative society. These originally developed out of anti-capitalist sentiment of the mid-nineteenth century as a means of providing good quality, competitively-priced food. Today the original 'Co-op' boasts a multi-billion pound turnover (and in 2014 £2.5 billion trading losses); millions of members; 3,000 food stores; factories; farms; travel agencies; funeral directors; and so on.

The economic climate of the early twenty-first century has seen a resurgence in the formation of consumer co-operative societies as a means of communities, particularly rural communities, taking over the management of vital community businesses such as pubs and village shops.

The consumer co-operative society belongs to its members and is run by an elected committee or board. The original idea of profits being returned to members in the form of cash dividends was long ago replaced by trading stamps (the precursor to loyalty cards or a points based discount scheme) and by reinvestment in areas intended to benefit the members, such as lower prices, higher quality and the like.

6.2.4 Workers co-operative

Also found in the not-for-profit sector is the workers' cooperative. Spanning a wide range of industries, including manufacturing, construction, engineering and retailing, in a workers' co-operative assets are owned and notionally controlled by the members, of which there must be a minimum of seven. Workers' co-operatives operate on democratic principles, membership being open to all employees of the organisation and every member having one share. As a result, it is theoretically possible for the senior management of a workers' co-operative to be voted out by the staff. In practice, workers' co-operatives and their assets are managed much like any other large-scale business and many such organisations appear as huge industrial and retail leviathans, indistinguishable from multinational, high-street, trading-names.

Surplus shares in a workers' co-operative are allocated by democratic agreement and ownership is restricted, both in terms of the number of shares available and because they are not available to trade on stock exchanges. Because of these restrictions workers' co-operatives are heavily reliant upon retained capital and loans and, although the focus is nominally on the employees, many of these businesses are long-standing, prudent and therefore cash-rich organisations.

> **NOT-FOR-PROFIT TRADING FORMS**
>
> - Charitable Incorporated Organisation
> - Company Limited by Guarantee
> - Consumer Cooperative Society
> - Workers' Cooperative

6.3 PUBLIC SECTOR ORGANISATIONS

By contrast to the private sector, where funding comes from shareholders or loans, the public sector is funded from the tax payer in the form of monies collected and distributed by central and/or local government. In the public sector the state owns assets of various forms and uses them to provide goods and services considered to be of public benefit, that is to say of benefit to its citizens, even if the provision of such goods and services results in a loss to the exchequer.

Public sector organisations come in a variety of forms including central government departments, for example the Department of the Environment, Food and Rural Affairs; local authorities such as Surrey County Council or Guildford Borough Council; regional bodies such as health authorities; quasi-autonomous non-governmental organisations (quangos) to which government has devolved power but still provides funding, for example the Arts Council; central government trading organisations, for example Her Majesty's Stationery Office; and public corporations comprising former nationalised industries such as British Coal, British Steel, British Telecom and so on, privatised in the 1980s and after.

Particular sections of the public sector, especially local authorities, have a long history of involvement in the marketing of goods and services, for example theatres; sports facilities; museums; and the activities that surround them. Public sector trading organisations were traditionally managed by local authority departments under the control of a chief operating officer but have increasingly been converted to companies and trusts. Companies and trusts provide a degree of independence from local authority control (considered beneficial in a competitive trading environment); access to market capital by an easing of central government restrictions on borrowing (particularly so with public/private finance initiatives); and an increase in competitiveness of the services by reducing or removing departmental overhead costs.

After successive governments concluded public services could be delivered more efficiently by commercial organisations, many public sector trading organisations have now been transferred into private ownership and management. Where private companies continue to provide vital public services, they are scrutinised by industry-specific regulatory bodies set up for the purpose, particularly in relation to the provision of essential utilities such as water, electricity and gas.

> **PUBLIC SECTOR TRADING FORMS**
>
> - Central Government Departments
> - Local Authorities
> - Regional Bodies
> - Quasi Autonomous Non-Governmental Organisations
> - Central Government Trading Organisations
> - Public Corporations

6.4　FINANCIAL ACCOUNTING

Within even the smallest of business organisations, the recording of financial transactions (sometimes referred to as book keeping) and day-to-day business operations are likely to be performed by different individuals with different skill sets. In small business organisations, it is likely that day-to-day recording of financial transactions will be dealt with in-house and an independent firm of accountants will prepare and finalise year-end financial statements and tax returns. In larger organisations, it is likely that in-house departments will deal with all financial accounting matters and firms of auditors will be employed to independently check and verify calculations; returns submitted; and the information available to shareholders, capital markets and bankers. One way or another, all business organisations are likely to require the input of an accountant at some stage, and it is imperative that business managers are able to correctly interpret the financial statements accountants produce.

Business manager(s) will be assisted in decision making and control activity by referring to the financial reports; shareholders, or potential investors, require information on the performance of their investments by reference to the income derived from their shareholding and how it has been achieved; creditors such as banks and suppliers need to know if the organisation can meet its financial obligations; and governments require financial information to formulate statistics and to ensure the correct amount of Corporation Tax and Income Tax are paid.

Some important conventions to note in relation to financial statements are that figures are presented for both the current and the previous trading period, thereby allowing interested parties to see at a glance whether financial performance has improved or declined during the current accounting period. Figures in brackets represent negative amounts and notes refer to comments on the financial statements generally presented elsewhere in the finalised reports.

6.4.1　Profit and loss accounts

Sometimes referred to as an 'income statement' as in Figure 6.1, a profit and loss account records 'sales revenue', that is to say the gross value of goods or services sold; 'cost of sales', that is the cost of materials and labour in the production of

Consolidated Income Statement for the year ended 31 March 2013

	Notes	2013 £m	2012 £m
Gross revenue (Group and share of joint ventures)		1,775.5	1,769.8
Revenue	2	1,705.2	1,711.1
Cost of sales		(1,088.7)	(1,097.1)
Gross profit		616.5	614.0
Administrative expenses		(512.4)	(476.8)
Operating profit	2	104.1	137.2
Comprising			
- Underlying operating profit		109.8	110.5
- Exceptional items	8	4.3	30.9
- Amortisation and impairment of acquired intangibles		(10.0)	(4.2)
		104.1	137.2
Profit on disposal of businesses/non-controlling interests	6	4.5	7.2
Share of post-tax profit from joint ventures	3	3.8	1.9
Profit before interest and tax		112.4	146.3
Finance income	4	3.4	4.1
Finance costs	4	(12.5)	(14.9)
Net finance costs	4	(9.1)	(10.8)
Profit before tax		103.3	135.5
Comprising			
- Underlying profit before tax		104.5	101.6
- Exceptional items	8	4.3	30.9
- Amortisation and impairment of acquired intangibles		(10.0)	(4.2)
- Profit on disposal of businesses/non-controlling interests		4.5	7.2
		103.3	135.5
Income tax expense	5	(14.9)	(28.7)
Profit for the year		88.4	106.8
Profit/(loss) attributable to:			
Owners of the parent		88.7	106.7
Non-controlling interests		(0.3)	0.1
		88.4	106.8
Earnings per share			
Basic earnings per share	10	91.0p	109.0p
Diluted earnings per share	10	88.8p	106.6p

Fig. 6.1 Sample Profit and Loss Account. Reproduced with permission of Atkins.

the goods and/or services sold; and 'administrative expenses', that is the cost of administering the business including such things as salaries paid to managers, vehicle costs, office rental, Information Technology, stationery, insurances, accountancy costs and so on. The intention is that 'sales revenue' should exceed the 'cost of sales' in order that a 'gross profit' is produced. Gross profits are, in turn, intended to exceed 'administrative expenses' in order for the business to produce a net or 'operating' profit to be returned to the shareholders of the business or reinvested in future performance.

As can be seen from Figure 6.1 the basic information contained in a profit and loss account; sales revenue; cost of sales; and administrative expenses, is further analysed to show particular items contributing to operating profit (in the example shown, these include such things as 'exceptional items' and 'profit on disposal of businesses/non-controlling interests') to arrive at 'profit before interest and tax'. Interest earned on investments and interest paid on borrowings, or 'net finance costs' are taken into account to arrive at 'profit before tax', which is again analysed. The amount payable in tax to the government (an often very complex calculation most often dealt with by the organisation's accountant and beyond the scope of this book) is then included as 'income tax expense' to arrive at 'profit for the year' and how this equates to 'profit per share' for the owners, that is to say the shareholders, of the business.

The profit and loss account is only one of the important documents that must be included with financial reports and it must be read in conjunction with other records because there are, in fact, a number of intrinsic problems associated with profit and loss accounts alone.

Profit and loss accounts are only a 'snapshot in time' based on the value of invoices raised for the goods and services provided by the business. The 'sales revenue' reported is therefore a measure of the amount invoiced and not what has actually been paid for. So what about if the customer doesn't pay? As the old maxim has it 'a sale is a gift until it's paid for'!

Similarly, 'cost of sales' is based upon the value of purchase invoices recorded at the time the financial reports are prepared and does not reflect what has *actually* been paid for by the business and goods or services procured by the business for which invoices have not yet been received.

In short, at the time the financial statements are prepared it is possible for the business to be illiquid, that is to say devoid of cash with which to continue to trade, despite a substantial sales volume or, alternatively, the business could have substantial amounts of cash until such time as purchase invoices are actually paid, with which it is doing nothing.

6.4.2   Balance sheets

The object of a 'balance sheet' is to provide information on the values of 'capital assets', that is to say assets not readily turned into cash such as buildings, vehicles and equipment; 'current assets' such as cash at the bank and amounts owed to the business in the form of unpaid invoices (referred to as 'trade and other receivables' in Figure 6.2); 'liabilities' in the form of amounts owed by the business (including those referred to as 'trade and other payables' in Figure 6.2) to arrive at 'net assets', that is to say, the 'total equity' value of the business and how the equity is accounted for at the time the financial statements were prepared.

6.4.3   Cash flow forecasting

For a business to trade successfully and profitably the business manager(s) need to know the current cash situation at any point in time. This is achieved by 'bank reconciliation' that is to say cross-referencing the detail included on bank

Consolidated Balance Sheet as at 31 March 2013

	Notes	2013 £m	2012 £m
Assets			
Non-current assets			
Goodwill	11	211.4	205.0
Other intangible assets	12	39.6	46.3
Property, plant and equipment		50.7	51.5
Investments in joint ventures	3b	7.1	3.5
Deferred income tax assets		92.2	84.2
Derivative financial instruments		0.3	0.3
Other receivables		20.0	18.2
		421.3	409.0
Assets of disposal group classified as held for sale	7	5.8	6.9
Current assets			
Inventories		0.2	1.1
Trade and other receivables		449.2	445.3
Financial assets at fair value through profit or loss		35.9	35.0
Available-for-sale financial assets		-	6.1
Cash and cash equivalents		201.5	167.0
Derivative financial instruments		0.5	0.4
		687.3	654.9
Liabilities			
Current liabilities			
Borrowings		(59.8)	(105.7)
Trade and other payables		(486.7)	(506.1)
Derivative financial instruments		(1.4)	(1.7)
Current income tax liabilities		(40.5)	(34.3)
Provisions for other liabilities and charges		(1.5)	(3.6)
		(589.9)	(651.4)
Liabilities of disposal group classified as held for sale	7	(5.2)	(0.1)
Net current assets		98.0	10.3
Non-current liabilities			
Borrowings		(49.4)	(4.9)
Provisions for other liabilities and charges		(4.4)	(6.8)
Post-employment benefit liabilities	13	(298.8)	(265.3)
Derivative financial instruments		(1.3)	(2.5)
Deferred income tax liabilities		(20.1)	(18.8)
Other non-current liabilities		(1.5)	(1.6)
		(375.5)	(299.9)
Net assets		143.8	119.4
Capital and reserves			
Ordinary shares	14	0.5	0.5
Share premium account		62.4	62.4
Merger reserve		8.9	8.9
Retained earnings		72.2	47.5
Equity attributable to owners of the parent		144.0	119.3
Non-controlling interests		(0.2)	0.1
Total equity		143.8	119.4

Fig. 6.2   Sample Balance Sheet. Reproduced with permission of Atkins.

statements with what business records show has been invoiced by suppliers (creditors) and invoiced to customers (debtors) to determine what payments have *actually* been made and received and what amount of cash is *actually* available at a given point in time. Though perhaps tedious, to be of any value bank reconciliation must be diligent, methodical and accurate.

Having established from the profit and loss account how much has been made in the most recently reported accounting period; from the balance sheet in what form the business assets are held; and from the bank reconciliation what is the current cash position, the business needs to be able to forecast how the current cash situation is likely to alter over a given period as a result of creditor invoices received and not yet paid and debtor invoices sent and not yet paid, or what is termed a 'cash flow forecast'.

The business might be in possession of substantial amounts of cash because of payments made that have not yet been presented to or cleared by the bank – cash that might be put to good short-term use by avoiding further borrowing, reducing existing overdraft facilities or obtaining short-term investment interest.

By regularly checking what has actually passed through the bank and what has not, the business manager, the book-keeper, the accounts department or whoever might be responsible, is able to determine whether the business needs to make a cash transfer to or from an interest-bearing account, whether the business needs to arrange a short-term overdraft and whether there is a major cash flow crisis looming. Not surprisingly, banks and other lenders tend to be more helpful and certainly charge less for their facilities if cash requirements are foreseen, discussed and prepared for in advance.

CHAPTER SUMMARY

- Private sector business organisations providing professional services consist of sole traders, partnerships, limited companies and public limited companies
- Not-for-profit business organisations providing professional services include charitable incorporated organisations, companies limited by guarantee, consumer co-operative societies and workers' co-operatives
- Public sector business organisations providing professional services include central government departments, local authorities, regional bodies, quasi-autonomous non-governmental organisations (quangos), central government trading organisations and public corporations comprising former nationalised industries
- A profit and loss account records 'sales revenue' against 'cost of sales' and will hope to show a 'gross profit' has been generated by the business
- Gross profits are intended to exceed the 'administrative expenses' in order that the business might produce a net profit to be returned to shareholders or reinvested
- The object of a balance sheet is to provide the business manager with information on the values of 'capital assets'; 'current assets'; and 'liabilities' to arrive at 'net assets' or the capital worth of the business
- Bank reconciliation and cash flow forecasting enables business manager(s) to accurately predict and prepare for cash demands or cash surpluses

7

Engaging a Landscape Professional

> THE AIMS OF THIS CHAPTER ARE TO:
>
> - Describe the range of services the landscape professional practitioner may be engaged to provide and how they relate to the work of other professionals
> - Explain the advantages and disadvantages of different forms of agreement for the provision of professional services
> - Explain the suite of professional engagement documents provided by the Landscape Institute to its members and how they should be used
> - Explain the advantages and disadvantages of different methods of calculating a fee proposal and when they might be used

7.1 SCOPE OF SERVICES

The extent of the professional practitioner's responsibilities will depend upon what has been agreed with the client. The professional practitioner may agree simply to produce a range of sketch proposals and develop that of the client's choosing to the master plan stage or to provide detailed planting plans (outside the remit of the present text); schedules (discussed in Chapter 11); specifications of materials and workmanship (discussed in Chapter 12); full contract documentation (discussed in Chapter 12) including conditions of contract (discussed in Chapter 13); to oversee the process of obtaining competitive quotations/tenders (discussed in Chapter 14); to administer the resultant contracts (discussed in Chapter 15); to provide quality control; or any or all of the above services.

Alternatively, having completed the design process, the professional practitioner may introduce a fellow professional specialising in project procurement and administration to produce contract documentation and undertake the processes of tendering and project management on behalf of the client.

In any event, the most successful professional relationships are those that proceed in an atmosphere of mutual trust and goodwill. The client has an important role to play in the working relationship by providing the professional practitioner with adequate information on the project, the site and the budget from the outset. Preliminary discussion with the client must provide sufficient information for the professional practitioner to determine whether the client's requirements are feasible within the client's available budget and preferred timescale.

7.2   FORM OF AGREEMENT

Whatever is agreed between the professional practitioner and the client, under a 'traditional' procurement strategy (discussed in Chapter 9) the agreement for the professional practitioner's fees is completely separate from agreements between the client and contractor(s) for implementation of the works, albeit such agreements are normally set up and administered by the professional practitioner acting as the client's agent (discussed in Chapter 2).

For an agreement to become legally binding there must be an offer; an acceptance; a consideration; and an intention to be contractually bound (discussed in Chapter 2). Whatever passes between the professional practitioner and a potential client during preliminary discussions, the terms of any agreement must be evidenced in writing; a verbal agreement or a 'gentleman's handshake' will simply not suffice.

In its simplest form, an agreement may be evidenced by an exchange of letters between the client and the professional practitioner. On small projects, especially those for 'domestic' as opposed to commercial clients, a simple exchange of letters may be sufficient, provided the letters clearly establish the extent of the professional practitioner's responsibilities and/or liabilities; the professional practitioner's fees and/or how the fees are to be calculated (discussed later in this chapter); at what stages fees are to be paid; under what circumstances the professional practitioner's commission may be terminated; and provisions for the resolution of any contractual disputes that might arise (discussed in Chapter 16).

An exchange of letters must be clear and concise. Any terms purporting to be 'standard' must be quoted in full. Neither party is entitled to assume the other party has access to the full text of 'standard' terms unless the parties have an established course of dealings by which it is clear those particular terms are understood.

Where an exchange of letters is deemed sufficient the professional practitioner may provide a duplicate copy of their offer letter for signing and returning by the client. By this means the client may indicate acceptance of the terms offered, provided the terms are sufficiently clear and capable of acceptance (as discussed in Chapter 2).

Unless the landscape professional practitioner is also a lawyer, an agreement based on an exchange of letters can be problematic. Care must be taken to ensure the terms in an exchange of letters are appropriate and legally enforceable; courts have broad ranging powers to interpret the meaning and content of contractual agreements and have a long-established history of so doing (discussed in Chapter 2).

Recourse to the courts in situations where the terms of agreement are not sufficiently clear rarely satisfies both parties, if indeed it satisfies either. There are always winners and losers in the court process. It is often said that the only real 'winners' are the lawyers who earn substantial fees for their trouble.

In practice, it is preferable and very much cheaper for the agreement between a professional practitioner and client to be based upon Conditions of Appointment and Memorandum of Agreement drafted by lawyers specifically for the purpose.

Whilst large multi-national practices may have their own Conditions of Appointment and Memorandum of Agreement and/or retained lawyers dealing with such matters on their behalf, it is much more common for standard Conditions of Appointment and Memorandum of Agreement to be used, such as those provided by the Landscape Institute to its members.

7.3   THE LANDSCAPE CONSULTANT'S APPOINTMENT

The Landscape Institute's *Landscape Consultant's Appointment* was first published in May 1988 and revised in May 1998. It was withdrawn in September 2011 due to legislative changes that made it invalid. The document was updated and re-issued in December 2013 aligning itself with the 'Plan of Work' introduced by the Royal Institute of Building Architects which itself is based upon a set of unified stages agreed through the Construction Industry Council.

The 'Plan of Work' incorporated in the 2013 version of the Landscape Institute's *Landscape Consultant's Appointment* incorporates 'Scopes of Services' S1 to S8. Helpfully, these new 'Scopes of Services' are cross-referenced to the former 'Work Stages' A to L for ease of use by professional practitioners more familiar with the earlier structure.

Whereas earlier versions of the Landscape Institute's *Landscape Consultant's Appointment* comprised a single document incorporating a Memorandum of Agreement; Appendix 1 detailing Work Stages A to L, of what 'Other Services' might comprise and the Conditions of Appointment; and Appendix II comprising a Schedule of Services to be undertaken and Fees to be charged, the 2013 version of *Landscape Consultant's Appointment* introduces an arguably unwieldy arrangement of separate, downloadable documents as follows:

   01 – Conditions of Appointment (which will apply to each appointment and will not be editable by the user)

   02 – Memorandum of Agreement (which is non-editable except for the details of the project; the parties to the agreement; the documents that comprise the agreement; and the signature sections)

   03 – Scopes of Services S1–S8 (fully editable documents intended to be flexible, so those sections not applicable to a particular project can be deleted

and those remaining may be personalised by the insertion of the professional practitioner's details or practice logo) comprising of:

S1: Landscape Design and Administrative/Post Contract Services

S2: Masterplanning Services

S3: Landscape and Visual Impact Assessment Services

S4: Landscape Planning Services

S5: Landscape Management Plan Services

S6: Stakeholder Engagement Service

S7: Landscape Maintenance – Design and Contract Administration Services

S8: Other Services

04 – Schedules of Fees and Expenses (fully editable documents intended to be used in conjunction with the Scopes of Services documents and to be amended so both sets of documents are consistent).

> **AIMS OF THE 2013 APPOINTMENT DOCUMENTS**
>
> (The Landscape Institute, December 2013):
>
> *The principal aims of the new appointment document are to:*
> - *Enable the Landscape Consultant and the Client to achieve a clear understanding of the services required by the Client;*
> - *Define the conditions concerning the provision of those services;*
> - *Set out the payment provisions relating to those services.*

According to the Landscape Institute's *Code of Standards of Conduct and Practice for Landscape Professionals* (referred to in Chapter 1) Landscape Institute members must not undertake a professional commission until they have agreed in writing the scope of the commission; the allocation of responsibilities and any limitations thereof; the fee or method of calculating the fee; provisions for termination of the agreement; and any provisions for dispute resolution. All four elements of the 2013 edition of The Landscape Institute's *Landscape Consultant's Appointment* are therefore required to provide what the Landscape Institute refers to as 'a fully enforceable contract' (The Landscape Institute, December 2013).

The Landscape Institute's *Landscape Consultant's Appointment* is not intended to be used for domestic clients without significant amendment. The Society of Garden Designers, however, provides documents specifically designed for such purpose.

7.4 THE PROFESSIONAL PRACTITIONER'S FEES

The Landscape Institute's *Engaging a Landscape Consultant – Guidance for Clients on Fees* published in 2002 was withdrawn because of inconsistencies with legislative changes.

Engaging a Landscape Consultant – Guidance for Clients on Fees offered guidance on alternative methods for charging fees, expenses and disbursements and was a valuable resource for inexperienced professional practitioners, not least because it included a method of calculating fees as a percentage of the overall project costs.

Whilst in the context of landscape projects, a fee graph based upon the Royal Institute of Building Architects model made little sense, since the value of landscape projects tends to be tiny by comparison with the construction costs of buildings or major engineering projects, nonetheless the fee graph contained within the 2002 *Engaging a Landscape Consultant – Guidance for Clients on Fees* was a means of obtaining a 'ball-park' figure or of contextualising fee bids calculated by other means.

According to The Landscape Institute (December, 2013) *Engaging a Landscape Consultant – Guidance for Clients on Fees* was withdrawn for several reasons, including because of 'alternative procurement methods currently available in the construction industry making the percentage fee scales, associated graph and complexity ratings obsolete'.

7.4.1 Calculating professional fees

Before considering alternative methods for charging fees, expenses and disbursements, and having gleaned from Chapter 6 something of trading forms and how the business manager might monitor and influence the financial performance of the business, it is necessary to consider how the professional practitioner should go about calculating the fees s/he actually needs to generate in order to make their business sustainable.

The income a professional practice needs to generate will differ substantially from one practice to another, not least because the large multi-national practice will expend huge amounts in 'overhead' costs, such as offices, administrative support staff, pensions, advertising and marketing, while the sole practitioner may well be working from their home at minimal expense.

Chapter 5 considered in some detail market appraisal and marketing tools and this too will influence, if not how much the professional practitioner needs to earn, how much the professional practitioner is able to charge for their services. For example, in London and the Home Counties the expectation is that professional fees are likely to be higher than in Wales or the North of England. To some extent this is a product of higher overhead costs, through larger salaries and more expensive offices, but allows the professional practitioner outside such areas to travel in order to earn higher fees.

In calculating what amount to charge for their services, the professional practitioner must firstly consider salaries, whether of the different levels of staff employed by a large practice or a public sector department or that of the sole practitioner. According to the Landscape Institute (July 2013) the most common salary range for chartered members in full time employment remains at £30,000–£39,000 although three per cent of Landscape Institute members reported earnings in excess of £100,000 per annum.

To the cost of salaries must be added employer's National Insurance contributions (broadly speaking 13.8 per cent on earnings in the 2014–2015 tax year) plus employee National Insurance (12 per cent on earnings between the primary threshold and the upper earnings limit in the 2014–2015 tax year) or the appropriate National Insurance rate for the self-employed sole trader.

The cost of funding a retirement pension is currently a topic of considerable debate. It is generally accepted that at least five per cent of gross earnings, that is to say earnings before the deduction of Income Tax and Employees National Insurance contributions, should be paid into a pension scheme to make adequate provision for retirement.

In calculating the fees needed to be earned, the professional practitioner must also make allowances for the cost of telephones; fax machines; broadband; mobile phones; tablets; desktop and/or laptop and/or notebook computers; appropriate software, which is likely to include Computer Aided Design; surveying equipment; desks; drawing boards; office storage; photocopying; postage costs; stationery; letterheads and business cards; advertising; protective clothing, such as waterproofs and boots; Professional Indemnity Insurance; Office Contents Insurance; Public Liability Insurance; Permanent Health Insurance (in case of long-term sickness, accident or incapacity); subscriptions to professional associations, journals and software licenses; annual accountancy and book-keeping costs; fees paid to credit agencies, factoring agencies and/or solicitors in respect of unpaid debts; office costs (whether rental or use of residence in the case of the sole trader); heating; lighting and maintenance.

As can be seen from the worked example in Figure 7.1 (based entirely upon notional figures that should not be relied upon) when all the business costs have been totalled up, an amount must be added for profit. The amount of 20 per cent used in Figure 7.1 is again a notional figure. The actual amount of profit to be included in the calculation of professional fees will be a 'balancing act' between that which the professional practitioner expects to make from their activities measured against what the particular market in which they operate will withstand in terms of the impact upon the rate per chargeable hour for their fees.

The 'Rate per Chargeable Hour' for fees in Figure 7.1 is a product of the 'Total Annualised Expenditure' divided by the number of chargeable working hours. The number of chargeable hours is arrived at by taking the number of working weeks after allowing for annual holidays (including eight days of bank holidays) and multiplying it by the average of 40 hours a week (albeit the hours actually worked in a week may be considerably more). This, however, is only part of the story, since allowance has to be made for hours worked that may well be productive but are non-remunerative.

Non-remunerative time includes travelling time, which is normally only charged one way or both ways but at half the hourly rate. Non-remunerative time will also

Professional Fees Calculation 2014/15 Tax Year

Salary	£ 40,000.00
Employer's National Insurance Contribution @ 13.8%	£ 5,520.00
Employee's National Insurance Contribution @ 12%	£ 4,800.00
Retirement Pension Contribution @ 5%	£ 2,000.00
Telephone/Fax/Broadband Costs	£ 468.00
Mobile Phone Contract	£ 420.00
Annualised Computer Costs	£ 1,600.00
Annualised Equipment Costs	£ 2,666.67
Copying Costs	£ 1,850.00
Postage Costs	£ 1,380.00
Stationery Costs	£ 1,800.00
Advertising & Marketing Costs	£ 15,000.00
Annualised Protective Clothing Costs	£ 266.67
Professional Indemnity Insurance	£ 800.00
Office Contents Insurance	£ 460.00
Public Liability Insurance	£ 250.00
Permanent Health Insurance	£ 324.00
Subscriptions	£ 1,800.00
Accountancy Fees	£ 4,600.00
Legal and Professional Fees	£ 2,000.00
Rental of Serviced Office	£ 12,000.00
Sub Total	£ 100,005.33
Gross Profit @ 20%	£ 20,001.07
Total Annualised Expenditure	£ 120,006.40
Rate Per Chargeable Hour	**£ 110.50**

Fig. 7.1 Worked Example of Calculating Professional Fees

include initial visits. These are vital to building relationships with clients and to gleaning information about potential commissions but are rarely paid for by the client. Such visits might be seen as business promotion and can be difficult to quantify. As can the time spent on business administration unless the professional practitioner employs somebody else to administer the business, in which case this is an identifiable 'Overhead' expense that could be included in the worked example at Figure 7.1. Similarly, the inexperienced practitioner is likely to take longer to complete a commission than a practitioner with years of experience. The former will have to reflect their relative inexperience either in their rate per chargeable hour or not charge for the full extent of their time in order to be competitive in their fees.

In reality, it is unlikely the professional practitioner will be able to charge for more than 25 out of every 40 hours worked. If the professional practitioner expects to take six weeks holidays a year and eight bank holidays, the total number of chargeable hours per year is therefore 1086.

Calculating the rate per chargeable hour as illustrated by the worked example in Figure 7.1 is prerequisite to the professional practitioner assessing the level of fees that must be charged for any particular commission.

The 2013 edition of The Landscape Institute's *Landscape Consultant's Appointment* recommends using one of three common methods of fee calculation adopted by other construction industry professionals, those being percentage fees, time charges, and lump sum fees. Each of these is dependent upon an understanding of the rate per chargeable hour and will now be considered in turn:

7.4.2 Percentage fees

For fees to be expressed as a percentage of the construction cost of a project the client and the professional practitioner must firstly agree the 'Scopes of Services' and the approximate construction budget for the total project or each stage thereof.

An agreed percentage can be applied to the total construction cost of the project or an agreed percentage for each 'Scope of Services' at each stage of the construction. In either case, the professional practitioner will have to estimate the likely number of hours required and multiply this by the rate per chargeable hour (discussed above) before converting the eventual total to a percentage of the total construction cost or the cost at each stage. For example, using the entirely fictional rate per chargeable hour calculated in Figure 7.1, if the professional practitioner estimated 280 hours' work (totaling £30,940.00) were required on a project with a projected construction cost of £350,000 then the percentage fee to be agreed would be 8.84 per cent of the construction cost.

Bearing in mind that the amount of work, relative to the cost of the project, is greater for smaller projects, percentage fees on small projects will generally be higher than on large projects.

Because construction costs of landscape schemes tend to be very much smaller than those for buildings or infrastructure projects, the landscape professional's fees quoted as a percentage of construction costs are normally considerably higher than those of building architects or engineers fees quoted as a percentage of construction costs for a building or major infrastructure.

Where there are numerous commissions on the same project, a separate percentage fee should be agreed for each separately identifiable commission, as the amount of work undertaken by the professional practitioner in total is likely to be greater than it would have been for a single commission with the same overall project budget.

The effect of phased implementation, or elements of a project being undertaken by different contractors under separate negotiations with the professional practitioner, can be a considerable increase in the percentage of the overall construction costs being charged as fees. For example, professional practitioner's fees amounting to 17.83 per cent on project construction costs of £160,000 where the project involved four or five separate commissions.

7.4.3 Time charged fees

Having calculated the rate per chargeable hour as illustrated by Figure 7.1, it becomes a very straightforward matter of whether or not this rate is an acceptable fee the client will agree to pay.

Time charged fees are generally applied where the cost of providing the professional practitioner's services cannot be related to construction costs. For example, where construction costs are not known when the professional practitioner's commission is agreed with the client. Likewise, when the Scopes of Services to be provided by the professional practitioner cannot be linked to an identifiable construction element. For example, where the professional practitioner is commissioned to undertake advisory or feasibility work in advance of any construction taking place.

In quoting time charged fees the professional practitioner must quote hourly rates for all levels of staff expected to be involved with a particular project, including, for example, the rate per chargeable hour for a Chartered Member of the Landscape Institute, a Quantity Surveyor, a Clerk of Works, and for administrative support staff. It is, of course, necessary to maintain records for the time expended by each member of the team in the event the commission is obtained in order to ensure the client is appropriately charged.

A quotation for time charged fees should include the dates on which the chargeable rates per hour for each member of the team are to be reviewed. For example, a long-running project might span one or more financial years and it is normal to recalculate the rate per chargeable hour each year in order to reflect changes in business overheads and/or expenditure.

Ultimately the client must decide whether the time charged fees quoted by the professional practitioner are acceptable or not. The realities of business mean some negotiation may be necessary. The professional practitioner may have to exercise commercial judgment. For example, a professional practitioner currently short of work might consider it prudent to offer their services at less than the chargeable rate per hour calculated in accordance with Figure 7.1 on the basis it is preferable to earn less per hour and be working than seeking a higher rate and unemployed; not least because many business overheads are fixed expenses whether the professional practitioner is working or not.

7.4.4 Lump sum fees

Lump sum fees can only be used where the Scopes of Services can be clearly defined. Only when it is clear what a commission involves can the professional practitioner estimate how many hours work are involved in completing the task and the members of the team likely to be involved.

In the same way as it would be unreasonable of a professional practitioner to expect a contractor to supply a 'fixed-price' quotation for a parcel of work not yet defined, so it is unreasonable of a client to expect a professional practitioner to quote a lump sum fee for a commission when the services required, the complexity and the amount of work are unclear.

Where lump sum fees are quoted it is important the parameters of variation are agreed at the outset. For example, the professional practitioner may quote for the production of three sketch proposals and developing one of the client's choosing to a master plan. If the client doesn't like any of the three sketch proposals and wants more options, or the client wants two different sketch proposals developed further, it must be clear this constitutes additional chargeable work over and above the lump sum fee; additional work normally to be agreed on a time charged basis.

Ultimately, the method of calculating fees to be used is a question of who takes what risk. Lump sum fees place all the risk on the professional practitioner and are only normally appropriate for straightforward commissions where, with experience, it is evident that what is involved in one project is pretty much the same as another.

Time charged fees place all risk on the client in undertaking to pay the professional practitioner at the agreed rate irrespective of how many hours work are involved.

Percentage fees arguably spread the risk between the parties. Although calculated by reference to the chargeable rate per hour, if the construction cost of the project turns out to be substantially less than expected the client will pay less in fees and the professional practitioner will earn less. The opposite is, of course, true. If project implementation costs increase, unless the professional practitioner's fee agreement allows for renegotiation, the client could end up paying considerably more than was expected and the professional practitioner earning considerably more.

METHODS OF CALCULATING PROFESSIONAL FEES:

- Percentage
- Time Charged
- Lump Sum

7.4.5 Expenses and disbursements

Expenses and disbursements incurred by the professional practitioner are usually charged to the client at cost, that is to say, at the amount paid by the professional practitioner without the addition of any profit, and in addition to the fees charged.

Expenses and disbursements include such items as printing, reprographics, postage, hotel and travelling expenses, and mileage charges in the professional practitioner's car. They also include fees to local authorities in respect of planning applications, the cost of procuring Ordnance Survey data, and, for example, the cost of soil testing.

Related professionals, such as Quantity Surveyors, Structural Engineers, Contract Administrators and Arboricultural Consultants, unless part of the professional practitioner's team, should all be paid separately (and preferably directly) by the client to avoid the professional practitioner being held accountable for failings in services outside his or her area of expertise. The professional practitioner may normally charge for any time they personally expend in the appointment of related professionals or the administration of their services.

Likewise, the professional practitioner may charge for time spent locating and managing suppliers but only where this activity does not reasonably fall within the Scopes of Services already commissioned by the client.

CHAPTER SUMMARY

- The extent of the professional practitioner's responsibilities will depend upon what has been agreed with their client

- Once the design process has been completed the professional practitioner may choose to introduce a fellow professional specialising in project procurement and administration to produce contract documentation and undertake the processes of tendering and project management

- Under a 'traditional' procurement strategy the agreement for the professional practitioner's fees is completely separate from agreements between the client and contractor(s) for implementation of the works

- The professional practitioner's commission must be agreed in writing with the client in advance of providing services

- The three common methods of fee calculation adopted by construction industry professionals are 'percentage', 'time charged' and 'lump sum'

- Expenses and disbursements incurred by the professional practitioner are usually charged to the client at cost

SECTION III
Legislative Bases of Assessment and Analysis

8

Development Control and Environmental Management

> THE AIMS OF THIS CHAPTER ARE TO:
>
> - Explain the importance of sustainable development in the context of the National Planning Policy Framework 2012
> - Define what is likely to be included within 'permitted development rights' and therefore not require an application under development control policy
> - Introduce the major pieces of legislation relevant to landscape, trees, heritage, woodlands, ecology and wildlife

Development control and environmental management legislation is a very large and complex subject, aspects of which have been and will continue to be covered in a great many authoritative texts. The present volume does not purport to provide a practical guide to the details of planning applications, appeals, environmental impact assessments or environmental protection measures; instead, it provides an overview of the major pieces of legislation upon which development control and environmental management are based so the professional practitioner might understand at what point practical interventions are required and ensure they have the necessary expertise with which to comply with the legislative requirements and their professional code of conduct.

The carrying out of building, engineering, mining or other operations in, on, over or under the land, or the making of any material change in the use of any building or land, for example change of use from agricultural land or woodland to a garden, is controlled by the planning process and generally requires planning permission.

The major pieces of legislation on which the planning process in England is based are the Town and Country Planning Act 1990, the Planning and Compulsory Purchase Act 2004, and the National Planning Policy Framework of 2012.

Applications for planning permission must generally be determined in accordance with the local development plan. Local planning authorities should have up-to-date development plans in place; should be guided by the National

Planning Policy Framework of 2012 in drawing up such plans; and the National Planning Policy Framework of 2012 should be a material consideration in the planning authority's decision making process.

The National Planning Policy Framework of 2012 indicates proposed development that accords with an up-to-date local development plan should be approved; proposals which do not accord with an up-to-date local development plan should be refused unless material considerations indicate otherwise; and that sustainable development should be at the heart of planning authority decision making and therefore of developer proposals.

> SUSTAINABLE DEVELOPMENT
>
> (Department for Communities and Local Government, March 2012, p. 2):
>
> *Resolution 42/187 of the United Nations General Assembly defined sustainable development as meeting the needs of the present without compromising the ability of future generations to meet their own needs. The UK Sustainable Development Strategy Securing the Future set out five 'guiding principles' of sustainable development: living within the planet's environmental limits; ensuring a strong, healthy and just society; achieving a sustainable economy; promoting good governance; and using sound science responsibly.*

In order that future development should be sustainable, according to the National Planning Policy Framework of 2012 the planning system must perform a number of roles: economic, social and environmental.

> PLANNING POLICY ROLES
>
> (Department for Communities and Local Government, March 2012, p. 2):
>
> - *An economic role – contributing to building a strong, responsive and competitive economy, by ensuring that sufficient land of the right type is available in the right places and at the right time to support growth and innovation; and by identifying and coordinating development requirements, including the provision of infrastructure;*
>
> - *A social role – supporting strong, vibrant and healthy communities, by providing the supply of housing required to meet the needs of present and future generations; and by creating a high quality built environment, with accessible local services that reflect the community's needs and support its health, social and cultural well-being;*
>
> - *An environmental role – contributing to protecting and enhancing our natural, built and historic environment; and, as part of this, helping to improve biodiversity, use natural resources prudently, minimise waste and pollution, and mitigate and adapt to climate change including moving to a low carbon economy.*

The implication of the National Planning Policy Framework of 2012 is that local planning authorities must positively seek opportunities to meet the objectively assessed development needs of their area; be sufficiently flexible to adapt to rapid change unless doing so would significantly outweigh the benefits when assessed against the National Planning Policy Framework of 2012; approve proposals that accord with the local development plan without delay; and where a local development plan does not exist, is silent or relevant policies are out of date, should grant permission for development unless doing so would significantly outweigh the benefits when assessed against the National Planning Policy Framework of 2012.

In response to the National Planning Policy Framework of 2012, communities are required to develop plans supporting the strategic development needs set out in the local development plan, including policies for housing and economic development, and shape development in their area that is outside the strategic element of the local development plan but accords with its objectives.

8.1   PERMITTED DEVELOPMENT

Permitted development rights are derived under the Town and Country Planning (General Permitted Development) Order 1995 and amount to a general planning permission for certain types of limited development granted not by the local planning authority but by Parliament.

In some designated areas of the country permitted development rights are restricted. For example in Conservation Areas, National Parks and Areas of Outstanding Natural Beauty. In such areas it will be necessary to seek planning permission for development that would otherwise fall within permitted development rights.

Local planning authorities may remove permitted development rights by issuing an Article 4 direction. Most common in conservation areas (discussed later in this chapter) Article 4 directions are made when the character of an important area may be threatened by development. The effect of an Article 4 direction is to require a planning application for proposed development that would otherwise fall within permitted development rights.

Schedule 2 of the Town and Country Planning (General Permitted Development) Order 1995 sets out classes of development that do not normally require a planning application, of which those most commonly encountered by the landscape professional practitioner include:

> Part 1: Class E – Any building or enclosure, swimming or other pool within the curtilage of residential premises, incidental to the enjoyment of the dwelling, including for the keeping of poultry, bees, pet animals, birds or other livestock for the domestic needs or personal enjoyment of the occupants of the dwelling and the maintenance, improvement or alteration of such a building or enclosure.

Part 1: Class E development may be taken to include the building of a garage, stable or loose-box and should be read to include any structure or erection constructed above or below ground, for example a greenhouse, summerhouse, shed, gazebo, arbour, swimming pool or pond.

Part 1: Class E development will not be permitted if the building or enclosure is itself a dwelling; is to be closer to any boundary highway than the part of the original dwelling nearest to the highway or at any point within 20 metres of that highway; the proposed building would have a capacity greater than ten cubic metres; any part of the proposed structure would be within five metres of any part of the dwelling; the height of the proposed structure will be greater than four metres in the case of a building with a ridged roof or otherwise three metres; or the total area of ground covered by structures would exceed 50 per cent of the total area of the land (excluding that of the original dwelling).

Part 1: Class F – A hard surface within the curtilage of residential premises used for any purpose incidental to the enjoyment of the dwelling, for example a hard standing for boat, caravan, trailer or car.

Part 1: Class G – A storage container for domestic heating oil, provided the capacity of the proposed container does not exceed 3,500 litres; no part of the proposed container would be more than three metres above ground level; and no part of the proposed container would be closer to any boundary highway than the part of the original dwelling nearest to the highway or at any point within 20 metres of that highway.

Part 2: Class A – Gates, fences, walls or other means of enclosure provided any such structure adjacent to a vehicular highway would not exceed one metre above ground level; not greater than two metres in areas not adjacent to a vehicular highway, and the proposed structure is not within the curtilage of or enclosing a listed building (in which case planning permission will always be required).

Part 2: Class B – A means of access to a highway which is not a trunk road or a classified road, where that access is required in connection with any other permitted development.

Part 2: Class C – Painting to the exterior of any structure provided such application of colour is not for the purpose of advertisement, announcement or direction.

Part 4: Class A – Temporary buildings, moveable structures, works, plant or machinery required for the duration of operations being carried out on, in, under or over land, or on land adjoining, provided the operations do not involve mining and that, if planning permission is required for the operations, such permission will have been granted.

Part 4: Class A temporary development is permitted subject to the conditions that, when the operations have been carried out, any building, structure, works, plant or machinery having been permitted, will be removed and that any adjoining land on which the operations were temporarily permitted will, as soon as reasonably practicable, be reinstated to its condition before the temporary operations took place.

Part 4: Class B – Use of any land for any purpose for not more than 28 days in total in any calendar year, of which no more than 14 days in any calendar year may be for the purpose of holding markets; motor racing including trials of speed and practising for such activities; and war games conducted with weapons designed not to injure (including paint balling) excluding military activities or training exercises organised by or with the authority of the Secretary of State for Defence.

Part 4: Class B activities are not permitted within the curtilage of a building; for the provision of a caravan site; if the land is within a site of special scientific interest and the intended activities include motor sports, clay pigeon shooting or any war gaming; or the use involves display of an advertisement.

Schedule 2 of the Town and Country Planning (General Permitted Development) Order 1995 is extensive. The schedule includes classes of permitted development for a range of specialist situations including agriculture, telecommunications, forestry and mining.

Any form of building, engineering, mining or other operations or the making of any material change in the use of any building or land, other than those listed in Schedule 2 as included within the presumed grant of planning permission by Parliament, will normally require an application for planning permission to the local planning authority.

8.2   ENVIRONMENTAL IMPACT ASSESSMENT

Environmental Impact Assessment has been a requirement for certain types of development since 1985. The aim of Environmental Impact Assessment is to ensure that planning authorities fully understand the likely effects on the environment of the proposed development. According to the Landscape Institute and the Institute of Environmental Management and Assessment (2013, p5) 'EIA is a way of ensuring that significant environmental effects are taken into account in decision making'.

> **DEFINITION OF A DEVELOPMENT PROJECT**
>
> (European Union Directive 2011/92/EU):
>
> *The execution of construction works or of other installations or schemes, or other interventions in the natural surroundings and landscape including those involving the extraction of mineral resources.*

Within defined limits, Annex I to European Union Directive 2011/92/EU *The Assessment of the Effects of Certain Public and Private Projects on the Environment* lists development projects for which Environmental Impact Assessment is a prerequisite as:

- Oil refineries
- Thermal power stations
- Nuclear power stations and installations connected with them
- Smelting installations
- Installations handling asbestos
- Chemical installations on an industrial scale
- Road, rail or air infrastructure projects
- Inland waterways and ports
- Waste disposal installations including landfill
- Large scale groundwater abstraction
- Large scale water transfer schemes
- Waste water treatment plants
- Facilities for the extraction of petroleum and natural gas
- Dams and other installations designed for the holding back or permanent storage of water
- Pipelines with a diameter of more than 800 mm and a length of more than 40 km

- Installations for the intensive rearing of poultry or pigs

- Industrial paper and timber milling plants

- Quarries and open-cast mining

- Overhead electrical power lines with a voltage of 220 kV or more

- Large scale storage of petroleum, petrochemical, or chemical products

- Carbon dioxide capture and storage

- Any change to or extension of such projects

Annex II to European Union Directive 2011/92/EU *The Assessment of the Effects of Certain Public and Private Projects on the Environment* lists development projects for which the requirement for Environmental Impact Assessment may be decided on a case-by-case basis or within thresholds set by individual European Union Member States as:

- Projects for the restructuring of rural land holdings; for the use of uncultivated land or semi-natural areas for intensive agricultural purposes; water management projects for agriculture, including irrigation and land drainage projects; initial afforestation and deforestation for the purposes of conversion to another type of land use; intensive livestock installations (projects not included in Annex I); intensive fish farming; and reclamation of land from the sea.

- Quarries, open-cast mining and peat extraction (projects not included in Annex I); underground mining; extraction of minerals by marine or fluvial dredging; deep drillings, in particular geothermal drilling, drilling for the storage of nuclear waste or for water supplies and with the exception of drillings for investigating soil stability; surface industrial installations for the extraction of coal, petroleum, natural gas and ores, as well as bituminous shale.

- Industrial installations for the production and carrying of electricity, steam and hot water (projects not included in Annex I); surface storage of natural gas and fossil fuels; underground storage of combustible gases; industrial briquetting of coal and lignite; installations for the processing and storage of radioactive waste (unless included in Annex I), for hydroelectric energy production, for the harnessing of wind power for energy production (wind farms) and for the capture and storage of carbon dioxide (installations not covered by Annex I).

- Installations for the production of iron or steel; processing of ferrous metals; smelting of non-ferrous metals; refining of recovered products; application of protective fused metal coats including surface treatment of metals and plastic using an electrolytic or chemical process; hot-rolling mills; smitheries with hammers; manufacture and assembly of motor vehicles and engines; shipyards; aircraft repair and construction; manufacture of railway equipment; swaging by explosives; and roasting and sintering of metallic ores.

- Installations for the manufacture of cement; production of asbestos and asbestos products (projects not included in Annex I); manufacture of glass and glass fibre; smelting of mineral substances including the production of mineral fibres; manufacture of ceramic products by burning, in particular roofing tiles, bricks, tiles, stoneware or porcelain; and coke ovens.

- Installations (not included in Annex I) for the production of chemicals, pesticides and pharmaceutical products, paint and varnishes, elastomers and peroxides; treatment of intermediate products; and storage facilities for petroleum, petrochemical and chemical products.

- Installations for the manufacture of vegetable and animal oils, fats, dairy products, confectionery, syrup and industrial starch; brewing and malting; animal slaughter; fish meal and fish oil factories; sugar factories; and the packing and canning of animal and vegetable products.

- Industrial installations for the production of paper and board (projects not included in Annex I); pre-treatment or dyeing of fibres or textiles; tanning of hides and skins; cellulose processing and production.

- Installations for the manufacture and treatment of elastomer-based (rubber) products.

- Infrastructure projects (not included in Annex I) including industrial estates; urban development projects; shopping centres; car parks; railways and intermodal transhipment facilities; airfields; roads, harbours and port installations; fishing harbours; inland waterways; canalisation and flood-relief works; dams and other installations designed to hold water or store it on a long-term basis; tramways, elevated and underground railways used exclusively or mainly for passenger transport; oil and gas pipeline installations and pipelines for the transport of carbon dioxide; long-distance aqueducts; coastal erosion defences and maritime constructions capable of altering the coast; groundwater abstraction; artificial groundwater recharge; and water transfer resources.

- Other projects (not included in Annex I) including installations for the disposal of waste; waste water treatment plants; sludge deposition sites; permanent racing and test tracks for motor vehicles; storage of scrap iron and scrap vehicles; test facilities for engines, turbines or reactors; for the manufacture of artificial mineral fibres; for the recovery or destruction of explosive substances; and knackers' yards.

- Ski runs, ski lifts, cable cars and associated developments; marinas; holiday villages and hotel complexes outside urban areas; permanent camping and caravan sites; theme parks.

- Any change or extension to projects listed in Annex I or Annex II, already authorised, executed or in the process of being executed, which may have significant adverse effects on the environment.

Where the requirement for Environmental Impact Assessment is decided on a case-by-case basis or within thresholds set by individual European Union Member States, the selection criteria that must be taken into account are set out in Annex III to European Union Directive 2011/92/EU *The Assessment of the Effects of Certain Public and Private Projects on the Environment* as:

- The characteristics of projects, in particular the size of the project; its cumulative effect; use of natural resources; production of waste; pollution and nuisances; and the risk of accidents, having regard to the particular substances or technologies being used.

- The environmental sensitivity of areas likely to be affected by the proposed development, having regard to the existing land use; the relative abundance, quality and regenerative capacity of natural resources in the area; the absorption capacity of the natural environment, especially wetlands, coastal zones, mountains, forests, nature reserves and parks; areas classified and/or protected under legislation and/or in which the environmental quality standards laid down in legislation have already been exceeded; densely populated areas; and landscapes of historical, cultural or archaeological significance.

- The potential effects of projects having regard to the extent of the impact (geographical area and size of the affected population); the trans-frontier nature of the impact; the magnitude, complexity, probability, duration, frequency and reversibility of the impact.

In those situations (defined above) where Environmental Impact Assessment is required, the assessment must identify, describe and evaluate the direct and indirect effects of the proposed development on human beings, fauna, flora, soil, water, air, climate, landscape, material assets and cultural heritage. The assessment must also consider the interactions between these factors.

The process of conducting Environmental Impact Assessment is beyond the scope of this book. For the present purpose it is sufficient for the professional practitioner to understand the circumstances in which Environmental Impact Assessment is or may be required.

The professional practitioner should bear in mind that landscape and visual impact assessment, while comprising part of Environmental Impact Assessment, is frequently carried out informally 'as a contribution to the appraisal of development proposals and planning applications' ('The Landscape Institute and the Institute of Environmental Management and Assessment', 2013, p. 4).

8.3   TREE PRESERVATION ORDERS

The power to make a Tree Preservation Order is contained in the Town and Country Planning Act 1990 and the Town and Country (Tree Preservation) (England) Regulations 2012 and is intended to protect trees and woodland in the interests of public amenity.

A Tree Preservation Order prohibits the cutting down, topping, lopping, uprooting, wilful damage or destruction of protected trees or woodlands without written permission of the local planning authority. The protection applies to all types of trees, including hedgerow trees but not hedges, bushes or shrubs and prohibits damage to roots as well as to stems and branches.

In deciding whether it is expedient to serve a Tree Preservation Order the local planning authority should make an objective assessment of the individual tree, group of trees or area of woodland to determine the impact it has upon the local landscape or to the general public. The planning authority may do so of its own volition or at the request of interested parties, who need not be, and frequently are not, the owners of the land on which the tree or trees are situated.

Under the Town and Country (Tree Preservation) (England) Regulations 2012 a Tree Preservation Order comes into force on the date it is served and lapses after six months, unless it has been confirmed by the local planning authority. If there are no objections to an order it will be confirmed by the planning authority without further consultation. Where objections are made within the prescribed period, which cannot be less than 28 days, the objections must be considered before the planning authority decides whether to confirm the order.

According to regulation 14 of the Town and Country Planning (Tree Preservation) (England) Regulations 2012 cutting down, topping, lopping or uprooting of a tree may exceptionally be undertaken on trees protected by a Tree Preservation Order where:

- The tree is dead and poses an immediate risk, in which case the planning authority must be given written notice of the works as soon as practicable after they become necessary. The onus is on the person authorising the work to prove the tree was dead and dangerous. This requirement is normally met by obtaining a report from a suitably qualified person before commencing the operations and, where there is no immediate risk, by informing the planning authority of the intended operations at least five working days before they are due to commence.

- The works are required by an Act of Parliament or in order to abate a legal nuisance, for example to prevent obstruction of a public highway.

- The works are requested by a statutory undertaker in connection with the inspection, repair or renewal of any sewers, mains, pipes, cables or other apparatus of the statutory undertaker or to enable the statutory undertaker to carry out development permitted by the Town and Country Planning (General Permitted Development) Order 1995.

- The works are urgently required for national security purposes.

- The works are to fruit trees provided the work is in the interests of the business of fruit production. This means that fruit trees are only exempt if they are actively cultivated for the purpose of a business.

- The works are necessary to implement a development approved by a detailed planning permission.

- The works are requested to enable the Environment Agency to carry out development permitted by the Town and Country Planning (General Permitted Development) Order 1995.

- The works are requested by a drainage body where the tree interferes, or is likely to interfere, with the maintenance, improvement or construction of watercourses or of drainage works.

- The works involve only the removal of dead branches from a living tree.

- The works are required to remove an immediate risk of serious harm, in which case the planning authority must be given written notice of the proposed works as soon as practicable after they become necessary. The onus is on the person authorising the work to prove there was an immediate risk of harm. This requirement is normally met by obtaining a report from a suitably qualified person before commencing the operations and/or or by obtaining the written consent of the local planning authority prior to the works being undertaken.

- The works concern no more than pruning, in accordance with good horticultural practice, of any tree cultivated for the production of fruit.

If a protected tree or woodland is removed without permission, there is a legal duty on the landowner to replace it. If permission is granted for a tree to be cut down the planning authority can require a replacement. Where a new tree is planted as a replacement for one that was removed because it was dead, the new tree will be protected within the same Tree Preservation Order as the original tree.

Anyone who contravenes a Tree Preservation Order may be liable, on conviction in a Magistrates Court, to a fine of up to a £20,000 and serious offences may be committed for trial at a Crown Court where, if convicted, the perpetrator may be subject to an unlimited fine. This is a very significant departure from the historical situation, where fines were such that unscrupulous developers blithely uprooted and destroyed protected trees safe in the understanding the paltry fines imposed would be far outweighed by the development profits derived from so doing.

8.4   CONSERVATION AREAS

Conservation areas, originally designated under the Civic Amenities Act 1967, provide for the establishment of 'areas of special architectural or historic interest the character of which it is desirable to preserve or enhance'. There are now over 8,000 conservation areas in England designated for their special architectural and historic interest.

Conservation areas may vary in character, form and size, from small groups of historic buildings to major parts of a town or city. While they may contain listed buildings, this is not always the case. Often it is the sense of place created by different components such as unlisted traditional buildings, historic street patterns, open spaces, trees, boundary walls, views or sites of human activity, such as market places, that combine to provide special character.

Under the Planning (Listed Building and Conservation Areas) Act 1990 the permission of the planning authority will normally be required to demolish buildings or to alter their appearance with cladding; replacement windows; satellite dishes; solar panels; conservatories; extensions; conversion of roof spaces; laying of paving; or building of walls within conservation areas. The Act places a statutory duty on local planning authorities to preserve and enhance conservation areas while undertaking their planning duties.

Within conservation areas, the local planning authority must be consulted at least six weeks in advance of any proposed works to cut down, lop, top, prune, destroy or uproot trees, regardless of their individual amenity value. This enables the planning authority to assess the contribution the tree or trees make to the character of the conservation area and decide whether to confer protection by issuing a Tree Preservation Order.

8.5   FORESTRY REGULATIONS

The Forestry Commission was established in 1919 to protect Britain's forests and encourage good forestry practice by setting standards, giving advice, providing information and by offering grants for expanding, regenerating and managing forests and woodlands. The Commission also controls the felling of trees through the issue of felling licences.

There is a general presumption under the Forestry Act (1967) that any felling of living trees will require a felling licence unless an exemption applies. Everyone involved in the felling of trees, whether owner; agent; professional practitioner; timber merchant; or contractor must ensure that a felling licence has been granted where one is required. If there is no valid permission, or if the wrong trees are felled, all involved may be prosecuted.

If the woodland is protected with a Tree Preservation Order the local planning authority must be consulted before carrying out any felling (as discussed above). Since almost all felling work in a woodland is licensed under the Forestry Act 1967, the local planning authority may advise applying for a felling licence from the Forestry Commission who will then decide whether to consult with the local planning authority.

Large individual trees standing in fields or hedgerows may also require a felling licence from the Forestry Commission. Advice should be sought from either the local planning authority or the Forestry Commission before any work is commenced.

According to The Forestry Commission (April 2007) in any calendar quarter it is permissible for a land owner to fell, or have felled, up to five cubic metres of timber on their property without a felling licence provided no more than two cubic metres are sold, that is to say the majority of the timber felled is for domestic use.

Under the Forestry Act 1967 (as amended) and related regulations, the only other categories of exemption to the requirement to obtain a felling licence are:

- Lopping and topping (which usually includes tree surgery, pruning and pollarding)

- Felling included in an approved Dedication Plan

- Felling fruit trees, or trees growing in a garden, orchard, churchyard or designated public open space

- Felling trees which, when measured at a height of 1.3 metres from the ground have a diameter of eight centimetres or less

- Cutting thinnings with a diameter of ten centimetres or less

- Cutting coppice or underwood with a diameter of 15 centimetres or less

- Felling for the purpose of development approved by planning permission under the Town and Country Planning Act 1990

- Essential felling at the request of statutory undertakers

- Felling necessary for the prevention of danger or abatement of a legal nuisance (wherever practicable seeking the agreement of the Forestry Commission in advance that the tree presents a real and immediate danger)

- Felling necessary to prevent the spread of a quarantine pest or disease in accordance with a notice served by a Forestry Commission Plant Health Officer under the Plant Health (Forestry) (Great Britain) Order 1993 (as amended)

- Felling imposed by or under an Act of Parliament

A Forestry Commission felling licence will normally include a condition that felled areas must be restocked and the newly planted trees maintained for a period not exceeding ten years. The Forestry Commission will discuss any proposed restocking condition with the applicant before a licence is issued. Only in exceptional circumstances will a felling licence be issued to fell trees without subsequent restocking. Such an application will be assessed under the Environmental Impact Assessment (Forestry) Regulations 1999. A felling licence for thinning woodland will be issued without a restocking condition.

8.6 HEDGEROWS REGULATIONS

The Hedgerows Regulations 1997 make provision for the protection of 'important' hedgerows including those in association with residential premises. The local planning authority must be consulted before removing or destroying hedgerows of at least 20 metres (66 feet) in length, more than 30 years old and of 'importance' as defined by the Regulations.

Part II of Schedule I to The Hedgerows Regulations 1997 is extensive but, in essence, a hedgerow may be considered 'important' if:

- It marks the boundary, or part of the boundary, of at least one parish or township existing before 1850

- It incorporates an archaeological feature which is a scheduled ancient monument

- It is situated wholly or partly within an archaeological site recorded as a scheduled ancient monument or on land adjacent to and associated with such a site

- It marks the boundary of a pre-1600 AD estate or manor or is visibly related to any building or other feature of such an estate or manor

- It is recorded as an integral part of a field system pre-dating the Enclosure Acts; is part of or visibly related to any building or other feature associated with such a system; that system is substantially complete; or is of a pattern recorded by the local planning authority as a 'key landscape characteristic'.

- It contains 'protected', 'endangered', 'extinct', 'rare' or 'vulnerable' species as categorised by sub-paragraph (3) of Part II of Schedule I to The Hedgerows Regulations 1997 or is recorded by the local planning authority as having done so, in the case of animals and birds, within the last five years and, in the case of plants, as having done so within the last ten years

- It contains at least seven woody species; six woody species and at least three of the features specified in sub-paragraph (4) of Part II of Schedule I to The Hedgerows Regulations 1997; at least six woody species including one or more of Black Poplar (*Populus nigra* ssp *betulifolia*), Large Leaved Lime (*Tilia platyphyllos*), Small Leaved Lime (*Tilia cordata*) or Wild Service Tree (*Sorbus torminalis*); at least five woody species and at least four of the features specified in sub-paragraph (4) of Part II of Schedule I to The Hedgerows Regulations 1997.

- It is adjacent to a bridleway or public footpath or byway open to all traffic; includes at least four woody species, ascertained in accordance with paragraph 7(3) of Part II of Schedule I to The Hedgerows Regulations 1997; and at least two of the features specified in paragraph 7(4)(a) to (g) of Part II of Schedule I to The Hedgerows Regulations 1997

The local planning authority must be given at least six weeks' notice of any intention to uproot or destroy an 'important' hedgerow in order that it might assess the importance of the hedgerow using the criteria set out in the Regulations. If no objection is received from the local planning authority, permission for the hedgerows removal is deemed to have been granted.

Regulation 6 of the Hedgerows Regulations 1997 permits certain types of work to be carried out to 'important' hedgerows, including the removal of such a hedgerow if the works or the removal are required:

- To make a new opening to land in substitution for an existing opening, provided the existing opening is filled by the planting of a similar hedge within eight months of making the new opening

- For obtaining temporary access to any land in order to give assistance in an emergency

- For obtaining access to land where another means of access is not available or is available only at disproportionate cost

- For the purposes of national defence

- For carrying out development for which planning permission has been granted or is deemed to have been granted

- For carrying out work required by statutory undertakers

- For preventing the spread of, or ensuring the eradication of, notifiable plant pests

- For the carrying out of works to a highway

- For the proper management of the hedgerow

The professional practitioner should bear in mind that the removal of any trees within a hedgerow may require a Forestry Commission felling licence (discussed above) and that trees within a hedgerow may also be protected by a Tree Preservation Order.

As a rule of thumb, if in doubt, the professional practitioner is well advised to check with the local planning authority and/or the Forestry Commission before proceeding with works concerned with the removal or destruction of potentially 'important' hedgerows.

8.7   HABITATS REGULATIONS

The Conservation (Natural Habitats, &c.) Regulations were introduced in 1994 and amended in 2007. Under the Regulations it is an offence to deliberately kill or cause significant disturbance to a protected species; to deliberately destroy their eggs; or to damage or destroy a breeding site or resting place used by such species, for example a bat roost or a dormouse nest.

Some of the most important protected species likely to be encountered by landscape professional practitioners in the UK are: all 17 species of bat, dormouse, great crested newt, otter, sand lizard, smooth snake, and natterjack toad as well as a whole range of plant species.

Before the 2007 amendments to The Conservation (Natural Habitats, &c.) Regulations, if damage was 'an incidental result of a lawful operation' and reasonable precautions had been taken, it would not have been an offence if damage occurred. Since the 2007 amendments it may now be a criminal offence if operations are carried out without making appropriate investigations, for example undertaking an ecological survey of an area likely to contain protected species, and obtaining appropriate permissions before carrying out operations likely to be detrimental to protected species and/or their habitats.

Professional practitioners need to consider the potential presence of protected species and follow good practice guidance to avoid committing an offence. In some cases management practices may need to be modified or rescheduled to a less sensitive time of year and, where this is not possible or adequate, a European Protected Species mitigation licence may need to be obtained from Natural England under the Habitats and Species Regulations 2010 in order to remain within the law.

> CHAPTER SUMMARY
>
> - The carrying out of building, engineering, mining or other operations in, on, over or under the land, or the making of any material change in the use of any building or land, generally requires planning permission
>
> - Environmental Impact Assessment must evaluate the effects of proposed development on human beings, fauna, flora, soil, water, air, climate, landscape, material assets and cultural heritage
>
> - A Tree Preservation Order prohibits the cutting down, topping, lopping, uprooting, wilful damage or destruction of protected trees
>
> - Within conservation areas the local planning authority must be consulted in advance of works to cut down, lop, top, prune, destroy or uproot any trees
>
> - Under the Forestry Act (1967) any felling of living trees will require a felling licence unless an exemption applies
>
> - The local planning authority must be consulted before removing or destroying 'important' hedgerows
>
> - It is an offence to deliberately kill or cause significant disturbance to a protected species, its breeding site or a resting place used by such species

SECTION IV
Project Implementation

9

Understanding Contractual Relationships

> THE AIMS OF THIS CHAPTER ARE TO:
>
> - Explain the roles and responsibilities of the main participants in landscape contracts
> - Explain how to identify client requirements and expectations and to establish and maintain a successful professional relationship
> - Describe the range of project procurement strategies that may be adopted and the pros and cons of each

9.1 ROLES AND RESPONSIBILITIES

In approaching project implementation, it is necessary to consider the roles and responsibilities of the three main protagonists within landscape contracts – client, professional practitioner and contractor – since being able to place each of these within their correct context is fundamental to understanding what follows thereafter. Smooth and efficient project implementation requires the professional practitioner to understand and fulfil their own obligations and to be clear what is required from other participants. The professional practitioner is frequently responsible for coordinating the project from start to finish, and must do all within their power to encourage the cooperation of all concerned.

9.1.1 The role of the client

The role of the client is paramount since it is they who 'set the train in motion' either by commissioning the services of a professional practitioner, often but not exclusively a Chartered Member of the Landscape Institute, or by entering into some form of agreement with a contractor.

It is perfectly possible and a frequent occurrence, for the client to reach agreement with a contractor without recourse to professional advice. It is, however, very much more common for the client to engage the services of a professional practitioner (discussed in Chapter 7). The professional practitioner then guides the development of the project proposals and contract documentation (discussed in Chapter 12); assists in the choice and appointment of suitable contractor(s) (discussed in Chapter 14); and administers the resultant contract(s) (discussed in Chapter 15).

The initial impetus for a project will come from the client providing an outline brief. The client must indicate the location of the works; this may be anything from an individual feature of a small domestic garden to the infrastructure of a major town centre redevelopment. Likewise the extent of the works; does the client require a professional practitioner to see a project through from inception to implementation and final completion (discussed in Chapter 7), or do they simply want a contractor to construct a new landscape feature such as a path or terrace? The client must indicate the intention of the project; the approach adopted when implementing landscape proposals as a condition of town and country planning legislation will be substantially different to that in respect of a client choosing to enhance the environs of their family home.

The client should be encouraged to provide as much information as they are willing to impart as regards their available budget. This can be a difficult issue on which the professional practitioner will frequently be required to offer sensible and sensitive advice. It is in the interests of all concerned to determine from the outset whether the client's aspirations are remotely achievable within the funds available. As might be imagined, this is an area in which it is all too easy to inadvertently cause offence. Not surprisingly, therefore, well-developed interpersonal skills can be a considerable asset to the successful professional practitioner.

It is essential that the client indicate their preferred timescale for the project and whether there are particular constraints to be considered. For example, the anticipated opening date of commercial facilities for which delay might prove very expensive. It is vital for the smooth and efficient running of a project (not to mention the ultimate satisfaction of the client) that consideration is given to achievability of such objectives from the outset.

Having entered into an agreement, whether for the provision of professional services or for implementation, the client is obliged to make the site available and to facilitate access so the commissioned services may be undertaken. That a client should make the site accessible may appear an obvious statement but it is, in fact, not uncommon for projects to be delayed even before they begin. Picture a client who wrongly anticipates the completion of one contractor's works upon which a second contractor's operations depend. The second contractor is, for example, unable to commence 'soft' landscaping works, perhaps the planting of trees, shrubs and ground cover, because the first contractor, engaged to construct 'hard' landscape elements, has yet to build the raised planters and beds into which the 'soft' components are to be placed. In circumstances such as these it is quite possible for the second contractor's works to be delayed by a few days, possibly weeks, or in extreme cases (particularly when dealing with bare-rooted nursery stock) until the next appropriate planting season.

Having entered into a contractual agreement, the client is required to pay for the services commissioned. Payment must be made at the agreed rates and intervals provided the works have been completed to the agreed standard. In general terms, the client's obligations in this respect are exactly the same whether in relation to the services of a contractor or those of the professional practitioner.

The precise detail of the client's obligations will very much depend upon the nature and content of each particular agreement, a subject covered in detail elsewhere in this book. For the present purpose, it is important simply to appreciate the professional and moral obligation of the professional practitioner to do all within their power to ensure the client fulfils those obligations.

That said, it should be noted that 'privity of contract' (discussed in Chapter 2) ensures the professional practitioner will not normally be held legally accountable should the client fail to perform any or all of their duties owed to a contractor or the supplier of goods or services.

> ROLES AND RESPONSIBILITIES OF THE CLIENT:
>
> - Commissioning of services
> - Outline brief
> - Facilitating access to the site
> - Payment for services rendered

9.1.2 The role of the contractor

A contractor will normally be appointed in order that their resources (labour, plant and equipment, technical expertise, and contacts with the manufacturers and suppliers of materials) may be deployed in project implementation. Project proposals may have been produced by the client, by their appointed professional practitioner, or by the contractor as part of a combined 'design and build' package, of which more will be said later in this chapter.

In simple terms, legally binding contractual agreements (discussed in Chapter 2) consist of an offer and an acceptance, together with evidence of an intention to be legally bound, and some form of consideration; most commonly a promise to pay for services rendered, goods supplied, or a combination of the two.

In submitting a formal quotation or tender (discussed in Chapter 14) a contractor is offering to undertake works as they have been described; to the standard requested; at the price quoted; and, unless indicating to the contrary, under the terms and conditions provided at the time of the invitation to tender or quote. For example, terms relating to timescale, quality of workmanship, materials and so on, must be adhered to. The client's acceptance of a quotation or tender indicates a binding promise to pay for the services rendered or goods supplied.

By the client's act of acceptance the contractor is bound. In simple terms this means legal action may be taken against a contractor for any failure to perform to the agreed standard, within agreed timescales, or to do so for the agreed amount. This is, in fact, very much an oversimplification and, as discussed in Chapter 15, the majority of contractual agreements provide for terms to be varied, by negotiation between the parties or by some pre-determined mechanism, to reflect the changing circumstances that frequently occur.

Once a formal agreement has been entered into, the contractor will ordinarily be responsible for the employment conditions and the payment of all their suppliers and sub-contractors according to the principle known as 'privity of contract' (discussed in Chapter 2). In short, only the parties to an agreement may be held accountable each to the other. Therefore the suppliers of goods and services cannot hold the client to account for failings on the part of the 'principal contractor', with whom they reached agreement, even though the client may be the ultimate beneficiary of the goods or services supplied.

An exception to the general rule (that the contractor will ordinarily be responsible for the employment conditions and the payment of all their suppliers and sub-contractors) arises where the client enters into a separate agreement directly with a particular supplier or sub-contractor, as here, too, privity of contract exists. For example, it may become necessary for the client to procure specialist nursery stock in advance of appointing a contractor; perhaps because the stock needs to be grown in the nursery for a season or two before it is suitable for use on the project. The client is likely to agree terms, including those concerning payment, directly with the supplier and therefore remains accountable in this respect. In these circumstances the accountability of any contractor eventually appointed will normally extend only to the handling and installation of the materials rather than their supply.

> ROLES AND RESPONSIBILITIES OF THE CONTRACTOR:
>
> - To undertake work as described
> - To the standard requested
> - At the agreed price
> - Under the terms and conditions provided
> - Within the agreed timescale
> - To employ and pay suppliers and sub-contractors as agreed

9.1.3 The role of the professional practitioner

The extent of the professional practitioner's responsibility will depend upon the detail of their specific commission. The professional practitioner may have been appointed simply to provide design proposals, alternatively to oversee a project from inception through implementation to final completion, or to undertake any or all of the intermediate Scopes of Services (discussed in Chapter 7).

Importantly, in selecting and appointing a professional practitioner, would-be clients should carefully consider qualifications and experience and, in particular, how these affect the limit of professional accountability placed upon the individual or practice. Within the landscape industry the only trading title with any form of legally protected status (and arguably therefore the only industry practitioners able to offer reassurance in respect of professional accountability) is the title of 'Chartered Member of the Landscape Institute' ('Chartered Landscape Architect' in the alternative), which only professionally qualified members of the Landscape Institute who obtain the Institute's chartered status are entitled to use (as discussed in Chapter 1).

As a result of the expertise that must be demonstrated in order to obtain Landscape Institute accreditation, Chartered Members of the Landscape Institute are regarded as the leading professionals within the landscape industry. There are however a great many 'quasi-professionals', less regulated and frequently less qualified than Landscape Institute members.

A plethora of trading titles are to be found within the landscape industry – 'landscape architect', 'garden designer' and 'landscape gardener' to name but a few. None of these titles have any form of legal status or protection and may be used freely by anyone, irrespective of professional qualifications or indeed of whether they hold any qualifications whatsoever.

The letters designate frequently conferred as a benefit of belonging to one or other industry association, unlike the 'CMLI' conferred upon Chartered Members of the Landscape Institute, do not necessarily indicate specific qualifications, experience, or compliance with a designated code of professional conduct.

The foregoing observations are not intended to diminish the efforts or the achievements of some very talented individuals but it is important, for the good of the industry as a whole, for potential clients to appreciate it is only the title of 'Chartered Member of the Landscape Institute' (as conferred by the Landscape Institute) on which they may rely for the provision of comprehensively regulated and rigorously accredited professional services.

Professional accountability is also affected by the extent to which Professional Indemnity Insurance (discussed in Chapter 3) underwrites the services provided. All professional practitioners should possess Professional Indemnity Insurance in order to ensure, in the event of what might be a considerable claim in negligence (discussed in Chapter 3) the individual's insurance, rather than the individual themselves, meets the cost of any damages awarded.

Would-be clients should note Professional Indemnity Insurance is not yet a legal requirement and is very specific as to what activities it covers. When, as often happens, an individual from a related discipline such as architecture is appointed to carry out the work of landscape architecture, care should be taken to ensure that cover in respect of one discipline extends to the other. If it does not, then in the event of a claim, for example resulting from damage to the foundations of a building caused by negligent positioning of an unsuitable tree species, there may be no valid insurance cover in place. Meanwhile, the individual concerned may lack the funds with which to personally satisfy the claim. This should sound a note of caution not only to would-be clients but also to responsible practitioners keen to ensure their personal assets are not put at risk in the event of an unfortunate lapse on their part.

The professional practitioner is frequently commissioned only to develop design proposals and, having done so, the terms of their engagement will have been fulfilled. More commonly, the commission will involve the provision of detailed development proposals, specifications of materials and workmanship, and contract documentation (discussed in Chapter 12).

The professional practitioner is also quite likely to administer the process of obtaining competitive quotations (discussed in Chapter 14) and to assume the contractual role of 'Contract Administrator', which normally includes responsibility for the supervision of contractors' activities and quality control (discussed in Chapter 15).

On more substantial projects it is common for the role of Contract Administrator to be undertaken by someone other than the landscape professional, for example a Resident Engineer if one has been appointed. Likewise, a technically competent individual situated on the site, such as a Clerk Of Works, may undertake the supervision of contractors and quality control elements of the project. Increasingly, even on smaller projects, a division of labour is occurring reflecting the particular expertise of the individuals concerned. A professional practitioner specialising in design may, for example, leave project procurement, contract administration and quality control elements to a fellow practitioner specialising in the management of such issues.

In essence, the professional practitioner is generally expected to carry out the particular services for which they have been engaged expeditiously, within the terms of what has been agreed in advance with the client, and within the parameters of their professional qualifications.

ROLES AND RESPONSIBILITIES OF THE PROFESSIONAL PRACTITIONER:

- Depend upon the detail of the specific commission but may include:
- Detailed design proposals
- Specification of materials and workmanship
- Preparation of contract documentation
- Administration of competitive processes
- Contract administration
- Supervision and quality control

9.2 PROCUREMENT STRATEGIES

In each and every project the concerns of the client will almost inevitably revolve around time, cost, performance and quality. Timing, or the period of the works, is likely to be important in relation to 'commencement'; that is to say, when must the client make the site available for works to begin and, perhaps more importantly, 'completion' or when the works are expected to be finished and the client to regain full control of the facilities.

Depending upon the extent to which the client's use of the site is excluded or restricted during the works the anticipated completion date can be a major factor. This is particularly so in the case of a commercial client, expecting to generate revenue from the site, or a public authority client whose management of the site is connected with the provision of a vital public service. In situations such as these, delay can lead to substantial overruns both in terms of time and cost.

Cost is a major factor as, perhaps not surprisingly, the majority of clients prefer to know from the outset what expenditure the project is likely to consume. Unforeseen expense, though often an inherent part of projects, can be extremely inconvenient, professionally embarrassing, and may require unwelcome compromise in order to stay within available budgets (discussed in Chapter 11). Cost overruns may even give rise to a client's inability to complete that which has begun.

The client's concerns regarding performance are likely to revolve around the perceived proficiency with which the project is carried out. It may be that works once commenced will continue unabated until they are completed. Alternatively, the client may have to endure long periods of inactivity as a result of the particular service provider opting to complete the project in stages. Measures may be taken to restrict the possibility of unnecessary breaks in continuity by the inclusion of appropriate clauses within the project specification and contractual agreement (discussed more fully in Chapters 12 and 13).

Quality issues relate to the finished standard of the works and the methods of construction used. The project should be completed within design parameters, and these parameters must ensure that finished components are reasonably likely to withstand the rigors of their eventual usage for a reasonable period of time. For example, a client may be justifiably dissatisfied if a newly constructed driveway collapses under the weight of vehicles, for which it was designed and constructed, within a few months of its completion.

The choice of procurement strategy, or the means of embracing all the activities with which a client may be concerned from inception to completion of a project, must address all these foregoing concerns whilst reflecting the client's policies, resources, organisational structure and preferences. A decision on the choice of procurement strategy will ordinarily be made after giving due consideration to the benefits, risks and financial constraints associated with each of the alternatives.

> **FACTORS INFLUENCING THE CHOICE OF PROCUREMENT STRATEGY:**
>
> - Timing or period of the works
> - Degree of uncertainty concerning costs
> - Performance management procedures
> - Quality control
> - Policies, resources, organisational structure and preferences of client
> - Benefits, risks and financial constraints of alternative strategies

9.2.1 Traditional procurement

Within the landscape industry 'traditional' is undoubtedly the most common form of procurement strategy. It has been similarly so within the construction industry for more than 150 years, following the emergence of general contracting firms and the establishment of independent consultants during the mid-nineteenth century.

As seen from Figure 9.1, the main distinguishing feature of 'traditional' procurement is that the client enters into an agreement with the professional practitioner for the provision of professional services (discussed in Chapter 7) and a *totally separate* agreement with a contractor or contractors for implementation of the works (discussed in Chapter 13). Consultative and implementation costs are therefore completely separate.

It should be noted in particular that suppliers or subcontractors appointed by the (principal) contractor generally have no direct relationship with the professional practitioner or the client; 'privity of contract' (discussed in Chapter 2) ensures agreements made between a contractor and their chosen suppliers or sub-contractors exist wholly between the parties to that particular agreement. Assuming the contractor wishes to sub-contract part of the work (discussed in Chapter 13) or to obtain materials or services from a particular supplier of their choosing, they (the contractor) remain wholly responsible for the employment conditions and payment of the parties with whom they form agreements, whether formally or informally.

It is not uncommon within 'traditional' procurement for the professional practitioner to limit the contractor's freedom of choice relating to sub-letting and supply through the use of specification clauses designed for the purpose (discussed in Chapter 12). These 'restrictive' clauses reserve the client's right to preclude sub-contracting or make it subject to approval in advance. Within a 'traditional' procurement strategy specifications frequently include a list of 'approved suppliers' and require the contractor to procure materials only from one or more of the sources identified.

Within a 'traditional' procurement strategy there exists an exception to the general rule (that suppliers or subcontractors appointed by the contractor generally have no direct relationship with the professional practitioner or the client) through

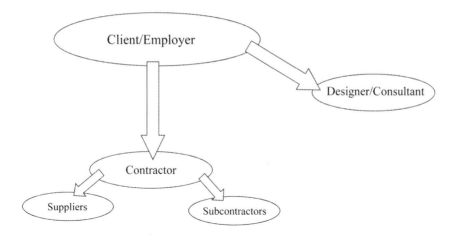

Fig. 9.1 Traditional Procurement

the use of 'nominated' sub-contractors or suppliers (discussed in Chapter 13). For the present purpose it is sufficient to say that measures thus taken compel the contractor to use only the sub-contractors or suppliers 'nominated' (or named) by the client, or their professional advisor, within the contract documents.

A further exception to the general rule (that the contractor is wholly responsible for the employment conditions and payment of sub-contractors and suppliers) frequently occurs when it is considered prudent to order materials in advance.

This often applies to nursery stock required in large numbers or at an extraordinarily large size. As the production of such material is likely to take several months (if not years) the nursery will need to commence the operation some considerable time in advance of the stock actually being required for the project. In these circumstances it is likely the nursery will require reassurance (that the stock will actually be required once it has been produced) and some form of financial security.

Security is frequently provided by the client entering into a separate contractual agreement with the nursery supplier and perhaps paying for the stock in advance. Because, in this scenario, the contractor is prevented from 'marking-up' the supply cost of items procured by the client under a separate contract (or from negotiating a trade discount) that would provide the profit they (the contractor) would normally, and quite reasonably, expect to make on the supply of the materials, it is not uncommon in these circumstances to permit the contractor a 'handling charge' reflecting their involvement in coordinating the delivery of pre-ordered materials and the handling of those materials once on site.

'Traditional' procurement normally involves the appointment of contractor(s) by a competitive process. The competitive process generally involves several contractors submitting quotations or tenders for the implementation of an identified package of work (discussed in Chapter 14). It is important to ensure the package of work is clearly identified and quantified in order that offers received are made on a 'like-for-like' basis. This in turn facilitates objective evaluation of the offers received.

It is not uncommon, particularly when a contractor and their standards of work are already known to a client, for an appointment to be made by negotiation. Negotiation may involve an additional package of work, perhaps a second phase, being agreed between the parties, often with the assistance of the professional practitioner, on terms similar to those for an earlier phase of works. Alternatively, negotiations with a particular contractor may concern works of a similar character to those already completed that are required to be undertaken on a separate project.

'Traditional' procurement generally places no design responsibility on the contractor, except in the case of specialist contractors who may need to provide drawings for their own materials or processes, for which purpose the JCLI Landscape Works Contract with Contractor's Design 2012 (discussed in Chapter 13) has been developed. The client generally has full control over the design, specified standards, and quality assurance, frequently choosing to appoint a professional practitioner to exercise this control by acting as the client's agent.

Design and construction are separate sequential processes, the former ordinarily being completed before moving on to the latter. As a result, the overall programme for a project procured by the 'traditional' method is likely to be relatively long.

Though it may be argued that making all design decisions before work commences on site brings with it a measure of inflexibility, standard forms of contract (discussed in Chapter 13) permit changes known as 'variations' to be implemented during the progress of the project.

Variations (discussed in Chapter 15) may involve the addition or removal of elements of the agreed works. The contractor is generally permitted to charge for variations on the basis of direct or related costs plus profit. Where the variation involves omitting part or all of an item, a contractor may be able to recover the profit that would otherwise have been made on that particular item by way of a contribution towards their fixed costs. In addition, an adjustment is normally made to the time period of the works in order to reflect the variation in the works to be carried out.

'Traditional' procurement has major advantages in that, with the exception of necessary variations, the client is reasonably certain of the extent and the cost of the works from the outset; a contract figure ordinarily being agreed in advance. Likewise, 'traditional' procurement contracts normally stipulate a period of time within which the works are to be completed. Although the contract documents will generally permit the date for completion to be extended in certain circumstances, usually under the control of the Contract Administrator (discussed in Chapter 15) the client can be reasonably certain from the outset what the likely period of the works will be. Furthermore, the conditions of contract generally permit the client to claim Liquidated Damages (discussed in Chapter 13) if and when losses arise from a contractor's failure to complete the works within the agreed timescale.

In terms of cost, design, and quality a 'traditional' procurement contract is therefore a relatively low-risk strategy for the client to adopt, particularly when the agreement has been established on the basis of a 'lump sum' rather than a 'measurement' contract. For the present purpose, it is sufficient to note that 'measurement' contracts bring with them a slightly higher level of risk for the client, as the quantity of work is re-measured on completion of the project. By contrast 'lump sum' contracts transfer the burden of risk to the contractor by requiring that they make their own assessment of what is required at the time of bidding for the work. With the exception of agreed variations no further alterations to a 'lump Sum' contract are permitted; therefore the risk of bidding errors remains firmly with the contractor.

FEATURES OF A 'TRADITIONAL' PROCUREMENT STRATEGY:

- Client has separate agreements with contractor(s) and the professional practitioner
- Contractor(s) responsible for employment of third parties
- Freedom of choice relating to sub-letting and supply may be restricted
- Appointments normally made on competitive basis
- Generally no design responsibility on contractor(s)
- Design and construction are sequential processes
- Overall programme relatively long and inflexible
- Client reasonably certain of costs from the outset
- Client generally permitted to claim damages for failure to perform
- Independent monitoring of quality

9.2.2 Design and build procurement

The primary distinction between 'design and build' and 'traditional' procurement, as seen from Figure 9.2, is that 'design and build' procurement generally removes the role of independent professional practitioner. That part of the professional practitioner's role (within 'traditional' procurement) concerned with design and specification becomes inseparable from the function of the contractor. Undoubtedly the most common exception to 'traditional' procurement, 'design and build' requires the client to enter into just a single agreement for both design and implementation of the project. 'Design and build' procurement is arguably therefore less complicated and can be more cost effective.

As with 'traditional' procurement, suppliers or subcontractors appointed by the (principal) contractor generally have no direct relationship with the client. Privity of

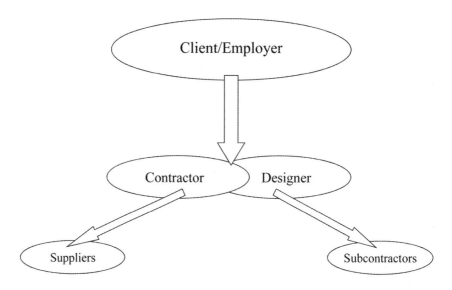

Fig. 9.2   Design and Build Procurement

contract (discussed in Chapter 2) ensures that should the contractor wish to sub-let part of the work, or obtain materials or services from a particular supplier of their choosing, they (the contractor) remain wholly responsible for the employment conditions and payment of the parties with whom they form agreements. However, unlike 'traditional' procurement, where the client or their professional advisor may influence the choice of sub-contractors and suppliers, in 'design and build' procurement such choices generally rest exclusively with the (principal) contractor. There is therefore little, if any, scope for 'nomination' (discussed in Chapter 13) of either suppliers or sub-contractors by the client or their representative.

'Design and build' procurement is often used within the engineering and construction industries for the commissioning of major buildings and infrastructure. The budgets for these projects are ordinarily many times greater than those for landscape projects and clients comfortably maintain teams of professional advisors to ensure contractor(s) comply with agreed standards in relation to materials, workmanship, timescale and budget.

Because budgets for landscape projects are relatively small, the role of professional practitioner is generally dispensed with in 'design and build' procurement of landscape projects and with it any form of independent verification of standards. For this reason 'design and build' procurement is very much less common within the landscape industry where the 'traditional' method of procurement is much more likely to be favoured as a means of commissioning services.

A curious exception to the general rule (that 'traditional' procurement is the preferred method of commissioning landscape services) occurs in the design and construction of 'domestic' gardens. Owners of residential premises, intent on making 'improvements' to their gardens, frequently engage a single contractor on a 'design and build' basis. One possible explanation seems to be that clients, unfamiliar with the industry and lacking technical expertise, often mistakenly believe they may obtain better value for money by avoiding professional fees. Regrettably this is rarely the case; a much more common outcome being poor-quality results brought about through design compromise together with a lack of supervision or professional accountability.

Readers of this book, if potential clients, are therefore urged to proceed with caution when considering the potential cost benefits of 'design and build' procurement; all too often what appears to be cost effective is ultimately found to be a false economy. Meanwhile readers who are, or aspire to be, professional practitioners are urged to do all within their power to promote the highest standards of professionalism which, it is generally held, is more likely to be achieved by maintaining a separation between the role of contractor and that of professional practitioner.

Where a contractor is appointed on a 'design and build' basis this should normally be a two-stage process. In order to maintain a competitive element, stage one requires a number of contractors to submit draft proposals and costings for consideration by the client. Evaluation at this stage is often difficult because the ensuing range of original design proposals generated, each quite different from the other, must be considered both in terms of merit and cost; comparison on a 'like-for-like' basis therefore being all but impossible. That said, there is arguably much greater scope for creativity within 'design and build' procurement through the application of competing creative energies though, as stated above, quality may sometimes be compromised in the process. Furthermore, originality of design can be achieved very effectively by introducing a competitive element into the initial selection of a professional practitioner in 'traditional' procurement. By this means the client may benefit from a diversity of creative energy whilst maintaining an appropriate level of professionalism and accountability.

Where 'design and build' is the preferred method of procurement, those contractors whose submissions are looked upon most favourably at stage one should be invited to submit detailed 'second stage' proposals. Second stage proposals may or may not require fully worked-up designs. Each contractor still 'in the race' must be given adequate time to prepare in sufficient detail to satisfy the client's requirements. By definition, each contractor in the second stage may be required to invest a considerable amount of time and resources in their submissions even though only one can eventually be awarded the contract; unfortunately the remaining bidders are unlikely to be remunerated in any way for their efforts. Competing for this form of procurement can therefore be an extremely costly undertaking for an unsuccessful contractor.

Once the competitive stages of 'design and build' procurement are complete the client will decide upon their preferred proposals and enter into an agreement with the successful contractor. The contractor assumes responsibility for detailed development of design proposals. As design is under the control of the contractor it frequently proceeds in parallel with construction of the project on site, thereby facilitating a shortening of the overall project programme.

The responsibilities of the parties in 'design and build' procurement are broadly similar to those within 'traditional' procurement; the main exception being the dual role created by the coming together of contractor and designer, thereby dispensing with the role of professional practitioner. More often than not this dual role is contractor led, being undertaken either by a contractor with 'in-house' design facilities or a contractor commissioning independent design consultants.

The fact that contractors undertaking work on a 'design and build' basis have need of design input provides a source of employment for professional practitioners beyond simply working directly for the client. However, when considering working for a contractor, the professional practitioner should reflect upon the degree to which their independence, and therefore their professional integrity, is likely to be compromised. Since the success of the contracting organisation will ultimately depend upon the profitability of project implementation, the professional practitioner should consider the degree to which they are likely to have to compromise professional standards in favour of the contractor's profits and ultimately their own employment.

From time to time the dual 'design and build' role is design-led, being undertaken by professional practitioners choosing to employ their own teams of construction workers or to sub-contract implementation of the project. This too can be fraught with difficulties, as the value of implementation (and therefore the financial risk of the project not going according to plan) is ordinarily much greater than the amount of the professional fees paid in respect of design. A scenario whereby 'design and build' procurement is design led is therefore quite unusual within the landscape industry and not normally recommended. Furthermore the code of conduct, to which members of the Landscape Institute must adhere (discussed in Chapter 1), though not actually prohibiting such involvements, does require Landscape Institute members to declare to potential clients any interest beyond landscape architecture before accepting a commission.

Whether led by contractor or professional practitioner 'design and build' procurement is quite likely to involve the professional practitioner in some form of direct financial interest beyond simply earning professional fees. Frequently the professional practitioner will be a director, an employee, or a partner in the organisation undertaking the project. Arguably therefore it is much more difficult for the professional practitioner to be impartial in their decision making, or to be perceived as such, since they inevitably have a vested interest in the profitability of the project.

Whereas the much greater budgets for engineering and construction projects permit professional integrity to be maintained, by the client employing their own teams of advisors independent of the contractor, the generally much smaller budgets of landscape projects undertaken using the 'design and build' form of procurement tend to ensure that no provision is made for appointing an independent contract administrator. Regrettably, therefore, once a landscape project has been got underway using the 'design and build' form of procurement, it is possible (and not uncommon) for unscrupulous operators to cut corners to increase the level of their organisation's profitability.

Within 'design and build' procurement, it is likely that contractors will have been required to submit a 'lump sum' price for their proposals. As a result the client can be reasonably certain of the cost, provided they refrain from making variations after the contract has been let. Alterations to the design or specification can be accommodated but the consequences in terms of direct costs and additional time are uncertain and largely a matter for the provider of the services to decide.

Within the landscape industry, 'design and build' procurement, though less complicated as a result of the client entering into only one agreement, is arguably more open to abuse, since it provides no independent verification of standards or quality control. The client may decide to address this issue by appointing an independent professional to act on their behalf, but standard forms of contract for this type of procurement generally do not recognise a role for such a person.

In terms of cost and time, 'design and build' procurement is a relatively low risk strategy for the client to adopt; speculative risks being borne largely by the contractor. There can however be uncertainty in matters of design and quality control, particularly if insufficient attention has been paid to preparation of the brief on behalf of the client and there is inadequate provision for the independent verification of the contractor's proposals.

> FEATURES OF A 'DESIGN AND BUILD' PROCUREMENT STRATEGY:
>
> - Generally removes the role of independent professional practitioner
> - Client enters into a single agreement
> - Contractor exclusively responsible for employment of third parties
> - Appointments normally made on a competitive basis
> - Design and specification inseparable from role of contractor
> - Design and implementation are parallel processes
> - Overall programme relatively short
> - Client reasonably certain of costs and timescale from outset
> - No independent verification of performance standards
> - No independent monitoring of quality
> - Evaluation of competitive bids may be difficult

9.2.3 Management procurement

A third major form of project procurement 'management' is, like 'design and build' procurement, common within the construction and engineering industries but less so within the landscape industry. 'Management' procurement, like its 'traditional' counterpart, involves the appointment of a professional practitioner to carry out the processes of design, specification and cost planning together with letting of a contract or contracts for project implementation.

Where 'management' procurement differs from 'traditional' procurement is that a contractor is appointed to *oversee* implementation rather than actually carry it out; the appointed contractor assuming responsibility for defining packages of work and 'managing' implementation through the letting of separate trades or works contracts.

The appointment of a management contractor is either by negotiation or competitive tender, with contractors submitting fee quotations for the management of the project. The submission of fee quotations is normally followed by interviews to determine the most appropriate contractor to appoint; the process being conducted on behalf of the client by the professional practitioner.

The involvement of a management contractor at an early stage in the project can be beneficial. Management contractors typically have extensive implementation experience enabling them to contribute considerably to issues of practicality, cost and programming of works. Once a management contractor has been appointed, it is likely that the packages of work will be offered on the basis of competitive tender.

'Management' procurement ensures overall responsibility for design, and specification remains with the client and their appointed advisors. Much of the design detail can proceed in parallel with construction, particularly that relating to specialist packages of work, and this enables the overall project period to be kept to a minimum.

'Management' procurement offers absolutely no certainty over costs at the outset as work proceeds purely on the basis of a cost plan or budget. Final costs will not be known until the last package of work is let and even this may be subject to variations as the work proceeds. The client is likely to address this issue by the appointment of a Quantity Surveyor to monitor progress against the budget and advise what action to take in the event of cost overruns. Design changes are not only possible as construction proceeds but are also quite probable as a means of reducing escalating costs. Care must be taken to ensure design changes do not affect work packages underway or those already completed as this may result in abortive work and costs.

Responsibility to ensure completion within the allotted timescale falls to the management contractor who, generally, may not permit individual contractors any extensions of time without first obtaining the approval of the client's appointed contract administrator.

In terms of design and quality, 'management' procurement is a relatively low-risk strategy, since the client maintains control through the design team. However there is a considerable degree of speculative risk associated with costs and time and these rest very much with the client.

> **FEATURES OF A 'MANAGEMENT' PROCUREMENT STRATEGY:**
>
> - Client has separate agreements with management contractor and professional practitioner
> - Management contractor responsible for employment of third parties
> - Freedom of choice relating to sub-letting and supply may be limited
> - Appointments normally made on a competitive basis
> - Responsibility for design and specification remains with the client
> - Design proceeds in parallel with construction
> - Project period may be kept to a minimum
> - No certainty of costs from the outset
> - Performance monitored and controlled by management contractor
> - Independent monitoring of quality by professional practitioner

In conclusion, 'traditional' procurement is, by far, the most common procurement strategy within the landscape industry. Though 'design and build' procurement is popular in the construction of 'domestic' gardens, the lack of an independent professional practitioner generally makes this form of procurement less desirable and hence less common within landscape projects. As for 'management' procurement, notwithstanding this form of procurement can be very efficient, it tends to be reserved for projects with very large budgets, where teams of professional advisors can be justified, and is therefore uncommon on landscape projects where budgets are generally relatively modest.

> **CHAPTER SUMMARY**
>
> - Smooth and efficient project implementation requires the professional practitioner to understand and fulfil their own obligations and to be clear what is required from other participants in landscape contracts
> - The role of the client is paramount since it is they who 'set the train in motion' either by commissioning the services of a professional practitioner or by entering into some form of agreement with a contractor
> - Contractor(s) will normally be appointed in order that their resources and technical expertise may be deployed in project implementation
> - The professional practitioner may be appointed simply to provide design proposals; to oversee a project from inception to final completion; or to undertake any or all of the intermediate Scopes of Services
> - The choice of procurement strategy must address time, cost and performance, as well as the client's policies, resources and organisational preferences
> - Within the landscape industry, 'traditional' is undoubtedly the most common form of procurement strategy
> - 'Design and build' procurement generally removes the role of independent professional practitioner
> - 'Management' procurement involves the appointment of a contractor to define packages of work and manage implementation

10

Construction Design and Management Regulations

> THE AIMS OF THIS CHAPTER ARE TO:
>
> - Introduce the Construction Design and Management Regulations
> - Explain how to determine when a project must be notified to the Health and Safety Executive
> - Describe the duties placed upon participants in construction projects
> - Explain the additional duties arising as a result of notification to the Health and Safety Executive

The Construction Design and Management Regulations were originally introduced in 1994. The Regulations required that health and safety be taken into account and managed throughout all stages of a construction project.

From conception, design and planning through site work and to subsequent maintenance and repair, the Construction Design and Management Regulations 1994 placed obligations upon everyone contributing to the construction process including client, designers/professional practitioners, contractors and the self-employed.

Where they applied, the Construction Design and Management Regulations 1994 required two specific roles to be filled, those of 'Planning Supervisor' and 'Principal Contractor', along with the production of a Pre-Tender Health and Safety Plan and a Health and Safety File.

In 2007 a supposedly simplified set of Construction Design and Management Regulations were introduced. The stated intentions of the new Regulations were to improve clarity and place the emphasis on practical planning and management of construction projects, so as to reduce health and safety risks, rather than the production of excessive paperwork, which had been the effect of the 1994 Construction Design and Management Regulations.

> **CONSTRUCTION DESIGN AND MANAGEMENT REGULATIONS 2007**
>
> - Part 1: Introduction
> - Part 2: General management duties applying to all construction projects
> - Part 3: Additional duties where projects are notifiable
> - Part 4: Worksite health and safety requirements
> - Part 5: General

The Construction Design and Management Regulations 2007 are supported by an Approved Code of Practice. The Regulations are intended to simplify procedures, not least by removing the separate Construction (Health, Safety and Welfare) Regulations 1996 which Part 4 of the Construction Design and Management Regulations 2007 replaces.

10.1 THE REQUIREMENT FOR NOTIFICATION

The Construction Design and Management Regulations 2007 apply to all construction work, but only projects for non-domestic clients, likely to last longer than 30 days or involve 500 or more person days of work, have to be notified to the Health and Safety Executive.

According to paragraph 13 of the Approved Code of Practice accompanying the Construction Design and Management Regulations 2007, tree planting and general horticultural work are not classified as construction work and are therefore exempt from any requirement for notification to the Health and Safety Executive.

> **DEFINITION OF CONSTRUCTION WORK**
>
> The Landscape Institute (June 2012):
>
> *The Health and Safety Executive have advised that 'construction work' as defined in the Construction Design and Management Regulations 2007 includes earthworks, all hard landscape works, installation of pipes and pipelines, demolition, dismantling, and preparation for such works (including site clearance and excavation). Demolition, dismantling and site clearance of 'construction work' are 'construction work' even when undertaken in preparation for tree planting and general horticultural work.*
>
> *The Health and Safety Executive have advised that tree planting and general horticultural work includes topsoiling, grading, amelioration, planting, grassing, agricultural fencing, tree work, soft landscape maintenance and associated preparation (including excavation and site clearance but excluding site clearance of 'construction work').*
>
> *The Health and Safety Executive have advised that where such works are carried out as part of a larger project including 'construction work' the tree planting and general horticultural work can be addressed separately.*

Notification is by submission (normally by the contractor) of Form F10 informing the Health and Safety Executive that potentially hazardous operations are being carried out on the site in order that the Health and Safety Executive may inspect if they so wish.

Notification triggers additional duties in accordance with Part 3 of the Construction Design and Management Regulations 2007; most notably the appointment of a 'Principal Contractor'; a 'Construction Design and Management Coordinator' (replacing the role of Planning Supervisor in the 1994 Regulations); the requirement to produce a 'Construction Phase Plan' (Pre-Tender Health and Safety Plan under the 1994 Regulations); and a 'Health and Safety File'.

The Health and Safety File is intended to be a record of useful site information that will help in managing health and safety risks during future maintenance, repair, construction or demolition work undertaken on the site. For example, the Health and Safety File ought to include drawings showing the precise locations and depths of any underground services installed on the site. The Health and Safety File should contain a full record of the site; what has been done; how it has been done; and why any residual (present or future) risks could not be designed out.

Most of the duties placed upon clients, designers/professional practitioners, contractors and the self-employed by the Construction Design and Management Regulations 2007 apply whether or not the project requires the Health and Safety Executive to be notified.

10.2   OBLIGATIONS OF THE CLIENT

Under the Construction Design and Management Regulations 2007 a 'client' is any individual or organisation who, in the course of business, has a construction project carried out or carries out construction work themselves. By definition, this excludes 'domestic' clients, that is to say, someone who lives, or will live, in the premises where the project is being carried out. It does not necessarily exclude domestic premises.

In order for domestic premises to be exempt from the requirement for notification under the Construction Design and Management Regulations 2007 the client must be paying for the project themselves. If construction work on domestic premises is being paid for by the client's company the 'domestic' exemption no longer applies. If the construction work is in connection with domestic premises that have not yet been occupied, that is to say a new build property, the project is similarly not exempt from the requirement for notification under the Regulations. The minimum thresholds set out above will however apply.

The duties placed on the client by the Construction Design and Management Regulations 2007 apply to domestic premises if the client is a local authority; landlord; housing association; charity; collective of leaseholders; or any other trade, business or undertaking (whether or not trading for profit).

If an insurance company (or its agent) arranges construction work under an insurance policy or warranty then the insurance company becomes the client for the purpose of the Construction Design and Management Regulations 2007. If the work undertaken is paid for by the insurance company but arranged by the insured, the role of client falls upon the insured who, if they are a domestic client (as defined above), is exempt from the requirement for notification to the Health and Safety Executive.

Where there are a number of clients for a project they may jointly agree in writing the identity of an individual or individuals who will assume the role of client(s). They may not appoint someone to act as client's agent as they could under the Construction Design and Management Regulations 1994.

For other than 'domestic' premises (as defined above) the client's responsibilities under the Construction Design and Management Regulations 2007 are to:

- Check the competence and resources of those they appoint in accordance with the Approved Code of Practice competence criteria

- Allow sufficient time and resources to complete the project with minimum risk

- Provide key information to designers and contractors and arrange for any gaps in information to be filled

- Ensure all those involved in the project cooperate and coordinate their activities

- Ensure that suitable management arrangements are in place according to the nature of the work being undertaken and the risks involved

- Ensure adequate personnel welfare facilities are provided on site

Additionally, under Part 3 of the Construction Design and Management Regulations 2007, on projects which must be notified to the Health and Safety Executive (as discussed above) clients must:

- Appoint a competent Construction Design and Management Coordinator

- Provide the Construction Design and Management Coordinator with key information including any existing Health and Safety File

- Appoint a competent Principal Contractor

- Ensure the construction phase of the project does not commence until suitable personnel welfare facilities are provided on site and a Construction Phase Health and Safety Plan has been produced

- Ensure a Health and Safety File is produced, that it is retained, revised with any new information and that access to the file is provided whenever it is reasonably required

The key advisor to clients on notifiable projects is the Construction Design and Management Coordinator. If a Construction Design and Management Coordinator or a Principal Contractor are not appointed on a notifiable project, the client will be deemed to have assumed the duties inherent in these roles themselves.

If the client reasonably judges the contractor's management arrangements to be suitable, based on the information available and the nature of the risks inherent in the project, clients will not be held accountable if the management arrangements subsequently prove to be inadequate or if the contractor fails to implement those arrangements without the client's knowledge.

Clients and Construction Design and Management Coordinators are not required to supervise construction work on site.

10.3 OBLIGATIONS OF THE CONSTRUCTION DESIGN AND MANAGEMENT COORDINATOR

The role of 'Construction Design and Management Coordinator' in the Construction Design and Management Regulations 2007 replaces that of 'Planning Supervisor' in the 1994 Regulations. The Construction Design and Management Coordinator's role is to advise the client on health and safety issues during the design and planning phases of construction work. The role of Construction Design and Management Coordinator is only required if the project is such that the Health and Safety Executive must be notified (as discussed above).

The early appointment of a Construction Design and Management Coordinator, where one is required, is key to successful implementation of the Construction Design and Management Regulations 2007. The Construction Design and Management Coordinator is expected to support the client in carrying out their duties, in particular to:

- Advise the client in the selection of competent designers and contractors

- Help identify what information will be needed by designers and contractors

- Coordinate health and safety provision within planning and design phases

- Ensure the Health and Safety Executive is notified of the project

- Advise on the suitability of the Construction Phase Health and Safety Plan

- Prepare a Health and Safety File

The duties of Construction Design and Management Coordinator may be carried out by the client (who is deemed to be Construction Design and Management Coordinator if no appointment is made); the Principal Contractor; the designer/professional practitioner; or a full-time Construction Design and Management Coordinator. On small projects combining the role of Construction Design and Management Coordinator and professional practitioner potentially advantages the client, by reducing bureaucracy and avoiding the generation of unnecessary paperwork, thereby reducing costs.

The role of Construction Design and Management Coordinator potentially provides an additional source of fees for suitably trained and competent professional practitioners, particularly those who specialise in the production of contract documentation and overseeing project implementation.

10.4 OBLIGATIONS OF DESIGNERS/PROFESSIONAL PRACTITIONERS

Anyone who designs or specifies construction work has duties under the Construction Design and Management Regulations 2007. These duties apply to all projects, including projects not required to be notified to the Health and Safety Executive (as discussed above) and projects carried out on domestic premises.

Where design work is undertaken by oversees designers, the duties under the Construction Design and Management Regulations 2007 fall on the client, or the person commissioning the design services provided they are in the United Kingdom.

Under the Construction Design and Management Regulations 2007 designers/professional practitioners are required to:

- Ensure clients are aware of their duties under the Regulations

- Ensure they are personally competent for the work they undertake

- Coordinate design operations with the work of other members of the project team as necessary to appropriately manage health and safety risks

- Provide information for the Health and Safety File

- As far as possible design out health and safety risks in the construction, cleaning, maintenance, proposed use (workplaces only) and ultimate removal of structures

- Reduce as far as possible the risks from hazards that cannot be designed out

- Prioritise collective risk reduction measures over individual measures, for example specifying plants that don't have irritant sap rather than specifying that those planting should wear gloves

- Take account of the Workplace (Health, Safety and Welfare) Regulations 1992 when designing a workplace structure

On projects required to be notified to the Health and Safety Executive (as discussed above) the designer/professional practitioner is additionally required to:

- Check that the client has appointed a Construction Design and Management Coordinator

- Cooperate with the Construction Design and Management Coordinator, Principal Contractor, other designers and/or other contractors so all parties may comply with their duties under the Construction Design and Management Regulations 2007

- Provide relevant design information for inclusion in the Health and Safety File

The amount of effort the designer/professional practitioner makes to design out risks is intended to be proportionate to the risks involved. The Construction Design and Management Regulations 2007 do not prescribe by what method designers/professional practitioners should communicate information concerning residual health and safety risks, that is to say risks it has not been possible to design out. Such information may be communicated by means of notes on drawings; written risk assessments (discussed in Chapter 4); and/or a suggested sequence of operations if felt necessary.

The Construction Design and Management Regulations 2007 do not require design risk assessment to produce excessive amounts of paperwork. There is no legal requirement to keep records of the design process and why key design decisions were made. In practice, written risk assessment (discussed in Chapter 4) is often the most methodical way to ensure the correct thought processes have been gone through in managing, or preferably eliminating, health and safety risks by the most efficient means but it is not prescribed within the Construction Design and Management Regulations 2007.

Risk assessment is fundamental to the management of health and safety risks, whether or not the project is notifiable under the Construction Design and Management Regulations 2007. Risk assessment involves consideration of hazards, for example the likelihood that a small child might fall into a pond; of the potential harm that might result; and of what might be done to eliminate or reduce the risk. Where it is not possible to design out a risk the contractor should be required to provide a method statement (discussed in Chapter 4) including their own assessment of the likely risk and how they intend to manage that risk.

Under the Construction Design and Management Regulations 2007 designers/professional practitioners are not required to control risks on site. This is generally the responsibility of the contractor(s); the professional practitioner being required only to influence that which is within their control and to take account of foreseeable risks. The designer/professional practitioner must think about inherent risks associated with each and every design detail, for example whether a large open expanse of water is a good idea where there are likely to be small children, and design out health and safety risks at source wherever possible.

10.5 OBLIGATIONS OF THE PRINCIPAL CONTRACTOR

In relation to the Principal Contractor's duties there is little change between the Construction Design and Management Regulations of 1994 and 2007.

On projects that require notification to the Health and Safety Executive (as discussed above) the client should ensure a Principal Contractor is appointed as soon as practicable. The Principal Contractor is thereafter required to:

- Ensure the client is aware of their duties

- Ensure a Construction Design and Management Coordinator has been appointed

- Ensure the Health and Safety Executive is notified

- Ensure other contractors they appoint are competent

- Ensure the construction phase of the project is properly planned, managed, monitored and resourced

- Inform contractors of the minimum time allowed for planning and preparation

- Provide relevant information to contractors

- Ensure safe working, coordination and cooperation between contractors

- Ensure the Construction Phase Health and Safety Plan is prepared and implemented, including contractors' risk assessments and method statements, product information (where appropriate), usage records and arrangements for managing risk tailored to the particular project (it is not acceptable to cut and paste a generic document)

- Ensure suitable welfare facilities are provided on site

- Instigate and enforce site rules aimed at ensuring safe working practices

- Give reasonable directions to contractors including client appointed contractors

- Prevent unauthorised entry to the site

- Provide access to the Construction Phase Health and Safety Plan for those who reasonably require it

- Promptly provide the Construction Design and Management Coordinator with information for inclusion in the Health and Safety File, for example updated construction drawings or service diagrams and application records for noxious substances

- Liaise with the Construction Design and Management Coordinator in relation to necessary design alternations

- Ensure all site personnel have been provided with suitable health and safety induction, information and training

The Construction Design and Management Regulations 2007 do not require the Principal Contractor to provide training to site personnel not employed or sub-contracted to themselves; this is the responsibility of the individual contractors by whom those personnel are employed. Neither do the Regulations require the Principal Contractor to undertake detailed supervision of other contractor's work.

10.6   OBLIGATIONS OF ALL CONTRACTORS AND THE SELF-EMPLOYED

To comply with the Construction Design and Management Regulations 2007 contractors and the self-employed on all projects, whether or not they are required to be notified to the Health and Safety Executive (as discussed above), are required to:

- Check clients are aware of their duties under the Construction Design and Management Regulations 2007

- Plan, manage and monitor health and safety risks in connection with the work they undertake

- Ensure they and those they appoint are competent and adequately resourced

- Inform any contractor they engage of the minimum time they have for planning and preparation

- Provide their workers (whether employed or self-employed) with induction, information and health and safety training as necessary

- Report to the client or Principal Contractor anything that is likely to endanger the health and safety of themselves or others

- Ensure any design work they undertake complies with the duties of the designer under the Construction Design and Management Regulations 2007

- Comply with site health and safety requirements

- Cooperate and coordinate with the project team as required

- Not begin work unless reasonable steps have been taken to prevent unauthorised access to the site

On projects required to be notified to the Health and Safety Executive (as discussed above) all contractors and the self-employed are additionally required to:

- Check that a Construction Design and Management Coordinator has been appointed and the Health and Safety Executive has been notified before commencing site operations

- Cooperate with the Principal Contractor, Construction Design and Management Coordinator and others working on the project

- Tell the Principal Contractor about risks to others created by their work

- Comply with any reasonable directions from the Principal Contractor

- Work in accordance with the Construction Phase Health and Safety Plan

- Inform the Principal Contractor of the identity of any contractor appointed

- Inform the Principal Contractor of any problems with the Construction Phase Health and Safety Plan or risks identified in connection with their operations that have significant implications for the management of health and safety risks on the project

- Inform the Principal Contractor about any death, injury, disease or dangerous occurrence on the site

- Provide information for the Health and Safety File as required

10.7 COMPETENCE AND TRAINING

The Construction Design and Management Regulations 2007 require all organisations and individuals involved in construction to be competent for the work they do. To be competent, an organisation or individual must have sufficient knowledge of the specific tasks to be undertaken, the risks such operations entail, sufficient experience to carry out those operations safely and to take appropriate actions to prevent harm to others working on the site or affected by the works.

All those who have duties under the Construction Design and Management Regulations 2007 should take reasonable steps to ensure persons who are appointed are competent; not arrange for anyone to carry out or manage design or construction work unless that person is competent; and not accept any appointment unless they are themselves competent for the task.

A key duty of the Construction Design and Management Coordinator is to advise the client about the competence of those to be engaged on the project. Assessment of competence should focus on the needs of the particular project and should be proportionate to the risk, size and complexity of the work to be undertaken.

In assessing the competence of an organisation it is necessary to consider the organisation's arrangements for health and safety as well as its experience and track record. Organisations will be expected to demonstrate the standards of competence required by the core criteria set out in the Approved Code of Practice included at Appendix 4 of the Construction Design and Management Regulations 2007. The core criteria have been agreed between the construction industry and the Health and Safety Executive.

In assessing the competence of an individual it is necessary to consider the individual's knowledge, training records and qualifications, including basic understanding of site risks, and the individual's past experience undertaking the type of operation they are being asked to undertake. Those new to construction work will need close supervision by a competent person until they can themselves demonstrate competence.

When assessing the competence of an individual designer/professional practitioner it is necessary to consider the individual's membership of a professional regulatory organisation, in the case of landscape professionals The Landscape Institute (as discussed in Chapter 1), along with evidence of the individual's past experience of similar work. It may be necessary to take into account the skills and knowledge of other designers/professional practitioners, if the work is to be carried out by a design team, in order to ensure that designers/professional practitioners are competent to:

- Identify hazards and understand how they can be eliminated where possible

- Identify significant residual risks and understand how they might be managed

- Design in accordance with the Workplace (Health, Safety and Welfare) Regulations 1992

- Communicate health and safety information effectively and appropriately to contractors

- Cooperate with the Principal Contractor and other members of the project team

Construction Design and Management Coordinators are key to compliance with the Construction Design and Management Regulations 2007. Construction Design and Management Coordinators need good interpersonal skills to encourage cooperation and coordination; they must understand the design process and the need to coordinate the work of individual designers; they must have excellent knowledge of health and safety in the context of construction projects; and must be able to identify the key information others need to know.

On smaller projects the competence of individual Construction Design and Management Coordinators can be assessed by considering the individual's knowledge of the design process and health and safety in construction, together with the individual's experience of applying that knowledge.

For larger projects or those involving more serious health and safety risks, the skills and knowledge of the Construction Design and Management Coordinator will need to reflect the complexity of the project and the specialist knowledge necessary to ensure that risks are properly controlled. Detailed guidance on such appointments is provided by the Agreed Code of Practice included at Appendix 5 of the Construction Design and Management Regulations 2007.

In relation to individual site workers, assessment of competence should focus upon the needs of the project proportionate to the risks. This means assessing the individual worker's knowledge and experience to carry out the required operations safely. This may be demonstrated by valid certificates of competence in, for example, herbicide application; use of chainsaws; use of lifting gear; and forklift driving. Supervision, training and instruction should be provided as necessary.

CONSTRUCTION DESIGN AND MANAGEMENT REGULATIONS

CHAPTER SUMMARY

- The Construction Design and Management Regulations require health and safety to be managed at all stages of a construction project

- The Regulations apply to all construction work but only projects for non-domestic clients, lasting longer than 30 days or involving 500 or more person days, have to be notified to the Health and Safety Executive

- Notification triggers the appointment of a 'Principal Contractor'; a 'Construction Design and Management Coordinator'; the requirement to produce a 'Construction Phase Plan'; and a 'Health and Safety File'

- Most of the duties placed upon clients, designers/professional practitioners, contractors and the self-employed apply whether or not the project requires the Health and Safety Executive to be notified

- A 'client' is any individual or organisation who, in the course of business, has construction work carried out or carries it out themselves

- The key advisor to clients on notifiable projects is the Construction Design and Management Coordinator

- The Construction Design and Management Coordinator's role is to advise the client on health and safety issues during the design and planning phases of construction work

- Anyone who designs or specifies construction work has duties that apply to all projects, including projects not required to be notified to the Health and Safety Executive and projects carried out on domestic premises

- Risk assessment is fundamental to the management of health and safety risks, whether or not the project is notifiable

11

Estimating Project Budgets

> THE AIMS OF THIS CHAPTER ARE TO:
>
> - Describe the processes by which a project budget is developed
> - Introduce sources by which to prepare a detailed project budget

The professional practitioner will normally be required to provide the client with an estimate of project implementation costs, that is to say, the expected cost of converting finished design proposals to a built landscape. A clear distinction must be made between the fees charged by the professional practitioner in respect of designing and overseeing the development of a project (discussed in Chapter 7) and the costs of converting finished design proposal to a completed project with which the present chapter is solely concerned.

In order to accurately estimate project implementation costs, it is preferable for the professional practitioner to have produced the comprehensive contract documentation (discussed in Chapter 12) that will eventually be required by landscape contractors quoting for the work. In practice, it is more often the case that the professional practitioner must estimate project implementation costs at an earlier stage in the project, in order that the client has something upon which to base a project budget and determine whether there are sufficient funds for the project to proceed.

Over time professional practitioners tend to develop a familiarity with the cost of particular commodities they frequently specify – for example, the average cost per square metre for stone paving or a specific type of lawn turf the use of which they favour. Knowledge of this form can be helpful in early discussions with clients who are frequently unfamiliar with the cost of landscape components and occasionally have unrealistic expectations of what can be achieved within a given amount of money.

An estimate of implementation costs prepared on behalf of the client and the quotation(s) eventually received from contractor(s) may be viewed as the two sides of a balance sheet and should be broadly comparable each to the other. To avoid embarrassment, or accusations of incompetence, the professional practitioner must ensure that any estimate of implementation costs accurately reflects prevailing market conditions. Whilst parity between an estimate and quotations from contractors cannot be guaranteed, and in practice the two are often substantially at odds, the professional practitioner must at least strive for accuracy and be able to substantiate and if necessary justify to the client, the estimates they have prepared.

To ensure that estimates of implementation costs are reasonably accurate, it is desirable, at the time of their preparation, for the client to have approved at least outline design proposals for the project. At this early stage it is quite possible, even likely, that final details of a project may not have been agreed. Estimates are therefore intended only as an indication of costs and may be subject to change as the design process develops. Nonetheless, in preparing client estimates, the professional practitioner must accurately reflect the design details, as far as they are known, and have access to current market prices. If the estimate is too high, the client may decide not to go ahead with the project; too low and the client may eventually find that the project costs a great deal more than expected when quotations are received from contractors.

Estimating project implementation costs should arguably be an intrinsic part of the design process, so the professional practitioner can ensure the finished scheme falls within the design parameters relating to cost. There is little point in a professional practitioner producing a finished design only to find that, once an estimate is prepared, its implementation is likely to cost considerably in excess of the client's available budget.

Estimates should always be given in writing and broken down into as much detail as reasonable and practicable. A detailed estimate provides not only a point of reference for future discussions but will also ensure there is no misunderstanding as to what has been included and what has not. Ensuring that estimates are broken down into a reasonable amount of detail will also enable the client to omit certain elements, or phase certain parts of the project, in the event the estimated implementation costs substantially exceed the available budget.

An estimate should set out any conditions and qualifications that must be considered. For example, the client should be made aware that the figures provided will be subject to change if the cost of particular components increases. Estimates should always be dated and preferably contain an indication of the period within which the figures might be expected to remain an accurate indication of project costs. Estimates should contain footnotes indicating any conditions or qualifications, for example: 'it is assumed all bulk materials will be delivered to site in full loads as part loads are likely to significantly increase costs'.

It is useful to note the sources of rates used when estimating since, although not necessarily of significant interest to the client, this information might serve as a useful aid to memory for the professional practitioner when the estimate is revisited, quite possibly some months after it was first prepared. Information concerning sources of rates need not be included on the estimating document presented to the client.

An estimate should be abundantly clear whether the rates used are inclusive of what are expected to be the contractor's overheads and profit. If not, an allowance must be made within the estimate for these items. It is always advisable to make an allowance for 'contingency items' when estimating. That is to say items it might subsequently transpire were unforeseen or under-estimated. Contingency sums should not, however, be regarded as sums intended to mask inaccuracies within an estimate. Hence, it is not ordinarily regarded as good practice to include contingency sums substantially in excess of 10–15 per cent of the overall project estimate.

Depending upon the size of the project and whether the contractor(s) it is anticipated will eventually carry out the works are expected to be registered with Her Majesty's Revenue and Customs for Value Added Tax purposes, that is to say whether the contractors will be required to charge Value Added Tax on the products and services they eventually provide, an allowance must be made in this respect when estimating project implementation costs. Although there are one or two minor exclusions, Value Added Tax is calculated as an overall percentage of the project costs, calculated using the rate of tax prevailing at the time the estimate is prepared (20 per cent in 2014–2015), which rate should be stated clearly on the estimate. Presenting the Value Added Tax element as a lump sum addition to an estimate, as opposed to including it within the individual unit rates, allows a client who is appropriately registered with Her Majesty's Customs and Excise and able to reclaim 'input tax' through their business, to readily see the amount by which the overall project implementation cost be reduced through the recovery of the Value Added Tax element.

ESTIMATING FUNDAMENTALS

- Estimates of project costs should:
- Ideally be based on comprehensive contract documentation
- Accurately reflect prevailing market conditions
- Be an intrinsic part of the design process
- Always be given in writing
- Be broken down into reasonable detail
- Set out any conditions and qualifications
- Be dated and indicate period for which figures expected to be current
- Allow for contractor's overheads and profit
- Allow for contingency items
- Show Value Added Tax as separate item and state the rate used

Estimation of project implementation costs requires the professional practitioner to undertake three stages: measuring approximate quantities and areas from the project drawings; preparing a schedule of operations together with approximate quantities; and attributing rates to the operations and approximate quantities listed. Each of these operations will now be considered.

11.1   MEASUREMENT

The first stage in preparing estimates of project implementation costs is the utilisation of one or more methods to measure approximate quantities and areas from the project drawing(s). Items such as specimen trees, numbered groups of plants or individual features may simply be counted. The majority of items are likely to be measured by area or volume utilising a variety of means.

A scale rule will enable approximate measurement of areas from the project drawings. In order to increase accuracy, it is advisable that informal areas are divided into geometric shapes; squares, rectangles, triangles and so on, as far as this is practicable. By this means the greater part of these informal areas can be accurately measured. Minor allowances should then be made in respect of those areas remaining outside of such geometric divisions.

Alternatively, a mechanical measuring device known as a planimeter (or platometer) may be used to measure areas. Planimeters are produced in a number of forms but each are intended to be used for carefully tracing around the perimeter or boundary of a given area of a plan. By utilising mathematical formulae provided with the planimeter, measurement of informal areas can accurately be achieved. The accuracy of this method of measurement is entirely dependent upon the skill and care with which the operator of the planimeter undertakes the task. It should however be said that the use of planimeters has, in practice, declined considerably since the advent of Computer Aided Design. Planimeters are nonetheless still in use and are an extremely valuable piece of drawing office equipment where plans are not available in a digital format or when working from printed copies thereof. Care should always be taken to ensure the scale of printed drawings is that which is printed on the plan and allowance should be made for minor inaccuracies due to paper stretch in the printing process.

It is not surprising to find that, since the 1980s when Computer Aided Design first became economically viable for use in the landscape industry, a vast array of software packages have been developed specifically for the landscape market. The software is now freely available and facilitates not only the drafting of plans in digital formats but ordinarily also allows the user to highlight and accurately measure areas and distances precisely and with consummate ease.

11.2   FORMULATING A SCHEDULE

The second stage in preparing estimates of implementation costs involves formulating a schedule of operations in respect of the project. Most commonly the schedule of operations will list the items of work to be undertaken, the approximate quantities of each item, unit rates and totals and will take the 'conventional' form illustrated in Figure 11.1.

No.	Item Description	Qty.	Unit	Rate	Total
	Preliminaries				
1	**All-in Cost:** of setting out hard and soft landscape elements and obtaining approval from landscape architect.		Site		
	Groundwork				
2	Excavate to reduced levels not exceeding 300mm for driveway and parking carefully preserving topsoil for re-use elsewhere on site as per specification clause ...	685	m2		
3	**Provisional Sum:** Disposal of excavated material off site to approved tip allowing for 20% bulking in excavations.	164	m3		
	Paving				
4	Supply and lay 'soldier course' brick edging on 50mm depth mortar bed as per specification clause ...	65	ml		
5	**Extra Over:** 'Soldier course' brick edgings to curves as per landscape architect's drawing and specification clause ...		Item		
	Structures				
6	**Provisional Sum:** Supply of pergola as per landscape architects drawing number ... and specification clause ...		Item		
7	**Extra Over:** Contractor's labour and overheads for arranging delivery and handling of pergola.		Item		
	Planting				
8	**PC Sum:** For supply of semi-mature tree grown off-site.		Item		
9	**All-in cost:** For contractor to take delivery of nursery stock		Item		

	SUB TOTAL £
Notes: Estimate prepared 23 September 2013.	**CONTINGENCIES @ 10% £**
Expected to be valid for 3 months from date of estimate.	
All rates will be subject to change according to fluctuations in the cost of materials and workmanship.	**VAT @ 20% £**
It is assumed all bulk materials will be delivered to site in full loads as part loads are likely to significantly increase costs.	
All rates are inclusive of contractor's overheads and profit.	**GRAND TOTAL £**

Fig. 11.1 Conventional Format for Schedule of Operations

The format in Figure 11.1 is similar to that used in what is known as a 'Bill of Quantities'. The term 'Bill of Quantities' should only be used when the schedule has been prepared strictly in accordance with the *Standard Method of Measurement* (Royal Institute of Chartered Surveyors, 1998); a task normally undertaken by a Quantity Surveyor assuming the project is large enough to warrant this additional expense.

On smaller projects that do not warrant the input of a Quantity Surveyor it is safer for the professional practitioner to prepare a 'Schedule of Operations' as opposed to a 'Bill of Quantities'. A Schedule of Operations is essentially a 'shopping list' noting the works to be undertaken, or commodities to be supplied, the quantities of each, and making provision for both individual rates and totals to be inserted in respect of each item. A Schedule of Operations in this format will enable the professional practitioner to produce a detailed estimate of project implementation costs.

A Schedule of Operations in the 'conventional' format shown in Figure 11.1 can be provided to contractors (minus the unit rates and totals inserted by the professional practitioner for the purpose of preparing an estimate) as one of the suite of contract documents (discussed in Chapter 12) upon which the contractors will base their quotations/tenders (discussed in Chapter 14). By providing an itemised Schedule of Operations the professional practitioner goes some way to ensuring that quotations subsequently received from contractors can be evaluated on a 'like for like' basis; that is to say, it is clear if any items have been omitted from a contractor's quotation or if there are significant anomalies in pricing between competing bids.

A variation of Figure 11.1 is where the schedule lists items of work and notional units rather than measured quantities. A schedule in this form is generally referred to as a 'Schedule of Rates'. The rate inserted in such a schedule is, for example, the rate to supply and lay one hundred square metres of cultivated lawn turf. The finished job is then measured, valued and paid for on the basis of the actual number of units used. A Schedule of Rates is often used for items not easily quantified at the design stage – items such as additional works the extent of which cannot yet be known or for maintenance operations.

Importantly, units adopted within a Schedule of Rates must reflect the scale, albeit not the precise quantity, of the works likely to be required. A Schedule of Rates should also accurately reflect the methods by which such works would normally be implemented. For example, it would not normally be considered reasonable to apply a rate per square metre for the mowing of sports pitches extending to several hectares. Since this work is most likely to be undertaken by means of large machinery a rate per hectare would normally be considered more appropriate. Similarly, it would normally be unreasonable to apply a rate per hectare for the hand digging of flowerbeds, since this operation is more appropriately measured in square metres. If inappropriate units of measurement were to be used, not only would rates for these items be difficult to find but contractors asked to bid for the works would find such units almost impossible to price.

As discussed above, although it is advisable to avoid the term 'Bill of Quantities' unless the services of a Quantity Surveyor have been employed, in preparing a schedule the professional practitioner should always follow the 'Common Arrangement of Work Sections' intended to ensure the suite of contract documents (discussed in Chapter 12) are related to each other by a common structure.

By adopting the 'Common Arrangement of Work Sections' in the preparation of schedules, the professional practitioner will ensure similar items are grouped together in a logical sequence. For example, even though the same paving (Common Arrangement of Work Sections Q25) is to be used in several areas of the site, the depth of sub-base (Common Arrangement of Work Sections Q20) and therefore the depth of excavations (Common Arrangement of Work Sections D20) could vary according to the anticipated loading, that is to say, whether the paving is designed for pedestrian or vehicular traffic.

By adopting the 'Common Arrangement of Work Sections' in the preparation of schedules, the professional practitioner will also ensure nothing is missed. This is a wise precaution, since errors and omissions coming to light only as implementation of the project proceeds are likely to cause a degree of embarrassment for the professional practitioner and potentially serious problems of additional expense; none of which will please the client.

Schedules should always be clear and concise containing only the outline information required, for example 'pre-cast concrete riven paving'. Full details of each item, for example the manufacturer of the paving; the colour; choice of bedding and pointing; and any specific requirements of workmanship, should all be included in the project specification (discussed in Chapter 12).

The reason only outline information is included in the schedule, apart from restricted space, is to discourage the contractor's on-site personnel from referring exclusively to the schedule in the event it becomes one of the contract documents; instead encouraging on-site personnel to consult the project specification where comprehensive details are to be found. To provide a further safeguard in this respect and to assist the contractor with cross referencing, it is common practise to state after each item contained in the schedule the words 'in accordance with specification clause …' in order to 'signpost' the way to the project specification and the detail therein.

11.3   ATTRIBUTING RATES

The final stage in estimating project implementation costs involves attributing rates to the items and approximate quantities measured from the project drawing(s) and making up the schedule. As can be seen from the example in Figure 11.1 the form of rates used may consist of any or all of the following, according to the level of information available to the professional practitioner at the time of preparing the estimate:

- 'Approximate all-in costs' comprise a reasonable estimate of, for example, the combined costs for all excavations, disposals, labour, materials and workmanship required for a particular item. Rates are normally applied per square metre, cubic metre or other appropriate unit.

- 'Measured works' normally account for the majority of items on a schedule of operations. This is a much more precise method of estimating costs in which, for example, excavations, disposals and materials are all treated as individual items and priced separately. Supply costs are normally obtained for the particular materials required. The supply costs will be based upon the exact quantity of material required and therefore reflect the precise cost of haulage and delivery. To each item must be added the cost of labour based upon an estimate of the time likely to be needed for the completion of each individual operation.

- 'Cost plus' also requires that the supply costs of materials are obtained for each item based upon the exact quantities required, to which the cost of labour is added according to the actual time required to complete each item. Since the majority of professional practitioners are unlikely to be familiar with the exact amount of labour required for each operation, this is a difficult basis on which to prepare estimates of implementation costs. Cost plus is therefore more commonly used for the retrospective valuation of additional items found necessary as the project progresses but not forming part of the original schedule. For example, if during excavations it is found necessary for the landscape contractor to re-route a drain not previously known to have existed. The professional practitioner should however take care as cost plus pricing can prove very lucrative for the unscrupulous contractor and rather expensive for the client.

- 'Prime cost' or 'PC' sums are included within the schedule of operations in circumstances where a particular product is to be used or a particular supplier has been specified – for example, where nursery stock has been produced in advance of project implementation. The amount inserted in the schedule will be the exact cost of supply only. The contractor will normally be permitted to add to PC Sums the cost of labour for delivery and handling; overheads; and profit. If PC Sums are used allowance must be made within the estimate for what are regarded as these 'on-costs'.

- 'Provisional sums' are used where an exact amount or a cost for a particular item cannot be determined, perhaps because the detail of the item has not yet been finalised. A 'provisional sum' represents an informed guess as to what the eventual cost might be. This may, for example, be the cost of a bespoke pergola that has not yet been fully detailed. Again it should be borne in mind it is normal for a contractor to add 'on-costs' so the professional practitioner must make an allowance in this respect when estimating.

- 'Extra over' items are additional amounts the client will be required to pay where a particular item requires extra work – for example, the additional cost per linear metre for laying brick edging to a curve rather than in a straight line. The additional cost arises as a result of the increased labour input and a greater amount of material wastage as a result of cutting.

11.4 SOURCES OF RATES

Particularly for the inexperienced or novice practitioner, it can be extremely difficult to prepare accurate estimates of project budgets and to know from where to obtain indicative costs when so doing. The following provides some indication of where guidance may be sought:

11.4.1 Previously quoted schemes

Schemes recently quoted by contractors are a valuable source of rates when the professional practitioner is preparing estimates of implementation costs. Previously quoted schemes enable the professional practitioner to develop a personal database of the average prices obtained for frequently specified items. However, it is important to remember that each job is subtly different to another and the costs associated with each project are likely to vary according to site conditions, location, quantities, and market considerations. For example, a contractor's quoted price for a particular item may vary considerably according to the amount of work they have at the time of submitting their quotation, that is to say the state of the contractor's order book.

11.4.2 Manufacturer's or supplier's costs

Manufacturer's or supplier's costs for particular items are a valuable source of information to the professional practitioner in estimating project implementation costs, since the precise cost of particular materials or components is the normal starting point when pricing. It should, however, be borne in mind that labour costs for handling, placing or fixing of materials and components, together with the contractor's overheads and profit, must be added to manufacturer's or supplier's costs for the purpose of estimating. Only by including these additional expenses can estimates based on manufacturer's or supplier's costs be relied upon to accurately reflect the price the client may eventually be expected to pay.

In addition, it is important to remember manufacturer's or supplier's costs may vary a great deal according to location, quantity, handling costs and so on and may be quickly out of date as a result of price changes.

The professional practitioner should aim to ensure accuracy in the estimating of project implementation costs. It is therefore advisable to obtain specific quotations from the manufacturer or supplier on each and every occasion rather than relying on averages of the prices obtained over a given period.

11.4.3 Indicative quotations from contractors

Indicative quotations from contractors can usefully be obtained for specific elements of a scheme. To obtain indicative quotations, the professional practitioner must, firstly, be able to provide sufficient detail of the particular elements in question and, secondly, be able to locate a contractor or contractors who are willing to commit time and resources to a project from which they may not ultimately obtain any paying work.

Indicative quotations enable relatively accurate estimating of costs and reflect market conditions at the time they are obtained.

Some contractors regard such assistance offered to a professional practitioner as a form of 'relationship' marketing, that is to say an opportunity for the contractor to establish a relationship with a professional practitioner based upon trust and goodwill. It would be naïve of the professional practitioner to conclude that the cooperation of contractors in providing indicative quotations is purely an exercise in goodwill or that it is entirely altruistic. In reality, contractors who cooperate in this respect are likely to do so in the hope that one or other project on which they assist will produce profitable business for them. It is quite likely, if a contractor provides indicative quotations on a number of occasions but fails to gain any profitable business when the schemes are offered for formal quotation or tender, the contractor's willingness to be helpful in this respect will diminish.

It is nonetheless true that the assistance of contractors in the form of indicative quotations is a valuable resource in estimating project implementation costs.

11.4.4   Spon's Landscape and External Works Price Book

Spon's Landscape and External Works Price Book is an annual publication produced to assist quantity surveyors, landscape professional practitioners and contractors estimating project costs. The publication follows the 'Common Arrangement of Work Sections' (discussed in Chapter 12).

Spon's Landscape and External Works Price Book uses an access code inside the cover of the book which serves as a license to gain updated information via the internet through its year of publication. Professional practitioners are expected to obtain a new edition every year in order to ensure estimating information remains up to date.

The 'Measured Works' section of *Spon's Landscape and External Works Price Book* is made up of rates for the majority of items likely to be encountered in the course of landscape professional practice. For example, the rates for different types and depths of sub-bases; paving; and planting. The professional practitioner should bear in mind the rates supplied are averages and therefore cannot reflect regional variations, such as the increased cost of operations in London, or site specific factors such as access and transport. Rates are inclusive of all labour and materials but are exclusive of Value Added Tax together with contractor's overheads and profit. An allowance must therefore be made in respect of these items.

It is essential for the professional practitioner to be familiar with the 'Common Arrangement of Work Sections' (discussed in Chapter 12) on which *Spon's Landscape and External Works Price Book* is based in order to understand what is and is not included within each item. For example, paving rates will *not* include excavation and sub-base costs priced separately and found elsewhere in the 'Measured Works' section of the book.

The 'Measured Works' section of *Spon's Landscape and External Works Price Book* comprises tables divided into a number of sections as illustrated by Figure 11.2. The column headings can be a little confusing to those unfamiliar with the publication and are explained below:

Prices for Measured Works

Q25 SLAB/BRICK/STONE/TIMBER PAVINGS

Item Excluding site overheads and profit	PC £	Labour hours	Labour £	Plant £	Material £	Unit	Total rate £
Clay brick pavings; 200 × 100 × 50 mm; laid to running stretcher or stack bond only; on prepared base (not included); bedding on cement: sand (1:4) pointing mortar as work proceeds							
PC £600.00/1000							
laid on edge	48.81	1.59	94.05	–	56.62	m^2	150.67
laid on edge but pavior 65 mm thick	41.00	1.27	75.24	–	48.81	m^2	124.05
laid flat	26.62	0.73	43.45	–	31.28	m^2	74.73
PC £500.00/1000							
laid on edge	40.67	1.59	94.05	–	48.49	m^2	142.54
laid on edge but pavior 65 mm thick	34.16	1.27	75.24	–	41.98	m^2	117.22
laid flat	22.19	0.73	43.45	–	26.84	m^2	70.29
PC £400.00/1000							
laid flat	17.75	0.73	43.45	–	22.41	m^2	65.86
laid on edge	32.54	1.59	94.05	–	40.35	m^2	134.40
laid on edge but pavior 65 mm thick	27.33	1.27	75.24	–	35.15	m^2	110.39
PC £300.00/1000							
laid on edge	24.40	1.59	94.05	–	32.22	m^2	126.27
laid on edge but pavior 65 mm thick	20.50	1.27	75.24	–	28.31	m^2	103.55
laid flat	13.31	0.73	43.45	–	17.97	m^2	61.42
Clay brick pavings; 200 × 100 × 50 mm; butt jointed laid herringbone or basketweave pattern only; on prepared base (not included); bedding on 50 mm sharp sand							
PC £600.00/1000							
laid flat	30.75	0.46	27.36	0.30	32.87	m^2	60.53
PC £500.00/1000							
laid flat	25.63	0.46	27.36	0.30	27.74	m^2	55.40
PC £400.00/1000							
laid flat	20.50	0.46	27.36	0.30	22.62	m^2	50.28
PC £300.00/1000							
laid flat	15.38	0.46	27.36	0.30	17.49	m^2	45.15
Clay brick pavings; 215 × 102.5 × 65 mm; on prepared base (not included); bedding on cement: sand (1:4) pointing mortar as work proceeds							
Paving bricks; PC £600.00/1000; herringbone bond							
laid on edge	36.44	1.19	70.21	–	43.31	m^2	113.52
laid flat	23.70	0.79	46.84	–	30.57	m^2	77.41
Paving bricks; PC £600.00/1000; basketweave bond							
laid on edge	36.44	0.79	46.81	–	43.31	m^2	90.12
laid flat	23.70	0.53	31.21	–	30.57	m^2	61.78

Fig. 11.2 *Spon's Landscape and External Works Price Book* 'Measured Works'

- 'PC £' indicates the supply cost of components required for the particular item in question. For example, the supply cost of bricks, based upon a rate per thousand, according to how the bricks are to be laid.

- 'Labour Hours' provides an indication of the time required to complete each unit. For example, 1.59 hours are indicated to be required for the laying of one square metre of clay brick pavings; on edge; on a prepared base (not included); bedded on sand and cement; and pointed as work proceeds.

- 'Labour £' is based upon an average wage rate multiplied by the number of labour hours indicated to be required per unit. The rate is deemed to include contractor's 'on-costs' associated directly with employees such as administration and National Insurance contributions.

- 'Plant £' is a term relating to machinery and equipment costs rather than any form of horticultural produce. Therefore the 'plant' cost associated with the laying of pre-cast concrete paving for example is that in relation to the hire or ownership, together with the running costs, of a disc cutter. These costs exclude fuel and transport expenses; costs normally considered within the separately priced 'preliminary items' section of the 'measured works' tables (Preliminary items will be explained in Chapter 12).

- 'Material £' represents the supply cost of components required for a particular item (as indicated in the 'PC £' column) plus the additional materials required for fixing; items such as sand, cement and so on, to arrive at an overall material cost.

- 'Unit' indicates the form of measurement used for a particular item, for example per square metre, cubic metre, linear metre and the like.

- 'Total Rate £' indicates the combined cost per unit of 'Labour £' (cost), 'Material £' (cost) and 'Plant £' (cost) to represent the overall figure to be used in estimating implementation costs, bearing in mind what has been said already that such rates do not allow for the contractor's overheads and profit which must be added.

The 'Approximate Estimates' section of *Spon's Landscape and External Works Price Book* is potentially a very useful source of information for professional practitioners. It provides an indication of cost for a complete operation, measured per unit, and including incidentals that would normally be measured separately. The professional practitioner should take care to remember that 'Approximate Estimates' being based upon 'Measured Works' similarly *exclude* contractor's overheads and profit, Value Added Tax and preliminary items (deemed to be measured elsewhere).

SOURCES OF RATES

- Previously quoted schemes
- Manufacturer's or supplier's costs
- Indicative quotations from contractors
- *Spon's Landscape and External Works Price Book*

CHAPTER SUMMARY

- The professional practitioner will normally be required to provide the client with an estimate of project implementation costs
- To ensure estimates of implementation costs are reasonably accurate it is desirable for the client to have approved outline design proposals
- Estimates should always be given in writing and broken down into as much detail as reasonable and practicable
- The process of preparing estimates of project implementation costs involves measuring approximate quantities; preparing a schedule of operations; and attributing rates to operations and approximate quantities
- Previously quoted schemes enable the professional practitioner to develop a database of the average prices obtained for frequently specified items
- Manufacturer's or supplier's costs are a valuable source of information
- Indicative quotations from contractors can usefully be obtained
- *Spon's Landscape and External Works Price Book* is an annual publication produced for use in estimating project costs

12

Specification Fundamentals

> THE AIMS OF THIS CHAPTER ARE TO:
>
> - Describe the range of contract documents
> - Introduce the concept of Building Information Modelling
> - Explain the layout and structure of a specification document
> - Introduce the Common Arrangement of Works Sections
> - Explain the meaning of preliminary/general conditions
> - Explain the key considerations in specifying materials and workmanship
> - Identify and explain the purpose of industry standard documents

The project specification is but one of a suite of contract documents examined in some detail throughout the remaining chapters of this book. For that reason the reader is invited to become familiar with the range of material contract documents embrace, the respective uses for the information contained therein and where this information might be sourced.

12.1 CONTRACT DOCUMENTATION

As illustrated by Figure 12.1 contract documentation falls broadly into two categories; that required by the client, amounting to a set of design drawings (beyond the scope of the present volume) and an estimate of implementation costs (discussed in Chapter 11) so the client might comment upon and approve both design proposals and an overall budget for the scheme; and that required by the contractor so that, once the client has approved design proposals and an overall budget, quotations of the *actual* cost of project implementation might be obtained (discussed in Chapter 14).

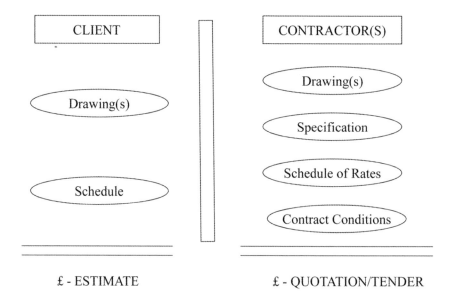

Fig. 12.1 Contract Documentation

To ensure that quotations for project implementation costs are accurate and the project is implemented to the required standard, contractors will normally require more comprehensive documentation than that required for the client to approve the design and the project budget.

Drawing(s) may amount to a single illustration of the site overlaid with the proposals of the professional practitioner; they may comprise a master plan with site survey and setting out information, individual planting and construction details or any combination thereof. The number and complexity of drawings is ultimately an individual decision driven by the needs of a particular project and the presentational style of the professional practitioner. Whilst the preparation of drawings is outside the scope of this book it is vital that, whatever range of drawings is employed, they are collectively the 'illustrative' representation of the professional practitioner's proposals for the layout of the scheme, for the assembly of materials and components and for the planting design.

Schedules list the specific operations or commodities required for project implementation and approximate quantities in respect of each item. Schedules are the 'quantitative' representation of the professional practitioner's proposals. The nature and composition of schedules has been dealt with in Chapter 11 so no more need be said here.

Specifications consist of detailed written descriptions relating to the standards of materials and workmanship required to implement the project. They are the 'qualitative' representation of the professional practitioner's proposals. It is with these 'qualitative' issues that the present chapter is solely concerned.

In addition, the contractor(s) will need to know the legal conditions under which the contract is to be awarded. These are discussed in detail in Chapter 13.

12.2 BUILDING INFORMATION MODELLING

Before looking at the detail of conventional project specifications it is important to consider the impact of Building Information Modelling. Building Information Modelling involves the collaborative generation and management of digital representations of physical and functional project characteristics. Rich in data that can be exchanged or networked to inform the decision making process and answer questions throughout the lifecycle of a project, Building Information Modelling potentially has far-reaching consequences for all areas of traditional construction processes particularly in the public sector. According to the Government Construction Client Group (Cabinet Office, May 2011, p14) Building Information Modelling is expected to be a requirement of all publicly funded projects by the end of 2016.

A Building Information Modelling Execution Plan and Employers Information Requirements are essential components of delivering a project compliant with Building Information Modelling. These documents reinforce established practice by adding formality. With a focus on project information requirements, methodology and deliverables, Building Information Modelling provides a sophisticated and structured model environment containing graphical representations, quantities and project specifications linked to increasingly intelligent Computer Aided Design; 'data' arguably being infinitely preferable to traditional contract 'documentation' including the project specification.

12.3 SPECIFICATION STRUCTURE

Whether in the virtual world of Building Information Modelling or as part of the 'traditional' suite of contract documents, specifications are the means by which the professional practitioner communicates the standards of materials and workmanship required on the project.

Specifications may consist of brief notes included on the contract drawing(s); a few pages appended to the contract drawing(s); or a comprehensive specification document. The decision as to what form of specification a project requires will depend upon the characteristics of a particular project; the choice of procurement strategy (discussed in Chapter 9); and to a lesser degree the skills and experience of the contractor(s) involved with the project which, in practice, can only be assumed at the time the project specification is drafted.

Specifications must always be clear and concise. The aim of a specification is to guide and to assist rather than to confuse. Specification clauses must be clear and unambiguous. In practice, contractors will be looking at many and varied specifications from multiple sources, whereas the professional practitioner is commonly dealing with variations of a single source document.

The professional practitioner should avoid vague phrases and be specific wherever possible or at least indicate a general standard. The specification should establish exactly what is required to complete the project. Contractors cannot be expected to be mind readers; if the specification doesn't specifically ask for whatever 'it' is, the professional practitioner has no right to complain when 'it' isn't produced.

A specification must be consistent. If the specification refers to a 'schedule of operations', the professional practitioner should ensure what is provided to the contractor is a 'schedule of operations' and not something entitled 'schedule' or 'Bill of Quantities'. If the project drawings refer to an 'extension to the York stone terrace' the proposed extension should not be referred to as a 'new patio' in the specification. To do otherwise will only lead to confusion.

The evidence of a well-crafted specification is that every contractor approached for a quotation is able to determine *exactly* what is required to complete the project. By that means all quotations received should be entirely comparable.

For reasons best known to themselves some professional practitioners choose not to be precise or to provide only limited detail in project specifications. In these circumstances the professional practitioner simply cannot be sure each contractor is quoting for the same. For example, one contractor might be quoting to lay paving on a concrete base and another on sand. Again there is nothing to be gained by imprecision. The same well-crafted specification will ultimately serve as a clear and unambiguous standard by which the professional practitioner can measure the materials and the workmanship eventually produced on site.

As discussed in Chapter 11, schedules of operations or schedules of rates should contain only basic information, for example 'x amount of pre-cast concrete paving' whilst full information contained within the specification should consist of the 'who' – for example, 'Marshalls'; 'what' – for example, 'riven York stone random paving 50mm thick'; and 'how' – for example, 'laid on a 100mm compacted limestone sub-base and full mortar bed'. The aim is to ensure the contractor reads carefully and understands what the professional practitioner requires and ensures this information is passed in full to those on site.

Provided the professional practitioner has selected, or intends to select, what they know to be reputable contractors to bid for the work (discussed in Chapter 14), it is fair to assume the contractors have a level of technical competence. For example, it should not be necessary to describe how to point brickwork but the professional practitioner *will* need to state which method of pointing is to be used, if this is considered an important feature of the finished work.

'Cover-all' clauses – for example, 'the contractor should build the wall to recognised standards' – are imprecise, unfair to contractors and to be avoided. The professional practitioner should specify to *what* 'recognised standard' the work is to be undertaken, for example 'to British Standard …' or in accordance with a stated code of practice. Furthermore, it is pointless to ask contractors to do something impractical, for example to use enormous pieces of rock on a site with only pedestrian access, but not unheard of for professional practitioners to do so.

In practice contractors often have considerably better technical knowledge than do professional practitioners. Lack of technical knowledge frequently results in the professional practitioner over-specifying materials or workmanship, thereby adding considerably to the cost, or providing a means for unscrupulous contractors to 'cut corners' by not providing the materials for which they have quoted. For example, is the professional practitioner able to recognise pressure treated timber from that which is untreated? Can the professional practitioner tell the difference between 18 and 19 gauge rabbit netting between which there is a substantial difference in price? Can the professional practitioner tell the difference between *Miscanthus zebrinus* which grows to 1.2 metres and sugar cane which grows to 2.7 metres?

A great deal of technical knowledge comes with experience. The inexperienced professional practitioner should look to more practiced colleagues for guidance and support. Alternatively, the professional practitioner might employ the services of a seasoned practitioner to draft the project specification and oversee project implementation. There are specialist practitioners, operating on a commercial basis, specifying and managing landscape projects. By employing the services of seasoned experts the inexperienced professional practitioner not only benefits but also learns.

A PROJECT SPECIFICATION MUST:

- Be clear and concise
- Be consistent
- Avoid vague phrases
- Avoid 'cover-all' clauses
- Establish exactly what is required to complete the project
- Specify to what standard works are to be undertaken

12.4 THE COMMON ARRANGEMENT OF WORK SECTIONS

Conventional specification structure is driven by the 'Common Arrangement of Work Sections', the product of a government initiative 'Coordinated Project Information' in 1979. The intention of Common Arrangement of Work Sections is to ensure that drawings, specifications, Bills of Quantity (where used) and schedules are related to each other by a common structure consisting of 25 sections broken down into a number of sub-sections.

The Common Arrangement of Work Sections are to be found within the *Standard Method of Measurement* (Royal Institute of Chartered Surveyors, 1998) and *Spon's Landscape and External Works Price Book* (each referred to in Chapter 11) along with other industry standard sources such as NBS Landscape (referred to later in this chapter as a useful starting point for the inexperienced practitioner drafting a project specification) and standard forms of agreement throughout the landscape and related industries.

Not all Common Arrangement of Work Sections are relevant to landscape contracts, and so landscape specifications conventionally begin with 'Preliminaries/General Conditions' based upon Common Arrangement of Work Section A, followed by those parts of Common Arrangement of Work Sections 'Materials & Workmanship' of relevance to the particular project.

12.5 PRELIMINARIES/GENERAL CONDITIONS

The Common Arrangement of Work Section A includes a number of sub-sections concerning preliminary information and general conditions relevant to a particular project. A non-exhaustive list of sub-sections commonly used by professional practitioners in the preparation of landscape specifications and the information each sub-section should contain is as follows.

12.5.1 Project particulars

In accordance with sub-section A10 of the Common Arrangement of Work Sections 'project particulars' should describe exactly where and what the project site consists of; what the expected start and finish dates of the project are (bearing in mind it is impossible to be certain of these at the stage of drafting a project specification); the details of the client/employer; and of the quantity surveyor, planning supervisor, structural engineer and so on, depending upon which, if any, of these are involved in the particular project.

12.5.2 Drawings

In accordance with sub-section A11 of the Common Arrangement of Work Sections, 'drawings' should comprise a list of the titles and numbers of all the drawings provided to the contractor(s) in relation to the particular project.

12.5.3 The site/existing buildings

In accordance with sub-section A12 of the Common Arrangement of Work Sections, 'the site/existing buildings' should comprise site information that may assist the contractor(s) in their assessment of the works for which they are being asked to quote. For example, the detail of boundaries, existing buildings on or adjacent to the site and services such as electricity, water and gas supply lines on, over or under the site.

12.5.4 Description of the work

In accordance with sub-section A13 of the Common Arrangement of Work Sections, the 'description of the work' should comprise a brief outline of the project. For example 'the project comprises re-grading and contouring of the site, the planting of trees, shrubs and conifers, together with the laying of cultivated lawn turf'.

12.5.5 Conditions of contract

In accordance with sub-section A20 of the Common Arrangement of Work Sections, 'conditions of contract' should make clear exactly the terms under which the contractor(s) are required to undertake the project. Conditions of contract should preferably be those contained within a standard form of agreement (discussed in Chapter 13) amended according to the requirements of the particular project.

If a sample copy of the conditions of contract with all the proposed amendments and additions (discussed in Chapter 13) is to be provided to the bidding contractor(s) it is not necessary to list each clause and each amendment within the specification document. If a sample copy of the conditions of contract is not to be provided to bidding contractors, the specification document must include a schedule of clause headings from the standard conditions of contract together with details of any special conditions or amendments that are to apply.

12.5.6 Employer's requirements: tendering sub-letting & supply

In accordance with sub-section A30 of Common Arrangement of Work Sections, the client/employer's requirements in relation to 'tendering sub-letting and supply' should comprise the instructions for tendering (discussed in Chapter 14), that is to say, to where the contractor(s) quotations are to be submitted, for whose attention and by what date. Bidding contractor(s) will also need to know for how long they are required to hold the price quoted; how any inaccuracies are to be dealt with; and whether a preliminary programme of works, method statement, safety policy and so on are to be returned with the contractor(s) quotation or tender.

As regards 'sub-letting and supply' the professional practitioner must state whether nominated sub-contractors (discussed in Chapter 13) are required to be used for elements of the project; under what circumstances the contractor(s) will be permitted to sub-let part or all of the works to domestic sub-contractors (discussed in Chapter 13), for example where specialist expertise is required for the laying of resin bonded gravel; and whether any of the materials have been procured in advance by the client (discussed in Chapter 11) for example advanced nursery stock.

12.5.7 Employer's requirements; management of the works

In accordance with sub-section A32 of the Common Arrangement of Work Sections, the client/employer's requirements as regards 'management of the works' should state whether there are specific requirements for supervision, for example whether the project requires the presence of a competent foreperson on site at all times; what is the expected frequency of monitoring visits and who needs to be in attendance, for example weekly meetings on site between the professional practitioner and the project manager appointed by the contractor; the amount of Public Liability Insurance required to cover accidents and/or injuries occurring to persons other than the contractor's personnel; any requirement for the contractor to maintain a site diary recording such things as weather, deliveries, number of men on site and so on; the requirement to submit and maintain a project programme; how progress is to be monitored; and how requests for extensions of time are to be dealt with if they should arise, for example whether such requests are to be dealt with by the quantity surveyor or the landscape professional practitioner.

12.5.8 Employer's requirements: quality standards/control

In accordance with sub-section A33 of the Common Arrangement of Work Sections, the client/employer's requirements as regards 'quality standards and control' should state by what quality standard materials are to be accepted or rejected and to what standards specified works are to be completed, for example any requirement for materials or stages of work such as excavations and foundations to be inspected and certified as satisfactory before work continues.

12.5.9 Employer's requirements: security/safety/protection

In accordance with sub-section A34 of the Common Arrangement of Work Sections, the client/employer's requirements as regards 'security safety and protection' should state what features are to be retained and how they are to be protected, for example existing trees are to be protected by temporary fencing or existing services by weight distribution; whether the contractor(s) may be permitted to burn on site, for example as a means of disposing of felled trees cleared from the site; and whether there are restrictions on noise, for example by the imposition of working hours on site.

12.5.10 Employer's requirements: facilities/temporary work/services

In accordance with sub-section A36 of the Common Arrangement of Work Sections, the client/employer's requirements as regards 'facilities temporary work and services' should state where on the site the contractor(s) facilities are to be located; where on the site the contractor(s) will be permitted to tip and store materials; whether the contractor(s) are required to provide on-site facilities such as washing, sanitary and rest accommodation or offices for site meetings; whether any secure storage is to be provided by the client/employer; and whether there are materials handling facilities available, for example if the client/employer is a farmer they may have a tele-handler they are prepared to make available for the contractor(s) use.

As regards temporary works, it must be made clear whether the contractor(s) are required to provide temporary access routes, protective fences, temporary screening and so on. These can be very expensive for contractor(s) to install, maintain and remove. Likewise, it should be clear whether contractor(s) will be permitted to display name boards on site or to use the project as a means of advertising in any other form, for example uploading photographs to a website.

As to services, it should be clear whether contractor(s) are required to provide their own supplies of electricity, water, telephone and so on, or if any such services are to be provided at the client/employer's expense.

The reader should bear in mind that 'Preliminaries/General Conditions' are intended to contain only the bare essentials of information and that the detail of, for example, quality standards as they relate to particular materials or workmanship should be contained within the second, generally more substantial, part of the specification.

For further information on the Common Arrangement of Work Sections, and the detail to be contained within each section of a specification see the *Standard Method of Measurement* (Royal Institute of Chartered Surveyors, 1998).

12.6   MATERIALS AND WORKMANSHIP

The second part of a specification concerns 'Materials and Workmanship' and is generally the much more substantial part of a specification, rich in detail, and therefore way beyond what can be included in the scope of the present text.

Suffice to say the 'Materials and Workmanship' section of a specification should also conform to the Common Arrangement of Work Sections and the detail of what information should be included within, for example, Section D 'Groundwork'; Section N 'Furniture/Equipment'; or Section Q 'Paving/Planting/Fencing/Site Furniture', is to be found in the *Standard Method of Measurement* (Royal Institute of Chartered Surveyors, 1998).

Within the limitations of the present text what will be offered here is general guidance as to what the professional practitioner should consider in approaching the 'Materials and Workmanship' section of a specification

12.6.1   Materials

The materials to be used on a project are likely to have become apparent during the design process. The object of specification clauses is to make clear to the contractor(s) the detail of what these materials are; to what standard the materials are to be supplied, for example Melcourt Ornamental Bark Chips; whether there are specific requirements for handling of materials, particularly in relation to durables such as nursery stock; whether particular materials are to be obtained from specific suppliers; and whether particular components have been pre-fabricated and if so by whom.

12.6.2   Workmanship

The specification should contain the precise detail of the workmanship required. For example, the depth and breadth of tree pits; at what stage in the planting process tree stakes are to be inserted; the measures that are to be taken to prevent damage during planting; by what means the trees are to be secured to the stakes; and the standard required on completion of planting, such as the soil level in relation to the nursery soil level, that trees and stakes are to be perpendicular and that footprints are to be removed.

Q31 External planting

To be read with Preliminaries/General conditions.

505   TREE PITS
- Sizes: 75 mm deeper than root system and wide enough to accommodate roots when fully spread.
- Sloping ground: Maintain horizontal bases and vertical sides with no less than minimum depth throughout.
- Pit bottoms: With slightly raised centre. Break up to a depth of 150 mm.
  - Treatment: Soil ameliorant worked into pit bottoms.
- Pit sides: Scarify.
- Backfilling material: Tree backfilling material.
- Accessories: Perforated plastics irrigation/ ventilation pipe and underground guying in accordance with BS 4043.

Fig. 12.2 Worked Example of Tree Pit Specification. Reproduced with permission of RIBA Enterprises Limited.

12.6.3 Quality assurance

The specification should state whether samples of particular components are to be provided for inspection. For example, reclaimed York stone paving can be endlessly variable in thickness and colour so the specification may require a sample area of paving to be laid for inspection by the professional practitioner, against which the standards of materials and workmanship can be measured as the project proceeds (such as that at Figure 12.3).

12.6.4 British Standards

British Standards are more commonly found in relation to materials though there are a few relating to workmanship for such things as tree surgery and fencing. A full list is available from the British Standards Institution or a list of those that apply to landscape projects is to be found in *Spon's Landscape and External Works Price Book*. It can be helpful to specify materials and workmanship by reference to the appropriate British Standard and perfectly reasonable to require the contractor(s) to provide samples and/or test certificates confirming that, for example, the topsoil supplied conforms to BS3882:2007.

12.6.5 Specification by type

Specification of materials and workmanship by type will suffice only when an item can be clearly defined and there is little scope for variation between one supplier and another. For example, it would normally be sufficient to specify a 'pressure treated five bar hunting gate' as there is generally little scope for variety of design, though it might still be advisable to specify a particular manufacturer, or a range of manufacturers, to ensure the quality of the product.

Q24 Interlocking brick/block roads/pavings

To be read with Preliminaries/ General Conditions
To be representative of colour and appearance.

230 CONTROL SAMPLES OF YORK STONE PAVING
- General: Carry out sample area of finished work:
  - Location: as drawing AZ/059/0035.
  - Size (minimum): 3.0 x 3.0 m.
  - Features to be included: Edging and Junction with building facade.
- Give notice: When ready for inspection.
- Timing: Obtain approval of appearance before proceeding.

505 REGULARITY OF PAVED SURFACES
- Maximum undulations in the surface of pavings (except tactile paving surfaces) under a 1 metre straight edge placed anywhere on the surface (where appropriate in relation to the geometry of the surface): 3 mm.
- Joints between paving units or utility access covers:
  - Joints flush with the surface: difference in level between adjacent units to be no more than twice the joint width (with a 5 mm max difference in level).
  - Recessed, filled joints: difference in level between adjacent units to be no greater than 2 mm; the recess to be no deeper than 5 mm.
  - Unfilled joints: difference in level between adjacent units to be no greater than 2 mm.
- Sudden irregularities: Not permitted.

Fig. 12.3 Worked Example of Specification for Paving Sample.
Reproduced with permission of RIBA Enterprises Limited.

12.6.6 Specification by proprietary name

Proprietary name can be an effective way of specifying a particular product provided the professional practitioner has thoroughly researched the requirements of the project and can be sure the product is exactly what is required. For example, is it necessary for the garden pergola to be treated with 'Sadolin Classic Dark Palisander', which is an expensive option, or will any dark brown wood preservative, other than creosote, suffice?

12.6.7 Specification by minimum standard

The specification should be clear as to any minimum standard that is acceptable. Contractor(s) may then supply a superior product if they so wish but must still gain approval for so doing.

It is worth remembering that, in a competitive situation, it is always in the client/ employer's interests to allow the contractor(s) maximum choice in the sourcing of materials. A contractor may be able to get a better deal from one supplier than from another and this should, in turn, be reflected in the price quoted for the job.

12.6.8 Specification by supplier

Nominating a particular supplier within the specification limits competition and denies contractor(s) a competitive 'edge' over their rivals. This may be advantageous, in that the contractor(s) are then competing purely on their own costs, but it also means the nominated suppliers of materials are protected from competition and can potentially name their price.

Nominated suppliers may be necessary where quality cannot be guaranteed simply by providing a specification. For example, the professional practitioner may wish to inspect plants on a particular nursery and, once satisfied as to their quality, require the plants are supplied only from that source.

Alternatively, the specification may provide a list of approved suppliers, consisting of a number of sources which the professional practitioner is satisfied can each supply a particular commodity to a similar standard, thereafter allowing the contractor(s) to negotiate the most favourable terms from one, other or a combination of the approved suppliers.

12.6.9 Specification by method

In specifying workmanship by method the professional practitioner needs to think logically about the processes involved and the sequence of operations. For example, whether it is preferable to have the tree stake driven into the bottom of the pit before the tree is planted, in which case will the roots allow the tree to be close enough to the stake for tying, or can the tree stake be driven in after planting, so it can be located as close to the stem as possible, without damaging the root system in so doing?

12.6.10 Specification by finished effect

Specification by finished effect can be extremely hazardous. For example, if the specification requires nothing more than that nursery stock should be planted, there is nothing to say that the pots should be removed; the roots teased out; the ground adequately cultivated and ameliorated; or the plants planted with sufficient room for the spread of their roots.

12.7 STANDARD SPECIFICATION CLAUSES

By now, the reader, especially if an inexperienced practitioner, may be wondering from where all the information required for a project specification might be gleaned, particularly if the reader does not work for a large established, professional practice or have experienced colleagues on whom they can rely for assistance.

Whilst a 'standard specification' simply does not exist, since each and every project is different in terms of site conditions and requirements, 'standard clauses' are common, since the majority of tasks are repetitive with only minor adjustments such as the depth of sub-base or the ratio of sand and cement in the mortar mix.

Standard clauses ensure familiarity, both from the point of view of the professional practitioner and contractors, and may be drawn from a number of sources:

Q31 External planting

To be read with Preliminaries/General conditions.

545 LONG SINGLE STAKING FOR FEATHERED TREES AND STANDARDS
- Staking: Position stake close to tree on windward side and drive vertically at least 300 mm into bottom of pit before planting.
  - Backfilling: Consolidate material around stake.
- Height of stakes: Cut off just below lowest branch of tree.
- Ties: Adjustable ties.
- Tying: Secure tree firmly but not rigidly to stake with at least two ties. Use three ties if necessary to prevent tree touching stake.
  - Position: Top tie within 25 mm of top of stake and lower tie approximately halfway down.

Fig. 12.4 Worked Example of Tree Staking Specification.
Reproduced with permission of RIBA Enterprises Limited.

12.7.1 NBS Landscape

NBS Landscape is a subscription-based, on-line resource library of clauses for selection and editing to produce project specifications for hard and soft landscaping. According to NBS Landscape (2013):

> NBS technical authors are continually researching to provide the best technical guidance and clause options to people writing specifications ... Customers receive updates on CD-ROM three times a year, and incremental updates are available to download online, so the information you are using is always up-to-date.

NBS Landscape provides a comprehensive set of clauses with detailed guidance appearing next to each clause on the screen. Whilst the on-screen guidance is intended to help select and edit the correct clauses, the NBS Landscape database is very large and is designed around the Common Arrangement of Work Sections. The user has to go through the library of clauses methodically, making choices as to which clauses are appropriate for a particular project and which are not. It is therefore very easy for the professional practitioner to over-specify and to end up with a specification document that is much larger than it needs to be.

To begin with the NBS Landscape process is time consuming and laborious. It is important for the professional practitioner to reproduce the specification clauses in full, as opposed to simply quoting clause numbers and assuming contractors will have access to the software and bother to look for the full text. In reality the professional practitioner will eventually build up a sub-set of their most commonly used clauses, to adapt each time they produce a specification document.

12.7.2 National Plant Specification

The introduction of a National Plant Specification was originally intended to address a lack of rigour in specifying plant material and disparate information on

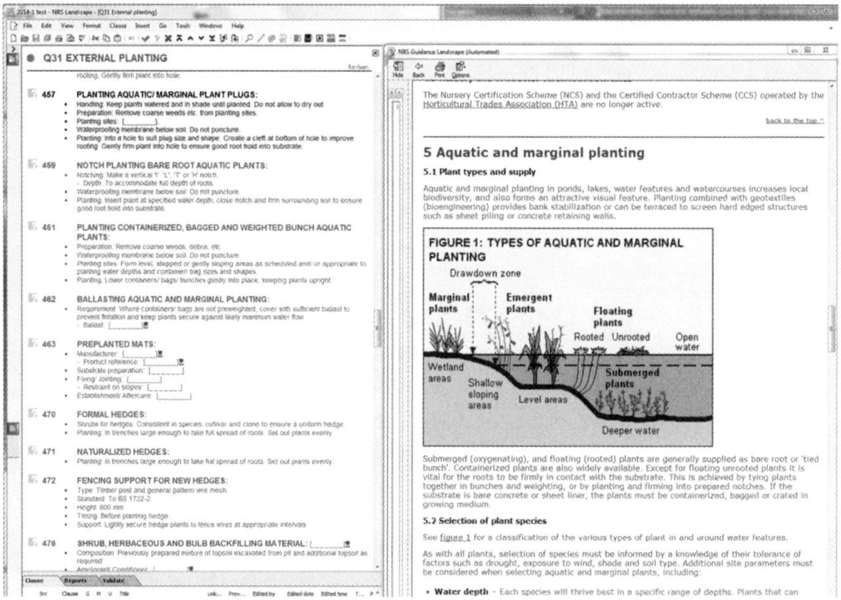

Fig. 12.5 Sample Screen Shot of NBS Landscape. Reproduced with permission of RIBA Enterprises Limited.

the subject, in order to provide an industry 'standard'. According to Helios Software Ltd (2013) the introduction of the National Plant Specification acknowledged and responded to the following:

1. British Standards contain much useful information; however, the rate of change occurring in production practices in the industry is so rapid that standards are quite quickly becoming out of date.

2. Changes within plant production have resulted in the production of specialist standards and these need to be incorporated into the industry wide documentation.

3. Plants are being bought and traded throughout Europe and grades and standards across the continent ought to respond to this.

4. Current standards provide general information on grades and conditions of product. Specific information on grades and conditions for a range of typical landscape plants would provide more particularly useful information.

Originally released in the 1990s, the National Plant Specification has been available exclusively as a web resource since 2007. The National Plant Specification database may be searched by plant characteristic (tree, shrub, herbaceous, etc.)

and provides information on form/habit; soil preference; aspect; and performance with recommendations as to the best or most suitable specification options.

National Plant Specification planting lists/palettes can be opened directly into Computer Aided Design programs for labelling, automatic plant number calculations, preparation of schedules, Bills of Quantity and project specifications. The National Plant Specification provides information for emerging Building Information Modelling content and processes relating to planting material and is expected to expand as a resource as Building Information Modelling for landscape develops.

Specification of plants can be particularly difficult for the professional practitioner as, unlike other commodities, plants are almost infinitely variable. Specification by 'type' is simply not sufficient. For example, one *Daphne odora 'Aureo Marginata'* can be very different from another in terms of its proportions, its quality and its general condition. The professional practitioner therefore needs to be much more specific.

In addition to specifying the height and spread of plants, when dealing with container grown stock it is essential for the professional practitioner to specify pot size, for example three litre, five litre and so on. Generally speaking plants produced in larger containers are bigger, better rooted and more mature than those in smaller containers. The professional practitioner should however be aware that plants in larger pot sizes have commensurately larger prices. Likewise, that it is not unusual for less reputable suppliers to provide recently potted specimens that, when removed from the pot, result in a considerably smaller rootball and a pile of loose potting compost, as opposed to a plant with a larger and more developed root system.

Where field grown, bare-rooted, nursery stock is concerned, 'age' is another common addition to the specific criteria employed by way of specification. Bare-rooted 'whips' usually being one year old; transplants being at least two years old and conventionally denoted as '1+1' or '1+2' depending on whether they have been grown on for one or two years after transplanting; 'feathered' denotes a transplant that has side shoots; and thereafter field grown stock is specified in terms of the girth measurement of its stem at one metre above ground in accordance with British Standard 3936 Part 1, that is 'light standard (6–8 cms); 'standard' (8–10 cms); 'select standard' (10–12 cms); 'heavy standard' (12–14 cms); 'extra heavy standard' (14–16 cms); 'advanced heavy standard' (16–18 cms); and 'semi mature' (18–20 cms+).

12.7.3 Code of Practice for Handling & Establishing Landscape Plants

In 1985 the Committee of Plant Supply and Establishment, previously a sub-committee of the Joint Council of Landscape Industries, published its *Code of Practice for Handling & Establishing Landscape Plants*. Aimed at improving establishment of plants, the code provided valuable information concerning appropriate methods of transporting, packaging, storage and handling – for example, practical methods of protecting plants from wind desiccation that could very usefully be incorporated into project specifications.

Having been asked by the President of the Landscape Institute to present *The Future Role of the Joint Council of Landscape Industries: A Strategic Review* (Fraser, 1998), the author of the present text recognised the Council's long-standing position of pre-eminence in the provision of industry standard documentation but concluded: 'It is clear that several of the organisation's objectives, in the light of developments which have taken place since its inception, are unrealistic and unlikely to be achieved.' The Strategic Review recommended building upon the Council's strengths, such that it took the lead in compiling and presenting market statistics; became the hub of members' interests across the industry; and the Inspectorate of national certification schemes. These recommendations were not followed. According to the Landscape Institute (2013), the Joint Council of Landscape Industries in 2004 'became the Joint Committee for Landscape Industries with a slightly different mission but was dissolved in 2010.' Whilst the demise of the Joint Council of Landscape Industries is, arguably, a regrettable loss to the industry, the *Code of Practice for Handling & Establishing Landscape Plants* was thankfully republished in 1995 and continues to be available online at http://www.gohelios.co.uk/nps/handling_establishment.aspx.

Following much of the format of the original, after being fully revised to take account of new research and techniques, the republished code continues to provide the professional practitioner with a useful resource in drafting project specification and in revised form, includes an expanded introduction; a list of further reading; and useful references on the subject of plant handling and establishment.

12.7.4 Other sources

In addition to the resources outlined above, most organisations will have, or will develop over time, their own library of 'standard' clauses and their own specification format. Similarly, many manufacturers and suppliers are very accommodating and readily provide detailed specifications for the use of their products. For example, Ennstone Breedon Limited provide an excellent product sheet giving detailed guidance on the specification of workmanship for the laying of its golden amber path gravel.

SPECIFICATION FUNDAMENTALS

CHAPTER SUMMARY

- The suite of contract documents comprise 'illustrative', 'quantitative', and 'qualitative' documents along with the conditions of contract
- Building Information Modelling contains graphical representations, quantities and project specifications linked to increasingly intelligent Computer Aided Design
- Specifications are the means by which the professional practitioner communicates the standards of materials and workmanship required
- The evidence of a well-crafted specification is that every contractor is able to determine exactly what is required to complete the project
- Conventional specification structure is driven by the 'Common Arrangement of Work Sections'
- Standard specification clauses ensure familiarity and may be drawn from a number of sources

13

Conditions of Contract

> THE AIMS OF THIS CHAPTER ARE TO:
>
> - Explain the difference between 'domestic' and 'nominated' sub-contracts
> - Explain the factors in selecting an appropriate form of agreement
> - Highlight the advantages of standard forms of agreement
> - Provide a step-by-step guide of the information required to complete a standard form of agreement using the JCLI Landscape Works Contract 2012

Chapter 12 introduced the idea that the project specification is but one of a suite of contract documents examined in some detail throughout the remaining chapters of this book. The reader was invited to familiarise themselves with the range of material embraced by contract documents and the respective uses for the information contained therein.

Figure 13.1 reiterates that contract documentation falls broadly into two categories; that required by the client to approve design proposals and an overall budget for the scheme; and that required by contractors in order to submit quotations for the cost of implementing the project proposals.

Chapter 12 explained that the contract documents required by contractors consist of a range of 'illustrative', 'quantitative' and 'qualitative' documents as well as the legal conditions under which any contract for project implementation is to be performed. Contractors will need all of this information in advance of quoting or tendering for the works (discussed in Chapter 14).

At this point it would be prudent to remind the reader that the 'traditional' form of project procurement (discussed in Chapter 9), which is the focus of the present volume, distinguishes the agreement between the professional practitioner and the client (discussed in Chapter 7) from the agreement between the client and contractor(s), in which the professional practitioner has no formal part other than as the client's agent (discussed in Chapter 2).

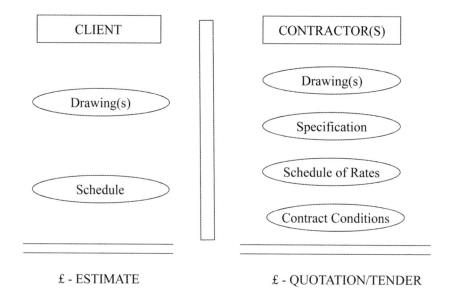

Fig. 13.1 Contract Documentation

The professional practitioner must consider the conditions of contract and any amendments to them in advance of seeking quotations for implementation of the works. Bidding contractors are normally advised of this information in the project specification (discussed in Chapter 12) and by means of a draft form of contract provided as part of the suite of contract documents on which the contractors are invited to submit their bids (discussed in Chapter 14). This same contract information comprises the legal agreement eventually set-up between the client and contractor(s) for implementation of the works. It is therefore the conditions of contract between the client and contractor(s) that form the substance of the present chapter.

13.1 SUB-CONTRACTS

It is not intended that any part of this book should deal with the detail of sub-contracts except insofar as to clarify one or two terms. The 'principal' or 'main' contractor might very well need or want to use the services of other contractors for elements of the work, that is to say, to 'sub-contract' to other suppliers of goods or services, or may be required to do so by the client and/or the professional practitioner.

The important distinction at this point is between 'domestic' sub-contracts, that is those contracts formed between a main contractor and any sub-contractors the main contractor might choose to employ; sub-contracts that are entirely the concern of the main contractor, in which the client and the professional practitioner have no part; and 'nominated' sub-contracts, that is to say, those with specialist suppliers of goods or services with whom the main contractor is obliged to enter into an agreement as a requirement of the main contractor's agreement with the client.

Once these distinctions are understood, it should be clear that, whether 'domestic' or 'nominated', sub-contracts are formed between the sub-contractor and the main contractor and (as discussed in Chapter 2) 'privity' of contract ensures they remain largely the concern of the main contractor.

Concerning the legal form of sub-contract agreements, it is worth noting at this point only that sub-contract agreements are variations on that which follows in the remainder of this chapter.

13.2   FORMS OF AGREEMENT

In every project the concerns of the client are likely to focus upon time, that is to say when the works are expected to start and finish; cost, as in how much the client expects to pay for the works; performance, in the sense of how is the contractor expected to carry out the works; and quality, that is to say, by what process is the contractor(s) work to be measured and approved.

The well-advised client will wish to set parameters in each of these respects at the outset of any contract for implementation of works.

Forming a contract by word of mouth is fraught with difficulties, not least the inability to determine the parameters or 'terms' of the alleged agreement as and when the need arises.

An exchange of letters, whilst somewhat better than word of mouth and often sufficient for very small and uncomplicated projects, can also be difficult. Since the vast majority of professional practitioners lack any form of legal training, when setting up agreements on behalf of clients, the professional practitioner can very easily and unintentionally miss something vital or include terms that are unenforceable at law.

Bespoke forms of agreement, that is agreements written by lawyers on behalf of clients with particular projects in mind, are common among large projects and large organisations with their own legal departments or advisors.

In the vast majority of situations within the landscape industry, where project budgets are generally modest when compared to construction or engineering budgets, the most appropriate and by far the most common method of setting up a legal agreement between the client and contractor(s) is by way of a standard form of agreement.

FORMS OF AGREEMENT:

- Word of mouth
- Exchange of letters
- Bespoke form of agreement
- Standard form of agreement

Standard forms of agreement are easy to use because they require the professional practitioner setting up a contract on behalf of the client to do no more than fill-in the blanks; directions in the form of footnotes and guidance notes being provided to assist with this task.

A standard form of agreement is generally readily understood because of the commonality of format and the terms used, making it widely accepted and familiar to the majority of those involved in the industry.

In essence a standard form of agreement concerns 'who' are the parties to the agreement; 'what' is the nature and extent of the project (for example, 'clearance and levelling of the site, provision of terrace, water feature, pergola, lawn and borders'); 'when' are works expected to commence and what is the anticipated time for completion; 'where' are the works to be undertaken; 'how much' are the works expected to cost; and 'what terms' are to be applied to the contract. Because standard forms of agreement are drafted by legal professionals on behalf of particular agencies, the terms used are tried and tested and may be relied upon to be reasonably enforceable at law.

ADVANTAGES OF STANDARD FORMS OF AGREEMENT:

- Easy to use
- Readily understood
- Widely accepted
- Tried and tested

The choice of which standard form of agreement to use is normally dictated by the person managing the project. In the 'traditional' procurement sense that is likely to be the professional practitioner who, on larger projects involving construction or engineering, is likely to be a fellow professional from an architectural or engineering discipline.

Within the landscape and construction industries the most common standard forms of agreement likely to be used to set up contracts between the client and contractor(s) are those produced by the Joint Contract Tribunal; the Infrastructure Conditions of Contract that replaced what was formerly known as the ICE Conditions of Contract (Institute of Civil Engineers, 2011); New Engineering Contract created by the Institute of Civil Engineers and recommended by the Construction Clients' Board (formerly Public Sector Clients' Forum) for use by public sector organisations procuring construction works; and that produced by the JCLI Contracts Forum for use on landscape projects, particularly those involving soft landscaping.

The reader wishing to understand in detail the differences between the standard forms of contract currently available within the construction industry is guided to Clamp, Cox, Lupton and Udom (2012) which considers the different forms of contract available in respect of 'traditional', 'design and build' and 'management' procurement strategies (discussed in Chapter 9).

As the JCLI Contracts Forum conditions of contract are drafted with the landscape professional practitioner specifically in mind it is with the JCLI standard form of agreement that the remainder of this chapter will be primarily concerned.

13.3 THE JCLI CONDITIONS OF CONTRACT

The most recent editions of the JCLI Contracts Forum conditions of contract comprise:

- The JCLI Landscape Works Contract 2012 (JCLI LWC)

- The JCLI Landscape Works Contract with Contractor's Design 2012 (JCLI LWCD)

- The JCLI Landscape Maintenance Works Contract 2012 (JCLI LMWC)

> ACCORDING TO JCLI PRACTICE NOTE NO 8
>
> (The Landscape Institute, June 2012):
>
> *The JCLI Landscape Works Contract and JCLI Landscape Works Contract with Contractor's Design are specifically for landscape projects which include soft landscape works. However, they are not appropriate for use on projects requiring named or nominated sub-contractors, planned phased commencement and/or completion, as well as not being appropriate for projects of over approximately £200,000. For projects requiring elements to be designed by the Contractor the JCLI Landscape Works Contract with Contractor's Design should be used rather than the JCLI Landscape Works Contract. However, the JCLI Landscape Works Contract with Contractor's Design is not appropriate for design and build projects.*

For projects where the JCLI forms of agreement are not appropriate, the professional practitioner should consider one of the other standard forms of agreement discussed above. As the JCLI Landscape Works Contract 2012 is based on the JCT Minor Works Building Contract 2011 and the JCT Intermediate Building Contract 2011 has provision for naming of sub-contractors which the JCLI forms of agreement do not, http://www.jctcontracts.com is a useful source of reference for the professional practitioner in determining what might be the appropriate JCT form of agreement to use as an alternative to the JCLI forms of agreement.

The information below provides a step-by-step guide to the blanks required to be filled and the alterations required to be made to the JCLI Landscape Works Contract 2012 when setting up an agreement between the client and contractor(s) for landscape works. Information required by other standard forms of agreement within the construction industry is similar, but Article, Recital and clause numbers will vary. In providing this step-by-step guide it is anticipated that the reader will have to hand a copy of the JCLI Landscape Works Contract 2012 and, if and when any required action remains unclear, the reader must refer to the footnotes and/or guidance notes contained therein.

13.3.1 Details of the parties

The Articles of Agreement comprising Articles, Recitals and Contract Particulars begin with the details of the parties (page 1 of the JCLI Landscape Works Contract 2012), that is to say, the name and address of the employer (client) together with registered office and company number (where the works are being carried out on behalf of an incorporated company) and similar details for the contractor. If either party is not a company incorporated under the Companies Acts, references to company number and registered office should be deleted by crossing through. The date to be inserted is the date on which the agreement is made and bears no relevance to the dates on which the works are expected to start or finish.

13.3.2 Nature and location of the works

The First Recital (page 2 of the JCLI Landscape Works Contract 2012) requires the insertion of a brief description of the nature and location of the intended works. For example, 'clearance and levelling of the site, provision of terrace, water feature, pergola, lawn and borders at 306 Park Lane, London, W1F 7DT'.

13.3.3 The contract documents

The Second Recital (page 2 of the JCLI Landscape Works Contract 2012) concerns the documents that comprise the contract documents (discussed in Chapter 12) namely:

- The titles and numbers of the contract drawings, or the schedule or other document listing the contract drawings (normally contained within the preliminary items section of the project specification)

- The project specification

- The work schedule(s) and/or Schedule(s) of Rates and/or Bill of Quantities if prepared in accordance with the *Standard Method of Measurement* (The Royal Institute of Chartered Surveyors, 1998)

13.3.4 The contract sum

Article 2 (page 3 of JCLI Landscape Works Contract 2012) requires the contract sum to be inserted in words and figures. The contract sum is the bid accepted by the client/employer, for the execution of the whole of the works comprising the contract (as discussed in Chapter 14) excluding any Value Added Tax.

The amount eventually paid to the contractor may be more or less than the contract sum stated at Article 2 of the JCLI Landscape Works Contract 2012 as a result of variations to the works ordered by the 'Landscape Architect/Contract Administrator' (discussed in Chapter 15).

Where Value Added Tax is properly chargeable by the contractor this will be added as a separate item to the contractor's invoices. This will enable the client/employer, if registered with Her Majesty's Revenue and Customs for the purposes of Value Added Tax, to reclaim the additional amounts charged through their business as input tax.

13.3.5 Professional practitioner's details

Article 3 (page 3 of JCLI Landscape Works Contract 2012) requires details of the professional practitioner appointed by the client/employer to advise on and administer the contract, to be inserted. It also requires the deletion by crossing through of one or other title according to whether the professional practitioner appointed to the role is a 'Landscape Architect' or a 'Contract Administrator' from another discipline.

The Landscape Architect/Contract Administrator is paid by the client/employer to act as their agent (discussed in Chapter 2) but is required to administer the contract between the client and the contractor fairly, independently and professionally.

Under the JCLI Landscape Works Contract 2012 only the Landscape Architect/Contract Administrator can issue instructions to the contractor. The client/employer is not entitled to issue instructions directly to the contractor and may do so only through the Landscape Architect/Contract Administrator.

13.3.6 The Construction Design and Management Regulations

Article 4 (page 3 of JCLI Landscape Works Contract 2012) and Article 5 (page 4 of JCLI Landscape Works Contract 2012) refer to The Construction Design and Management Regulations 2007. Article 4 and Article 5 will be relevant only if the Construction Design and Management Regulations 2007 require the project to be notified to the Health and Safety Executive (discussed in Chapter 10).

If the project is notifiable under the Construction Design and Management Regulations 2007 the first two lines of Article 4 of the JCLI Landscape Works Contract 2012 assume the 'Construction Design and Management Coordinator' to be the Landscape Architect/Contract Administrator, in which case the remainder of Article 4 should be deleted by crossing through. If the Construction Design and Management Coordinator is not to be the Landscape Architect/Contract Administrator then the details of the person to assume the Construction Design and Management Coordinator role must be inserted in Article 4.

If the project is notifiable under the Construction Design and Management Regulations 2007 Article 5 of the JCLI Landscape Works Contract 2012 assumes the 'Principal Contractor' to be the contractor named in the Articles of Agreement (page 1 of the JCLI Landscape Works Contract 2012) in which case the remainder of Article 5 should be deleted by crossing through. If the Principal Contractor is other than the contractor named in the Articles of Agreement then the details of the Principal Contractor must be inserted in Article 5.

If the project is *not* notifiable under the Construction Design and Management Regulations 2007 then Article 4 and Article 5 of the JCLI Landscape Works Contract 2012 should be deleted in their entirety by crossing through.

The Fifth Recital of the Contract Particulars (page 5 of the JCLI Landscape Works Contract 2012) must be completed in any event, deleting by crossing through two of the three asterisked clauses to leave only the one applicable clause remaining.

13.3.7 Dispute resolution

Article 6, Article 7 and Article 8 (page 4 of JCLI Landscape Works Contract 2012) clause 7.2 and Schedule 1 of the Contract Particulars (page 8 of the JCLI Landscape Works Contract 2012) all concern the method adopted for resolving contractual disputes (discussed in Chapter 16).

As with all construction contracts in accordance with the Housing Grants, Construction and Regeneration Act 1996, Article 6 of the JCLI Landscape Works Contract 2012 provides a statutory right for either party to refer contractual disputes to an adjudicator, in which case the name of the adjudicator may be inserted in clause 7.2 of the Contract Particulars. An individual adjudicator should not be named in the contract without their prior agreement, and it should be recognised that if and when a dispute arises the particular individual named may not be available.

If the method of resolving contractual disputes is to be adjudication but no adjudicator is to be named, that part of clause 7.2 of the Contract Particulars and all but the preferred nominating body from the list of asterisked bodies at clause 7.2 of the Contract Particulars should be deleted by crossing though.

If the method of resolving contractual disputes is to be adjudication and no nominating body has been agreed, the nominating body shall be one of the asterisked bodies listed in clause 7.2 of the Contract Particulars selected by the party at the time that party requires the dispute to be referred to adjudication.

Not all landscape contracts are required to include adjudication provisions. In particular, where the client/employer is a residential occupier within the meaning of section 106 of the Housing Grants, Construction and Regeneration Act 1996 the provisions do not apply. Unless Article 6 and clause 7.2 of the Contract Particulars are deleted in their entirety by crossing through, a residential occupier entering into the JCLI Landscape Works Contract 2012 will be accepting adjudication as the preferred means of resolving contractual disputes.

In the limited circumstances in which the Housing Grants, Construction and Regeneration Act 1996 does not apply, for example in the case of a client/employer who is a residential occupier within the meaning of section 106 of the Housing Grants, Construction and Regeneration Act 1996; in circumstances where either or both parties are dissatisfied with the outcome of adjudication; or where neither party wishes to have the dispute adjudicated, arbitration or legal proceedings may be nominated as the method of resolving contractual disputes. If arbitration is adopted as the method of resolving contractual disputes Article 7 of the Contract Particulars must be amended by selective deletion to read 'Article 7 and Schedule 1 (Arbitration) apply'.

Where the client/employer is entering into a contract outside their business interests the Unfair Terms in Consumer Contracts Regulations 1994 state that excluding or hindering the consumer's rights to bring legal proceedings or exercise any other legal remedy, particularly by requiring them to take contractual disputes exclusively to arbitration, represents an unfair contract term.

In the limited circumstances outlined above in which the Housing Grants, Construction and Regeneration Act 1996 does not apply; where either or both parties are dissatisfied with the outcome of adjudication; or where neither party wishes to have the dispute adjudicated, legal proceedings may be nominated as the method of resolving contractual disputes. In this case it is not necessary to make amendments to the JCLI Landscape Works Contract 2012 since, if neither entry at Article 7 is deleted, Article 7 and Schedule 1 do *not* apply and legal proceedings will be the default method of resolving contractual disputes.

13.3.8 Construction Industry Scheme

The Fourth Recital of the Contract Particulars (page 5 of the JCLI Landscape Works Contract 2012) concerns whether the client/employer is classified as a 'contractor' for the purposes of Her Majesty's Revenue and Customs' Construction Industry Scheme at the 'Base Date' inserted.

> ACCORDING TO HER MAJESTY'S REVENUE AND CUSTOMS
>
> (January 2013, p. 6):
>
> *A contractor is a business or other concern that pays subcontractors for construction work. Contractors may be construction companies and building firms, but may also be government departments, local authorities and many other businesses that are normally known in the industry as 'clients'. Some businesses or other concerns are counted as contractors if their average annual expenditure on construction operations over a period of three years is £1m or more. Private householders are not counted as contractors so are not covered by the scheme ... A subcontractor is a business that carries out construction work for a contractor.*

Where the client/employer is a 'contractor' as defined by Her Majesty's Revenue and Customs Construction Industry Scheme the contractor entering into a JCLI Landscape Works Contract 2012 will be deemed to be a 'subcontractor' under the Construction Industry Scheme. The client/employer must therefore deduct Income Tax from any payments made to the (sub) contractor and pay that tax to

Her Majesty's Revenue and Customs, unless the (sub) contractor can satisfy Her Majesty's Revenue and Customs that it qualifies to be paid gross.

Because it is important for a contractor entering into a JCLI Landscape Works Contract 2012 to know the status of the client/employer at the 'Base Date' this date must be inserted in the Fourth Recital of the Contract Particulars. The Base Date is generally that, or around that, date stated for submission of tenders (discussed in Chapter 14). A Base Date must be adopted on which the client/employer can be certain of its status in relation to the Construction Industry Scheme so tenderers need not deal with last minute changes to the contract particulars.

13.3.9 Supplemental provisions

The Sixth and Seventh Recitals of the Contract Particulars (page 5 of the JCLI Landscape Works Contract 2012) and Schedule 3 (pages 35 and 36 of the JCLI Landscape Works Contract 2012) concern supplemental provisions which Guidance Note 20 (page 40 of the JCLI Landscape Works Contract 2012) states reflect 'principles adopted by the Office of Government Commerce in the Achieving Excellence in Construction initiatives'.

The supplemental provisions detailed at Schedule 3 of the JCLI Landscape Works Contract 2012 are intended to ensure both the smooth running of the project and that the contractor's experience and industry contacts can be put to best use. The choice of which of the supplemental provisions are to apply is made in the Seventh Recital of the Contract Particulars.

The supplemental provisions detailed in Schedule 3 of the JCLI Landscape Works Contract 2012 are generally intended to apply unless there is a 'Framework Agreement' or some other contract document that makes similar provision, in which case the details of the Framework Agreement and/or other document should be inserted in the Sixth Recital of the Contract Particulars.

Where there is no Framework Agreement and/or the supplemental provisions in Schedule 3 of the JCLI Landscape Works Contract 2012 are intended to apply, the Sixth Recital of the Contract Particulars should be deleted in its entirety by crossing through and the words *'does not apply'* in relation to each of the supplemental provisions in the Seventh Recital of the Contract Particulars should also be deleted by crossing through.

Alternatively, where the supplemental provisions of Schedule 3 of the JCLI Landscape Works Contract 2012 *are* intended to apply, the Seventh Recital of the Contract Particulars need not be amended in any way as, where neither entry against an item is deleted, the default position is that the relevant supplemental provision detailed in Schedule 3 of the JCLI Landscape Works Contract 2012 will be taken to apply.

In the unlikely event that the supplemental provisions of Schedule 3 of the JCLI Landscape Works Contract 2012 are intended *not* to apply, the Seventh Recital of the Contract Particulars *must* be amended so as to delete the word 'applies' by crossing it through in each case.

Supplemental provision 6 of Schedule 3 of the JCLI Landscape Works Contract 2012 concerns the avoidance or early resolution of contractual disputes by negotiation (discussed in Chapter 16) between the parties. Where supplemental provision 6 is intended to apply the name of the senior executive nominated by each party to conduct such negotiations must be inserted in the Seventh Recital of the Contract Particulars.

Where supplemental provision 6 of Schedule 3 of the JCLI Landscape Works Contract 2012 is *not* intended to apply, apart from deleting by crossing through the word 'applies' in relation to paragraph 6 in the Seventh Recital of the Contract Particulars, for completeness it is advisable to delete by crossing through the continuation of the Seventh Recital of the Contract Particulars in its entirety.

13.3.10 Construction Design and Management planning period

Clause 1.1 of the Contract Particulars (page 6 of the JCLI Landscape Works Contract 2012) is applicable only where the project is notifiable to the Health and Safety Executive under the Construction Design and Management Regulations 2007 (discussed in Chapter 10).

The Construction Design and Management Regulations 2007 require the client/employer to allow sufficient time prior to commencement of operations on site to enable Construction Design and Management planning and preparatory operations to be carried out.

Where the project is notifiable to the Health and Safety Executive under the Construction Design and Management Regulations 2007 the period (in days or weeks) must be inserted in clause 1.1 of the Contract Particulars along with the date the Construction Design and Management Planning Period will begin or end. Where marked by an asterisk a choice must be made and that which does not apply must be deleted by crossing through.

Where the project is *not* required to be notified to the Health and Safety Executive under the Construction Design and Management Regulations 2007 clause 1.1 of the Contract Particulars should be deleted in its entirety by crossing through.

13.3.11 Duration of the works

Clause 2.1 and clause 2.2 of the Contract Particulars (pages 6 of the JCLI Landscape Works Contract 2012) require the date for commencement and the date for completion of the works, respectively, to be inserted.

The date for completion of the works should be the target date. Insertion of such a date in clause 2.2 of the Contact Particulars does not preclude any subsequent extension of time by order of the Landscape Architect/Contract Administrator named in Article 3 of JCLI Landscape Works Contract 2012 (discussed in Chapter 15).

13.3.12 Liquidated damages

Clause 2.8 of the Contract Particulars (page 6 of the JCLI Landscape Woks Contract 2012) concerns 'Liquidated Damages' or the amount to be charged to the contractor in the event of non-completion, or delayed completion, of the contract other than by extension of time granted by the Landscape Architect/ Contract Administrator named in Article 3 of the JCLI Landscape Works Contract 2012 (discussed in Chapter 15).

Liquidated damages must be calculated prior to inviting tenders (discussed in Chapter 14) and the tenderers advised of the amount, which must never be punitive. Liquidated damages are not intended to be a 'stick' with which to beat the contractor and should, instead, be the sum of three figures: the cost of administering the contract during the period of delay, that is to say the Landscape Architect/ Contract Administrator's fees; notional interest which is normally the estimated value of the project (discussed in Chapter 11) multiplied by the bank base rate plus 2 per cent; and losses that are expected to flow from the delay which will depend on the nature of the project and must be provable. For example, loss of revenue if the client/employer's facilities are unable to open due to non-completion in which case the expected losses might be temporary hire of alternative facilities.

Liquidated damages may be charged per day, week or month and the appropriate rate and period must be inserted at clause 2.8 of the Contract Particulars.

13.3.13 Defects and establishment of plants

Clause 2.10A and clause 2.10B of the Contract Particulars (page 6 of the JCLI Landscape Works Contract 2012) concern rectification of defects detected in the works post 'Practical Completion' – that is to say, after the date on which the Landscape Architect/Contract Administrator named in Article 3 of JCLI Landscape Works Contract 2012 certificates that the contractor has fulfilled its obligations under the implementation phase of the contract (discussed in Chapter 15).

Defects in hard landscaping elements are often detectable during the progress of the works, in the course of a practical completion inspection by the Landscape Architect/Contract Administrator or within a relatively short time thereafter. By contrast, soft landscaping elements are much more likely to require an establishment period, of at least 12 months and preferably more, in which to determine which, if any, of the plants (and grass) have died or failed to thrive.

It is generally preferable that the same contractor who carried out the installation works is also contracted to carry out establishment maintenance. The care of trees, shrubs, grass and other plants after practical completion is excluded from the JCLI Landscape Works Contract 2012 but the JCLI Landscape Maintenance Works Contract 2012 has been drafted with the specific intent that it should be used 'back-to-back' with either the JCLI Landscape Works Contract 2012 or the JCLI Landscape Works Contract with Contractor's Design 2012.

The advantage of making the same contractor who carried out the installation works responsible for the establishment maintenance is that it provides the contractor with the maximum incentive to undertake the installation to a high standard.

Assuming the establishment maintenance is to be carried out by the same contractor, then clause 2.10A of the Contract Particulars applies; clause 2.10B of the Contract Particulars must be deleted in its entirety by crossing through;

a 'Rectification Period' should be stated (page 6 of the JCLI Landscape Works Contract 2012) if the period is to be anything other than the default 12 months; a 'back-to-back' JCLI Landscape Maintenance Works Contract 2012 must be set-up, the duration of which cannot be less than the Rectification Period stated; and the contractor will be responsible for replacing any plants or grass that have died, or failed to thrive, at the end of the Rectification Period (other than as a result of theft and/or malicious and/or vehicular damage) at no cost to the client/employer.

Where the same contractor is *not* to be used for establishment maintenance, clause 2.10B of the Contract Particulars applies and clause 2.10A of the Contract Particulars must be deleted in its entirety by crossing through. In these circumstances the client/employer is responsible for the care and replacement of any trees, shrubs, grass and other plants which fail to thrive following practical completion, whether by its own labour force or by paying another contractor. Adoption of clause 2.10B of the Contract Particulars is not recommended because of the absence of a plant guarantee and due to the difficulty assessing plant health at practical completion, particularly in the dormant season.

Whichever of clause 2.10A or clause 2.10B of the Contract Particulars is adopted, the contractor remains responsible for defects in anything other than trees, shrubs, grass and other plants, due to defective materials, goods or workmanship at the end of the Rectification Period stated at page 6 of the JCLI Landscape Works Contract 2012.

13.3.14 Theft or malicious damage

Most commonly, the contractor is responsible for losses arising from theft or malicious damage prior to practical completion. This comes at a cost to the client/employer as the contractor will make its own assessment of the likelihood of loss/damage occurring and/or the cost of securing the site so loss/damage is reduced and build this cost into its tendered sum. The contract sum will be commensurately increased and the loss/damage may not actually occur. The question is therefore one of risk and who is to take it.

Clause 2.13 of the Contract Particulars (page 7 of the JCLI Landscape Works Contract 2012) is generally only used when the likelihood of losses and/or damage prior to practical completion is small, for example in a secure domestic garden, or when the likelihood of theft and/or malicious damage is extremely high, for example an open space that cannot be closed to the public and is situated in an area of high vandalism.

If clause 2.13 of the Contract Particulars is used, a 'Provisional Sum' to be expended on the instruction of the Landscape Architect/Contract Administrator named at Article 3 of the JCLI Landscape Works Contract 2012 must be inserted in the blank provided.

If clause 2.13 of the Contract Particulars is used, the project specification (discussed in Chapter 12) should require the contractor to report malicious damage and/or theft as soon as it occurs in order that the theft and/or damage might be verified by the Landscape Architect/Contract Administrator.

13.3.15 Retentions

Clause 4.3.1 and clause 4.4.1 of the Contract Particulars (page 7 of the JCLI Landscape Works Contract 2012) concern interim payments made to the contractor up to practical completion and those on or after practical completion, specifically the amounts to be withheld from payments pending satisfactory performance of the contract.

During the period of the works, the contractor is entitled to interim payments (discussed in Chapter 15) to cover works properly completed and the value of materials and goods held on site for the purpose of the works. From these interim payments, a retention amount is deducted, meaning the contractor is never paid for the entirety of the works or materials vested in the site until the works are certificated as finally complete (discussed in Chapter 15).

The default amount retained from interim payments is 5 per cent and if this is acceptable, clause 4.3.1 of the Contract Particulars need be amended only to the extent of deleting the blank by crossing through. If a different amount is to be retained from interim payments a figure must be inserted in the blank at clause 4.3.1 of the Contract Particulars. It should be noted that this figure will be the total percentage the contractor can expect to be paid on interim valuations *not* the percentage to be retained. The amount the contractor can expect to be paid on interim valuations might be reduced if, for example, the project involves a high proportion of planting or high value items such as semi-mature trees where the retention might otherwise not be enough to cover any losses sustained.

The amounts retained from interim valuations are normally released in part when the Landscape Architect/Contract Administrator named in Article 3 of the JCLI Landscape Works Contract 2012 issues a Certificate of Practical Completion (discussed in Chapter 15). The default amount the contractor is entitled to have been paid following practical completion is 97.5 per cent of the contract sum. If the default position is to be adopted, clause 4.4.1 of the Contract Particulars need be amended only to the extent of deleting the blank by crossing through.

The object of the retention following practical completion is to ensure sufficient funds are withheld, so the contractor has an incentive to return to site and fulfil its obligations to remedy defects at the end of the Rectification Period stated in clause 2.10A or 2.10B of the Contract Particulars (page 6 of the JCLI Landscape Works Contract 2012) or, in the event the contractor reneges on its duties in this respect, that sufficient funds are withheld to remedy any defects. If the amount to be retained following practical completion is to be greater than the default 2.5 per cent of the contract sum – for example, if the project involves a high proportion of planting or high value items such as semi-mature trees where the retention might otherwise not be enough to cover any losses sustained – an alternative amount must be inserted at clause 4.4.1 of the Contract Particulars. It should be noted that this figure will be the total percentage of the contract sum the contractor can expect to have been paid following the issue of a Certificate of Practical Completion (discussed in Chapter 15), *not* the percentage of the contract sum to be retained.

The amount to be retained following practical completion is generally only increased where the contractor is responsible for establishment maintenance during the Rectification Period stated in clause 2.10A or 2.10B of the Contract Particulars (page 6 of the JCLI Landscape Works Contract 2012) and has entered, or will enter, a 'back-to-back' contract for establishment maintenance on the JCLI Landscape Maintenance Works Contract 2012 form or similar.

In any event, the percentage of the contract sum stated at clause 4.4.1 of the Contract Particulars as payable to the contractor following the issue of a Certificate of Practical Completion (discussed in Chapter 15) cannot be less than the percentage of the contract sum to be included on interim valuations stated at clause 4.3.1 of the Contract Particulars (page 7 of the JCLI Landscape Works Contract 2012).

13.3.16 Supply of documents

Clause 4.8.1 of the Contract Particulars (page 7 of the JCLI Landscape Works Contract 2012) concerns the period following practical completion, at the end of which the contractor must provide any documentation required for the Landscape Architect/Contract Administrator named at Article 3 of the JCLI Landscape Works Contract 2012, to compute the amount of the Final Certificate (discussed in Chapter 15).

The default position is that this period will be the same as the Rectification Period stated at clause 2.10A/2.10B of the Contract Particulars (page 6 of the JCLI Landscape Works Contract 2012), in which case clause 4.8.1 of the Contract Particulars need be amended only to the extent of deleting the blank by crossing through. If clause 2.10A/2.10B of the Contract Particulars has been amended to anything other than the default 12 months, then the same figure used in clause 2.10A/2.10B would normally be inserted at clause 4.8.1 of the Contract Particulars.

13.3.17 Contribution, levy and tax changes

Clause 4.11 of the Contract Particulars (page 7 of the JCLI Landscape Works Contract 2012) and Schedule 2 (pages 32–5 of the JCLI Landscape Works Contract 2012) concern changes in rates of contribution, levy or tax payable by the contractor during the period of the works.

Given the Chancellor of the Exchequer normally announces changes in the rates of contribution, levy and tax on employees at least 12 months in advance of the changes being implemented, clause 4.11 of the Contract Particulars and Schedule 2 are generally inappropriate and should be deleted in their entirety by crossing through.

In the unlikely event the period of the works is such that the contractor is unable to foresee any changes in the rates of contribution, levy or tax payable on employees at the time of tendering, the words *'does not apply'* must be deleted from clause 4.11 of the Contract Particulars by crossing through and a percentage addition for 'Fluctuations Option', sufficient to cover the fluctuation in the contractor's overhead costs as a result of changes in the contribution, levy or tax payable on employees, should be inserted in accordance with paragraph 13 of Schedule 2 of the JCLI Landscape Works Contract 2012.

13.3.18 Contractor's liability insurance

Clause 5.3.2 of the Contract Particulars (page 7 of the JCLI Landscape Works Contract 2012) concerns the level of insurance cover the contractor is required to provide in respect of loss or damage occurring to persons or property during the course of the works.

The contractor is required to provide evidence of insurance cover against any negligence, breach of statutory duty, omission or default on the part of any person employed or engaged on the works by the contractor (including any subcontractors).

The amount of liability cover the contractor is required to hold should be inserted at clause 5.3.2 of the Contract Particulars and is generally a minimum of five million pounds in respect of any one occurrence but, depending on the nature of the project, the client and the insurance available, it could be considerably more.

13.3.19 Insurance of the works

Clause 5.4 of the Contract Particulars (page 7 of the JCLI Landscape Works Contract 2012) provides three alternative provisions according to who will be responsible for insuring against loss or damage to the works and/or materials held on site up to practical completion (discussed in Chapter 15).

Clause 5.4A and clause 5.4B of the Contract Particulars both refer to insurance of the works in joint names; in clause 5.4A such insurance provided by the contractor; and in clause 5.4B the insurance provided by the client/employer. Paragraph 29 of the Guidance Notes (page 41 of the JCLI Landscape Works Contract 2012) states: 'There is normally no substantial difficulty in obtaining Joint Names insurance for the Works but, in cases that involve residential occupiers, it is difficult to obtain Joint Names insurance for existing structures and contents'.

The author, who has many years' experience of the contracts industry, both managing contracts and as professional practitioner, begs to differ. In the author's experience it is unusual to find any insurer who will provide insurance in the joint names of the contractor and the client/employer. The far more common scenario is that the client/employer, who quite possibly already has the site and existing structures insured, extends its existing insurance to cover the increased risk to existing structures during the period of the works. The contractor provides insurance (ordinarily in its sole name) for the full cost of reinstating the works (including the removal and disposal of any debris from the lost and/or damaged works) plus the percentage stated at clause 5.4 of the Contract Particulars to cover professional fees incurred in overseeing the reinstatement of the lost and/or damaged works.

In the scenario outlined above, clause 5.4B of the Contract Particulars is deleted in its entirety by crossing through; clause 5.4C remains unaltered; clause 5.4A is altered to the extent of deleting the words 'in joint names' by crossing through; and a percentage figure to cover professional fees is inserted if it is to be anything other than the default 15 per cent. If the default 15 per cent to cover professional fees is adopted the space in which to insert an alternative percentage should be deleted by crossing through.

13.3.20 Attestation

The term 'attestation' refers to witnessing of a signature or sealing of a contract document. If the client/employer and the contractor are individuals or sole traders, it is normal for attestation to be by the signature of the parties, or their authorised representatives, in the presence of witnesses who then sign and set out their names and addresses in the spaces provided (page 11 of the JCLI Landscape Works Contract 2012).

Public and private companies incorporated under the Companies Act (discussed in Chapter 6) often require attestation to be in the form of a deed, that is to say a written document executed with formality, by which the interest or rights conferred by the contract, or the obligations contained therein, are confirmed and become binding. Execution as a deed may be in one of a number of forms (page 13 and page 14 of the JCLI Landscape Works Contract 2012):

A. Through signature by one Director and the Company Secretary or by two Directors;

B. By affixing the company's 'common seal' incorporating the registered details of the company in the presence of one Director and the Company Secretary, or of two Directors or of other officers authorised by the company to perform such functions;

C. Through signature by one Director of the company in the presence of a witness who then signs the deed and sets out their name and address in the spaces provided.

Occasionally, where the employer or the contractor is an individual or sole trader (discussed in Chapter 6), the preference is for attestation in the form of a deed. In this case attestation should be by form (D) (page 13 and page 14 of JCLI Landscape Works Contract 2012) requiring each individual or sole trader to sign, where indicated, in the presence of a witness who then signs and sets out his/her name and address in the spaces provided.

It should go without saying that, once attested in whatever form, a copy of the executed form of contract should be provided to both parties for their records.

CHAPTER SUMMARY

- The conditions of contract and any amendments to them must be agreed between the client and the professional practitioner before seeking quotations for implementation of the works
- The choice of which form of agreement to use is normally dictated by the person managing the project in consultation with the client
- Contractors must be advised of the conditions under which the contract is to be offered before bidding for the works
- It is preferable to use a standard form of agreement for setting up a contract on behalf of the client for implementation of the works

14

Single Stage Selective Tendering

> THE AIMS OF THIS CHAPTER ARE TO:
>
> - Explain the alternative methods of obtaining quotations from contractors
> - Explain how to identify and evaluate potential contractors
> - Introduce the concept of single stage selective tendering
> - Explain what information is required for an invitation to tender
> - Describe the key principles of administering a fair tender process
> - Explain how to evaluate the tenders submitted

In the 'traditional' procurement scenario (discussed in Chapter 9), once the client has approved the project designs and the estimate of implementation costs (discussed in Chapter 11), it will be necessary to obtain the *actual* costs of implementation from contractor(s).

It is not uncommon, particularly when a contractor and their standards of work are already known to a client, for an appointment to be made by negotiation. Negotiation may involve an additional package of work, perhaps a second phase, being agreed between the parties, often with the assistance of the professional practitioner, on terms similar to those for an earlier phase of works. Alternatively, negotiations with a particular contractor may concern works of a similar character to those already completed that are required to be undertaken on a separate project.

More commonly, the appointment of contractor(s) will be on a competitive basis, that is to say by a process involving several contractors submitting quotations or tenders for the works. In order to respect the key values of fairness, clarity, simplicity and accountability contractors can only reasonably be expected to quote for packages of work that have been clearly defined by reference to the suite of documents discussed in Chapter 12, that is to say 'illustrative' drawings;

'qualitative' specification; 'quantitative' schedules; and a form of agreement stating the conditions under which the contract is to be awarded (discussed in Chapter 13). As discussed in Chapter 12, these need not necessarily be extensive or complex documents but, by following this general rule, the professional practitioner will be doing all s/he can to ensure quotations are received from contractors on a comparative 'like-for-like' basis and, in turn, will facilitate objective evaluation of the offers received.

The process of tendering is a formalised method of obtaining and evaluating competitive quotations for clearly defined packages of work. Managed according to a pre-determined programme, the tendering process is intended to ensure confidentiality and fairness; to avoid collusion and/or corruption or any suggestion thereof; and obtain the best quality/price balance.

> THE QUALITY/PRICE BALANCE
>
> Finch (2011):
>
> *The principle of tendering is to ensure that true competition is achieved, as it is evaluated by applying certain criteria. These criteria may be expressed in terms of financial matters, comprising a simple assessment related to tender sums, or more complex financial evaluation, including consideration of projected costs over the life cycle of the completed project. It could also address other non-financial factors such as time and proposed methods or levels of capability; or sometimes a mixture of both – collectively referred to as a 'quality/price balance' or 'matrix'. European legislation describes this concept as the assessment of the most 'economically advantageous' option.*

Whilst the 'most economically advantageous option' ought to reflect both quality and price, it is most often the case that the contractor who submits the lowest priced tender will be awarded the contract. For this reason it is essential the professional practitioner does all s/he can to introduce a pre-tender element of evaluation into the procedure in order to satisfy themselves of individual contractors' credentials and industry standing before offering them the opportunity to quote for the works.

14.1   PRE-TENDER EVALUATION

The starting point in any tendering process is approving a list of contractors to be invited to bid for the work. Pre-tender evaluation enables the professional practitioner to be confident each contractor chosen for the approved list is able to meet specified eligibility criteria and should be able to carry out the work successfully if appointed.

The aim is to arrive at a short-list of suitable contractors for the project under consideration. Most codes of practice recommend a maximum of six tenderers and fewer where the work is specialist in nature. An excessively large number of tenderers may lead to reluctance to bid on the part of contractors, who will be only too well aware the likelihood of bidding successfully is statistically remote. Excessive numbers of tenderers will also require the professional practitioner to expend large amounts of time evaluating tenders received and increase the client's costs.

The process of pre-tender evaluation begins by informing contractors of likely projects for which they may wish to bid. On large public sector projects the requirement for public notification of forthcoming contracts is prescribed by legislation. In any event, it makes sense to inform contractors of forthcoming projects in order that they might indicate whether they wish to bid.

For the majority of landscape contracts it will be sufficient to inform contractors of forthcoming projects by telephone call, letter, email or by advertisement in the trade press. In doing so, care should be taken to show no favouritism nor to disclose any competitively sensitive information, that is to say information that may give one contractor a competitive advantage over another.

Contractors expressing an interest in the project are invited to complete a pre-qualification questionnaire unless they are already known to the professional practitioner and/or client. The pre-qualification questionnaire is intended to establish that potential contractors possess or have access to the governance; qualifications and references; expertise; competence; health and safety/environmental/financial standing; and other essential criteria, to the extent necessary for them to be considered suitable to undertake works for the client. By obtaining suitability information in advance, the professional practitioner is able to ensure that information eventually submitted with a tender can be entirely project specific.

Throughout the construction industry, potential suppliers of goods and services are frequently required to submit to pre-qualification processes involving a plethora of different qualification forms. This leads to considerable effort and wasted time and money, not only for those seeking to demonstrate their suitability for delivering goods and services but also for the professional practitioner who has to read and evaluate varied information provided in many different formats. This proliferation of pre-qualification questionnaire formats is due, in part, to commercial clients and well-established professional practices often having their own supposedly 'standard' pre-qualification questionnaires that are, by definition, very far from 'standard'. For contractors and suppliers, the number and variety of questionnaires they are presented with can be a considerable drain on resources.

There is currently a movement, spearheaded by the British Standards Institution, for a publicly available specification setting out the content, format and use of questions widely applicable to pre-qualification for construction industry tendering. According to the British Standards Institution (March 2013):

> The consistent use of a set of common questions in all construction related pre-qualification activity would not only significantly reduce the resources invested by suppliers in such activity but would also enable assessment providers and procurement officers to more reliably source suppliers.

Though perhaps rather complex, *PAS 91:2013 Construction Prequalification Questionnaires* is free to download from the British Standards Institution http://shop.bsigroup.com/en/Navigate-by/PAS/PAS-91-2013/ and provides detailed guidance, questions that might be included in a pre-qualification questionnaire and information that should be sought from contractors. From the professional practitioner's point of view, it will be necessary to consider the level of information it is appropriate or necessary to require from contractors or suppliers for each project. The British Standards Institution would like to see its questions forming the basis of a database of approved suppliers and contractors to the construction industry. Whilst this is a debatable position and one that is unlikely to be achieved in the foreseeable future, PAS 91:2013 does provide a useful reference point for the professional practitioner and presents some very cogent, thought-provoking arguments for a move towards standardisation of pre-qualification questionnaires.

PRE-QUALIFICATION QUESTIONNAIRE INFORMATION

(The British Standards Institution, March 2013):

- Supplier identity, key roles and contact information
- Financial information
- Business and professional standing
- Health and safety policy and capability
- Equal opportunity and diversity policy and capability
- Environmental management policy and capability
- Quality management policy and capability
- Building Information Modelling policy and capability
- Mandatory exclusion from public sector procurement (if applicable)
- Discretionary exclusion from public sector procurement (if applicable)
- Organisational technical and/or professional capability

In addition to pre-qualification questionnaires it may be appropriate to seek confidential references from third parties as to the standing of contractors and/or to invite interested contractors to interview if it becomes necessary to clarify specific responses to the pre-qualification questionnaire.

Pre-qualification should not be confused with two-stage tendering, favoured in large, complex, projects where the successful contractor may have significant design input. The present volume is concerned only with single stage selective tendering which is, by far, the most likely process the landscape professional practitioner will encounter in the UK.

14.2 PRELIMINARY ENQUIRY

Having arrived at a short-list of suitable contractors for the project under consideration, it is advisable and courteous for the professional practitioner to confirm that individual contractors remain willing to bid for the work before sending out the formal invitation to tender.

> THE PRELIMINARY ENQUIRY SHOULD INCLUDE DETAILS OF:
>
> - Employer
> - Professional practitioner(s)
> - Construction Design and Management Coordinator
> - Principal Contractor
> - Location of the project
> - Description of the work
> - Proposed form of contract and amendments
> - Proposed commencement and completion dates
> - Tendering timescales
> - Number of tenders to be invited
> - Basis of tender evaluation
> - Requirement for bonds, guarantees and warranties
> - Date, address and format for response to enquiry
> - Where contract documents may be inspected
> - Other significant requirements

In the period between pre-tender evaluation and preliminary enquiry it is entirely possible the circumstances of some of the preferred contractors will have changed, for example because of other work taken on, such that certain contractors are no longer willing or able to comply with the tendering timetable or other requirements.

When drawing up the short-list of suitable contractors for the project under consideration, it is therefore advisable for the professional practitioner to have the details of one or two more approved contractors than the number from whom it is intended to obtain tenders, to allow for those contractors who are unwilling or unable to comply with the request to submit a tender at the preliminary enquiry stage. It is not in the interests of the client, nor is it professional, to put a contractor in the position where it feels its only option is 'cover pricing'.

> **COVER PRICING**
>
> Finch (2011):
>
> *Occurs when a tenderer finds itself unable to submit a bid, but rather than prejudice the possibility of subsequent work from an employer, will submit a bid which has not been properly programmed or quantified, accepting that it is calculated so as not to be the lowest or most acceptable. Unfortunately, in some thankfully rare circumstances, tenderers have colluded with each other in order to ensure that this was the case; in extreme occasions bribes were offered to ensure that the outcome of the tendering process was artificially controlled.*

It is far more satisfactory, for all concerned, that a contractor should be permitted to decline at the preliminary enquiry stage. In this case, the contractor must be assured by the professional practitioner that their refusal to bid will not prejudice any future opportunities to do so.

14.3   INVITATION TO TENDER

As can be seen from the example at Figure 14.1, the information included in the invitation to tender will replicate much of what was included in the preliminary enquiry (discussed above). The professional practitioner may be tempted to refer to the preliminary enquiry rather than reproduce the information for tendering purposes but must not do so.

While there should be no inconsistencies between the preliminary enquiry and the invitation to tender, the information provided with the invitation to tender should comprise that which was provided with the preliminary enquiry but *must* be accompanied by the entire suite of documents referred to in Chapter 12 (and at the beginning of this chapter) to which the preliminary enquiry will only have referred. In short, the invitation to tender should provide bidding contractors with *all* the documentary information required to prepare a tender.

The instructions to tenderers, contained within the invitation to tender, explain to the contractors how the formal process will be handled and managed. These instructions will normally also form part of the project specification. In accordance with the preliminaries/general conditions of the Common Arrangement of Work Sections (discussed in Chapter 12) the instructions to tenderers should include the client/employer's requirements in relation to 'tendering sub-letting and supply'; where the contractors quotations are to be submitted; for whose attention; and by what date; for how long contractors are required to hold the price quoted; how any inaccuracies are to be dealt with; and whether a preliminary programme of works, method statement and safety policy are to be returned with the tender.

Finch (2011) provides a worked example of preliminary clauses within a specification document, relating to instructions to tenderers, which is drawn from the National Building Specification referred to in Chapter 12 in connection with National Building Specification Landscape.

Employer: *[insert name of Client/Employer]*

Project: *[insert location of the works]*

Description: *[insert brief description of the works]*

Having responded to our tender enquiry of *[insert date]* indicating you wish to tender for these works we enclose the following documents:

- Project drawings numbered *[insert drawing numbers]*
- Two copies of schedule of works to be priced (one to be returned with completed tender)
- Project specification *[insert reference]*
- Copy of the JCLI Standard Form of Agreement (with amendments)
- An addressed envelope in which tender is to be returned (no other envelope to be used)

The completed form of tender, sealed in the envelope provided, should reach this office no later than 12 noon on *[insert date for tender return]*.

The tender is to be accompanied by your method statements in respect of the following *[insert those operations requiring method statements]* and your proposed programme of works.

The site may be inspected by arrangement with *[insert name]* at this office who can be contacted on *[insert contact telephone numbers]* with whom any queries may be raised.

The tendered sum will be taken to be fully compliant with the Client/Employer's requirements as indicated in the tender documents and no correction of errors and/or omissions will be permitted.

The Client/Employer is not bound to accept the lowest or any tender.

....

I/We have read the documents referred to above, inspected the drawings and the site as I/we deem necessary and offer to complete the whole of the works, as detailed, in accordance with the conditions of contract provided for the sum of:

£ *[insert amount in figures]* and in words *[insert amount in words]*.

I/We expect to complete the works within *[insert number]* weeks from the date of site possession.

This tender remains open for consideration for *[insert number]* days from the date fixed for the return of tenders.

Signed .... On behalf of ....

Name: *[print name in full]* ....

Fig. 14.1 Worked Example of Invitation to Tender Letter

14.4 TENDER EVALUATION

Tenders should be opened as soon as possible after the time for receipt specified in the invitation to tender. The specification and the invitation should both have identified any documentation and supporting information required to be returned with the tender.

The first stage in evaluating the individual tenders will be to check that everything requested has been submitted. If, as is quite likely, the tenders include a priced schedule or Bill of Quantities, this should be subjected to an arithmetical check and careful scrutiny to ensure no items have been missed. Errors discovered in preliminary evaluation of tenders may be dealt with in one of two ways. The tenderers should have been advised which of the two is to be applied in the invitation to tender.

> DEALING WITH ERRORS AND/OR OMISSIONS
>
> Option 1: The tender will be treated as fully compliant with the specified requirements and the price tendered as though there were no errors and/or omissions. The tenderer will be given the opportunity to accept full liability for the cost of errors and/or omissions or to withdraw from the bidding process
>
> Option 2: The tenderer will be given the opportunity to correct genuine errors and/or omissions in its tendered bid

Once satisfied that all the tenders are arithmetically and technically correct, or that individual tenderers have accepted full liability in this respect, a second stage tender evaluation takes place to consider such things as method statements for particular aspects of the work (where these were requested). It could be that as part of the second stage evaluation process clarification is sought from individual tenderers on particular aspects of their bid. However, it is important to ensure all tenderers are treated fairly, equally and that such discussions do not disclose any sensitive information as regards competing bids.

Once the tender evaluation is complete, the professional practitioner should prepare a report for the client commenting upon aspects of each tender submitted and making a recommendation as to which of the tenders should be accepted. The final decision to accept or reject an offer, though guided by the professional practitioner, will always be made by the client.

It is possible that even the lowest-priced tender submitted may exceed the client's budget though, if the professional practitioner provided an *accurate* estimate of project costs (discussed in Chapter 11) this should rarely be the case.

In circumstances where the tendered bids all exceed the client's budget, it will be necessary to decide with the client whether the project budget can be increased. If the project budget cannot be increased, the professional practitioner may be required to seek a reduction in the tendered price.

Negotiation with contractors after tenders have been submitted and evaluated can be fraught with difficulty. For example, if the preferred contractor is unwilling or unable to reduce its tendered price, it may be necessary for the professional practitioner to go to one or other of the remaining tenderers to see if there is room for negotiation with them. This is a situation that will often leave the professional practitioner feeling most uncomfortable and is to be avoided if at all possible.

In the final analysis, in a situation where the tendered bids exceed the available budget, it may be necessary to abandon the tendering exercise altogether, or repeat it within different parameters (having revised aspects of the project). Alternatively it may be necessary to invite re-tenders on the basis of the project being completed in a number of phases as the client's funds permit. Any requirement to re-tender is less than satisfactory, as it will inevitably lead to increased costs.

For all these reasons, as discussed in Chapter 11, the professional practitioner must do their best to ensure accuracy when providing an estimate of project implementation costs.

14.5   TENDER OUTCOME

It is good practice (not to mention good manners) for the client's decision to be confirmed in writing to all those contractors who submitted tenders, rather than just the successful bidder. In doing so, the professional practitioner may determine what amount of information to impart.

Frequently, unsuccessful bidders are simply informed of this fact and no more. In practice, it is helpful for all concerned and common to provide a list of the bids received and a *separate* list of the contractors who submitted tenders, thereby ensuring neither one can be linked to the other. Such information enables contractors to see how competitive their bid was against rival bids and might encourage individual contractors to be more competitive next time.

Assuming a contract is to be entered into with one or other contractor following the tender procedure, the formalities discussed in Chapter 13 should be observed in setting up the contract and the procedures discussed in Chapter 15 should be followed when administering the contract.

CHAPTER SUMMARY

- Contractors can only be expected to quote for packages of work that have been clearly defined

- Pre-tender evaluation enables the professional practitioner to establish each contractor chosen for the approved list is able to carry out the work

- The invitation to tender should provide bidding contractors with all the documentary information required to prepare a tender

- Once the tender evaluation is complete, the professional practitioner should make recommendation as to which of the tenders should be accepted

- The final decision to accept or reject an offer will always be the client's

- It is good practice to advise all bidding contractors of the outcome of the tender process

15

Contract Administration

> THE AIMS OF THIS CHAPTER ARE TO:
>
> - Explain how to successfully monitor and control projects
> - Explain at what stages of project implementation the professional practitioner should certificate performance
> - Explain where to obtain model certificates and how they should be used
> - Introduce the concept and significance of variations to the contract
> - Explain the processes and significance of practical completion
> - Explain the importance of defects/establishment maintenance and the process of certificating final completion
> - Describe the range of drawing office records and their importance to successful professional practice

Once the suite of contract documents (discussed in Chapter 12) has been prepared; quotations/tenders have been obtained for implementation of the works and suitable contractor(s) selected (discussed in Chapter 14); and formal contract(s) set up (discussed in Chapter 13) in a 'traditional' procurement strategy (discussed in Chapter 9), it will normally fall to the professional practitioner to administer the resultant contract(s).

Administration of contracts it likely to include instructing necessary variations to the works and documenting performance of the contract(s) at various stages, that is to say certificating pre-determined stages of implementation as the works proceed.

15.1 CERTIFICATION

Assuming a standard form (discussed in Chapter 13) has been used to set up agreement(s) between the client and contractor(s) for implementation of the works, the standard form of agreement will be accompanied by model certificates for use as the works proceed. In the case of the JCLI Landscape Works Contract 2012 and the JCLI Landscape Works Contract with Contractor's Design 2012 (discussed in Chapter 13) model forms may be downloaded free at http://www.landscapeinstitute.org by Landscape Institute members. The Landscape Architect/Contract Administrator should use the basic layout and format of the model forms provided; producing their own forms, or those of their practice, by adding to the basic layout and format their practice information and/or company logo.

For the purposes of the Housing Grants, Construction and Regeneration Act 1996, as amended by the Local Democracy, Economic Development and Construction Act 2009, the Eighth Recital (page 2 of the JCLI Landscape Works Contract 2012) cites the Landscape Architect/Contract Administrator named in Article 3 (page 3 of the JCLI Landscape Works Contract 2012) as the person specified by the client/employer to issue certificates.

> ANY CERTIFICATE ONCE ISSUED SHOULD BE COPIED TO:
> - File
> - Client/Employer
> - Contractor
> - Quantity Surveyor
> - Project Manager
> - Construction Design and Management Coordinator

The Landscape Architect/Contract Administrator may be required to issue any or all of the following forms of certification:

- Landscape Architect's/Contract Administrator's Instruction
- Interim Payment Certificate(s)
- Payless Notice(s) (Type 1)
- Payless Notice(s) (Type 2)
- Certificate of Practical Completion
- Certificate of Making Good
- Final Certificate

CONTRACT ADMINISTRATION   217

Each of these forms of certification will now be considered in turn, together with the detail of the certification required to be issued at each stage of project implementation, by reference to the model forms provided by the Landscape Institute and referred to above.

15.1.1   Landscape Architect's/Contract Administrator's Instruction

The Landscape Architect's/Contract Administrator's Instruction relates to 'Variations' made in accordance with clause 3.6 (page 20 of the JCLI Landscape Works Contract 2012).

Without invalidating the agreement, the Landscape Architect/Contract Administrator named in Article 3 of the JCLI Landscape Works Contract 2012 may issue instructions for additions to, omissions from or other changes to the works, including the order or period in which the works are to be implemented.

It may be necessary to change the way an operation is carried out, for example the depth of excavations and material to be excavated, because only once the contractor has commenced operations do the remains of a former road running under the site become apparent.

It may be necessary to vary the contract period as a result of additions or omissions, and this may have a significant effect on the contractor's preliminary items (discussed in Chapter 12). For example, the contractor may have temporary facilities on site which are being paid for by the week and these may need to be on site for longer than originally expected.

The Landscape Architect/Contract Administrator should attempt to agree the value of any variation with the contractor before the variation works are carried out. If it is not possible to agree the value of the variation, clause 3.6 of the JCLI Landscape Works Contract 2012 permits the Landscape Architect/Contract Administrator named in Article 3 of the JCLI Landscape Works Contract 2012 to place a reasonable value on the variation.

In valuing a variation to the contract in accordance with clause 3.6 of the JCLI Landscape Works Contract 2012 the Landscape Architect/Contract Administrator may use only relevant prices taken from the quotation/tender submitted by the contractor (discussed in Chapter 14) from which the contract sum at Article 2 (page 3 of the JCLI Landscape Works Contract 2012) is derived.

The value placed upon any variation to the contract, whether by agreement or by the Landscape Architect/Contract Administrator in accordance with clause 3.6 of the JCLI Landscape Works Contract 2012, will be deemed to include any loss and/or expense incurred by the contractor due to the expected progress or sequence of the works being altered to accommodate the variation.

The model Landscape Architect's/Contract Administrator's Instruction provided by the Landscape Institute (referred to above) has columns headed 'omit' and 'add' both of which have a '£' sign attached to them. That is to say, additions and omissions each have a value. The Landscape Architect/Contract Administrator should also bear in mind that the contractor may be entitled to loss of profit and/

or a contribution towards its overhead expenses if the overall value of a contract is substantially reduced as a result of variations.

The model Landscape Architect's/Contract Administrator's Instruction provided by the Landscape Institute (referred to above) has a summation at the bottom. The summation consists of: the contract sum taken from Article 2 of the JCLI Landscape Works Contract 2012; the value of any previous Landscape Architect's/Contract Administrator's Instruction(s); and the value of the current instruction to arrive at an adjusted total, that is to say a revised contract sum; information both the client/employer and the contractor are likely to consider important but for very different reasons.

15.1.2 Interim Payment Certificate

According to clause 4.3 (page 22 of the JCLI Landscape Works Contract 2012) contractor(s) are entitled to interim payments at four-week intervals from the 'Date for Commencement of the Works' stated at clause 2.2 of the Contract Particulars (page 6 of the JCLI Landscape Works Contract 2012) until practical completion (discussed below).

Not later than five days after each 'due date', the Landscape Architect/Contract Administrator named in Article 3 of the JCLI Landscape Works Contract 2012 must issue Interim Payment Certificates, even if no money is due to the contractor at that time.

The amount of an Interim Payment Certificate should be the value of work the Landscape Architect/Contract Administrator considers to have been properly implemented and the value of materials and goods on site considered by the Landscape Architect/Contract Administrator to be properly intended for the works at the due date, less the retention percentage determined by reference to clause 4.3.1 (page 7 of the JCLI Landscape Works Contract 2012).

From the sum of works completed and materials on site less the retention must be deducted the total of amounts previously certificated (if any). It is important these are 'bottom line' amounts the Landscape Architect/Contract Administrator has previously certificated for payment as these figures will reflect retentions previously held against the works and avoid deducting the same retention amount twice.

From the sum of works completed and materials on site, less retentions, less amounts previously certificated, must be deducted the total of any amounts notified as overdue by the contractor in accordance with clause 4.5.2 (page 23 of the JCLI Landscape Works Contract 2012) if and when the Landscape Architect/Contract Administrator has previously failed to issue an Interim Payment Certificate in accordance with clause 4.3 of the JCLI Landscape Works Contract 2012 following a due date.

The value of contractor's payment notices issued in accordance with clause 4.5.2 of the JCLI Landscape Works Contract 2012 must be adjusted to reflect any 'Payless Notice' issued by the Landscape Architect/Contract Administrator in accordance with clause 4.5.4 (page 23 of the JCLI Landscape Works Contract 2012) and discussed below.

From the sum of works completed and materials on site, less retentions, less amounts previously certificated and amounts notified as overdue by the contractor, must be deducted the difference between the value of any 'Payless Notice' issued against previous Interim Payment Certificates under clause 4.5.4 of the JCLI Landscape Works Contract 2012 (discussed below) and the value of the Interim Payment Certificate to which the 'Payless Notice' applies, to arrive at the 'bottom line' valuation of the current interim certificate.

In practice at each due date the contractor(s) normally provide written valuations of the works considered complete and the value of materials and goods on site, to which the Landscape Architect/Contract Administrator responds by verifying quality, completeness and that goods and materials on site are properly intended for the works, before preparing a valuation (by the method stated above) and issuing an Interim Payment Certificate.

In accordance with clause 4.3 of the JCLI Landscape Works Contract 2012, subject to any 'Payless Notice' later issued by the Landscape Architect/Contract Administrator in accordance with clause 4.5.4 of the JCLI Landscape Works Contract 2012 (discussed below) the sum stated as due to the contractor on the Interim Payment Certificate plus any Value Added Tax properly chargeable must be paid to the contractor no later than the final date for payment, that is to say 14 days after the due date for the valuation.

If the client/employer fails to pay the contractor by the final date for payment, the amount owed will attract interest in accordance with clause 4.6 (page 23 of the JCLI Landscape Works Contract 2012) until the amount due is finally paid.

Should the client/employer fail to pay the contractor by the final date for payment, that is to say 14 days after the due date for the valuation, the contractor is entitled to serve notice on the client/employer and the Landscape Architect/Contract Administrator of its intention to suspend performance of its obligations under the contract, in accordance with clause 4.7 (page 23 of the JCLI Landscape Works Contract 2012). Should the amount owed to the contractor remain unpaid seven days after serving such notice, the contractor is entitled to suspend performance of the contract until such time as the debt is paid in full, or, alternatively, to terminate the agreement in accordance with clause 6.8 (page 29 of the JCLI Landscape Works Contract 2012).

Each Interim Payment Certificate records the cumulative value of works implemented to date; the cumulative value of retentions held against the works; and provides a running total of expenditure as the project proceeds. Each Interim Payment Certificate enables comparison to be made against the project budget estimated by the professional practitioner (discussed in Chapter 11) and allows the client/employer to keep track of its finances.

By using the model certificate provided by the Landscape Institute (discussed above) and consecutively numbering Interim Payment Certificates, the Landscape Architect/Contract Administrator maintains an audit trail that may be re-visited if a problem arises. For example, if the Landscape Architect/Contract Administrator inadvertently certificates the same element of the project twice.

15.1.3 Payless Notice(s) (Type 1)

Payless Notices are issued by the Landscape Architect/Contract Administrator named in Article 3 of the JCLI Landscape Works Contract 2012 if the client/employer wishes to deduct an amount from an Interim Payment Certificate; a Final Certificate; or to reduce the amount claimed on a contractor's payment notice issued in accordance with clause 4.5.2 of the JCLI Landscape Works Contract 2012 (discussed below).

A Payless Notice (Type 1) may be issued by the Landscape Architect/Contract Administrator in accordance with clause 4.5.4 (page 23 of the JCLI Landscape Works Contract 2012) only when it has become necessary to deduct the 'Liquidated Damages' stated in clause 2.8 of the Contract Particulars (page 6 of the JCLI Landscape Works Contract 2012) (discussed in Chapter 13) or an Interim Payment Certificate/Final Certificate requires adjustment for some other legitimate reason. For example, a miscalculation of the value of materials and goods held on site.

The Landscape Architect/Contract Administrator may only issue a Payless Notice after receiving written authorisation from the client/employer for each individual deduction it is proposed to make and the reasons for making such deduction.

> ACCORDING TO JCLI PRACTICE NOTE NO. 8
>
> (The Landscape Institute, June 2012, p. 8):
>
> *The Landscape Architect/Contract Administrator can issue a payless notice not less than 5 days before the final date for payment, against either a payment certificate or a Contractor's notice. The payless notice states the amount due at the date of the notice and has to be paid by the Employer by the final date for payment, instead of the amount on the certificate or Contractor's notice*

15.1.4 Payless Notice(s) (Type 2)

The difference between a Payless Notice (Type 2) and the Payless Notice (Type 1) discussed above, is that a Payless Notice (Type 2) is specifically intended to be issued by the Landscape Architect/Contract Administrator when the client/employer justifiably wishes to reduce the amount to be paid in response to a contractor's payment notice issued in accordance with clause 4.5.2 (page 23 of the JCLI Landscape Works Contract 2012). A contractor's payment notice is issued in accordance with clause 4.5.2 when the Landscape Architect/Contract Administrator has failed to issue any payment certificate on time.

> **ACCORDING TO JCLI PRACTICE NOTE NO. 8**
>
> (The Landscape Institute, June 2012, p. 8):
>
> *If a payment certificate is not issued on time the Contractor can issue a payment notice … The final date for payment is extended by the number of days between the end of the 5 day period above and the date of the Contractor's notice. Hence, since the final date for payment in the JCLI Contracts is 14 days after the due date, the final date for payment is extended to 9 days after the date of the Contractor's notice.*

Clause 4.5.4 (page 23 of the JCLI Landscape Works Contract 2012) requires the Landscape Architect/Contract Administrator named in Article 3 of the JCLI Landscape Works Contract 2012 to serve any Payless Notice (Type 2) on the contractor not less than five days before the final date for payment. Since the final date for payment is extended to nine days following the issue of the contractor's payment notice, any Payless Notice (Type 2) must be served on the contractor within four days of the date on which the contractor's payment notice was served. Time is therefore very much of the essence. Neither the client/employer nor the Landscape Architect/Contract Administrator can afford to delay.

15.1.5 Certificate of Practical Completion

Practical Completion is very significant in the administration of contracts. In accordance with clause 4.4.1 of the Contract Particulars (page 7 of the JCLI Landscape Works Contract 2012) 50 per cent of the retentions held in accordance with clause 4.3.1 of the Contract Particulars (page 7 of the JCLI Landscape Works Contract 2012) are ordinarily released for payment to the contractor with the issue of a Certificate of Practical Completion.

Regardless of whichever provision in clause 5.4 of the Contract Particulars (page 7 of the JCLI Landscape Works Contract 2012) has been adopted, responsibility for theft or malicious damage will pass to the employer after a Certificate of Practical Completion has been issued.

A Certificate of Practical Completion confirms the works comprising the contract have, by the date of the certificate, been substantially completed to the satisfaction of the Landscape Architect/Contract Administrator named in Article 3 of the JCLI Landscape Works Contract 2012 who remains the arbiter of such matters.

Since the object of the retentions following the issue of a Certificate of Practical Completion is to ensure the contractor has an incentive to remedy defects at the end of the Rectification Period specified in clause 2.10A or 2.10B of the Contract Particulars (page 6 of the JCLI Landscape Works Contract 2012) or, if the contractor reneges on its duties in this regard that sufficient funds have been retained to remedy the defects, the Landscape Architect/Contract Administrator named in Article 3 of the JCLI Landscape Works Contract 2012 must take great care to ensure they are satisfied with the works before issuing a Certificate of Practical Completion.

A Certificate of Practical Completion may be issued subject to a schedule of minor works that remain outstanding – for example, because of seasonal requirements, unforeseeable delay in supply or unfavourable conditions. If a Certificate of Practical Completion is to be issued subject to a schedule of outstanding works, in accordance with Guidance Note 26 (page 41 of the JCLI Landscape Works Contract 2012) the contractor must provide a written undertaking to complete the outstanding works within an agreed timescale.

The model Certificate of Practical Completion supplied to its members by the Landscape Institute permits the Landscape Architect/Contract Administrator named in Article 3 of the JCLI Landscape Works Contract 2012 to refer to a schedule of outstanding works. A copy of the schedule should be attached to the certificate.

The model Certificate of Practical Completion supplied to its members by the Landscape Institute permits the Landscape Architect/Contract Administrator named in Article 3 of the JCLI Landscape Works Contract 2012 to state the date on which the Rectification Period in clause number 2.10A or 2.10B of the Contract Particulars (page 6 of the JCLI Landscape Works Contract 2012) expires. If the Certificate of Practical Completion is being issued subject to a schedule of outstanding work, the date to be inserted will be the Rectification Period stated in clause 2.10A or 2.10B extended by the amount of time agreed with the contractor in which to complete the outstanding works.

In accordance with clause 2.12 (page 19 of the JCLI Landscape Works Contract 2012) with the consent of the contractor, the client/employer may take 'Partial Possession' of that part of the works which the Landscape Architect/Contract Administrator named in Article 3 of the JCLI Landscape Works Contract 2012 is willing to certificate as practically complete.

In the case of partial possession by the client/employer, the model form for Certificate of Practical Completion provided to its members by the Landscape Institute may be issued after amending the title to read 'Certificate of Practical Completion of Part of the Works'; amending the first sentence to describe that part of the works which is to be certificated as practically complete; and by adding a serial number to indicate there will be more than one Certificate of Practical Completion in relation to the particular project.

15.1.6 Certificate of Making Good

The Landscape Architect/Contract Administrator named in Article 3 of the JCLI Landscape Works Contract 2012 is required to notify the contractor of any defects in the works not later than 14 days after the end of the Rectification Period stated in clause 2.10A or 2.10B of the Contract Particulars (page 6 of the JCLI Landscape Works Contract 2012).

If clause 2.10A of the Contract Particulars has been adopted, the contractor is responsible for rectifying all defects in the works and undertaking a separate maintenance contract for at least the duration of the Rectification Period stated, whether on the basis of the JCLI Landscape Maintenance Works Contract 2012 or some other form of contract.

If clause 2.10B of the Contract Particulars has been adopted, the contractor is responsible for rectifying defects in the works excluding trees, shrubs, grass and other plants and will not be responsible for subsequent maintenance (as discussed in Chapter 13).

Where there has been partial possession of the works by the client/employer in accordance with clause 2.12 (page 19 of the JCLI Landscape Works Contract 2012) (discussed above) the Landscape Architect/Contract Administrator named in Article 3 of the JCLI Landscape Works Contract 2012 must issue a Certificate of Making Good for each part of the works for which a Certificate of Practical Completion was issued. By definition, where partial possession by the client/employer arose from the need to complete outstanding works in the appropriate season, the Certificate of Making Good relating to different parts of the works are likely to be issued at different times.

A Final Certificate cannot be issued until all the defects have been remedied and a Certificate of Making Good, specifying the date on which the contractor's responsibilities in this regard were discharged, has been issued in respect of each and every part of the works.

15.1.7 Final Certificate

At the end of the period stated at clause 4.8.1 of the Contract Particulars (page 7 of the JCLI Landscape Works Contract 2012), which will ordinarily coincide with the Rectification Period stated in clause 2.10A or 2.10B of the Contract Particulars (page 6 of the JCLI Landscape Works Contract 2012), the contractor must provide all the documentation the Landscape Architect/Contract Administrator named in Article 3 of the JCLI Landscape Works Contract 2012 reasonably requires to compute the final valuation.

In accordance with clause 4.8.1 of the Conditions of Contract (page 24 of the JCLI Landscape Works Contract 2012), the due date for the final valuation by the Landscape Architect/Contract Administrator named in Article 3 of the JCLI Landscape Works Contract 2012 is 28 days after receipt of the documentation from the contractor or, if later, 28 days from the date the contractor discharged its responsibilities in relation to rectification of defects, as stated on the last of the Certificates of Making Good issued by the Landscape Architect/Contract Administrator.

Not later than five days after the due date for computing the final valuation, the Landscape Architect/Contract Administrator named in Article 3 of the JCLI Landscape Works Contract 2012 must issue a Final Certificate stating the amount due either to the contractor or to the client/employer. This amount will include the release of all outstanding retentions held in accordance with clause 4.4.1 (page 7 of the JCLI Landscape Works Contract 2012), that is to say the contractor must be paid the full value of the works.

On issuing a Final Certificate, the Landscape Architect/Contract Administrator named in Article 3 of the JCLI Landscape Works Contract 2012 is confirming that the works are complete and to their entire satisfaction.

If the client/employer wishes to deduct Liquidated Damages resulting from delay from the Final Certificate in accordance with clause 2.8 of the Contract Particulars (page 6 of the JCLI Landscape Works Contract 2012), a Payless Notice (Type 1) in accordance with clause 4.5.4 (page 23 of the JCLI Landscape Works Contract 2012) (discussed above) must be issued in advance of, or at the same time as, issuing the Final Certificate.

In accordance with clause 4.8.2 (page 24 of the JCLI Landscape Works Contract 2012), the sum stated to be due on the Final Certificate plus any Value Added Tax properly chargeable must be paid by the paying party no later than the final date for payment, that is to say 14 days after the due date for the valuation.

Where a Payless Notice has been issued in accordance with clause 4.5.4 of the JCLI Landscape Works Contract 2012 (discussed above) a payment of not less than the amount indicated on the Payless Notice must be made on or before the final date for payment.

If the paying party fails to pay the amount due by the final date for payment, the amount owed will attract interest in accordance with clause 4.9 (page 24 of the JCLI Landscape Works Contract 2012) until the debt is finally paid and the party to whom the money is owed will be entitled to instigate dispute resolution procedures in accordance with whichever of Article 6, Article 7 and Article 8 (page 4 of JCLI Landscape Works Contract 2012) and/or clause 7.2 and/or Schedule 1 of the Contract Particulars (page 8 of the JCLI Landscape Works Contract 2012) are deemed to apply (discussed in Chapter 13).

15.2   DRAWING OFFICE RECORDS

In order to maintain a successful practice and correctly administer contracts, the professional practitioner must be diligent and methodical in the keeping of drawing office records. The records likely to have to be maintained consist of:

- Job lists

- Contract documentation

- Valuations, certificates and variations

- Correspondence

- Practice timesheets and invoices

Each of these will now be considered briefly in turn.

15.2.1   Job lists

It is essential for the purposes of practice administration and marketing (discussed in Chapters 5 and 6) that the professional practitioner keeps up-to-date job lists recording who a job is for; the nature of the project; where the project is located;

the professional fees expected to be earned; and the stage of the project's implementation.

The professional practitioner must be systematic and consistent in record keeping. Each new commission should be allocated its own unique job reference number. This unique number (or a derivative of it) should be used on all records relating to that particular job, for example contract documents, variations, valuations, certificates, correspondence, practice time sheets and invoices.

The job list should be regularly updated with the current status of each job from the practice point of view, that is to say the value of professional fees earned to date; the expected value of fees yet to be earned (information vital for cash flow forecasts discussed in Chapter 6); and estimated completion dates (information vital to managing the practice workload).

15.2.2 Contract documentation

The range and purpose of contract documentation has been discussed at length in Chapter 12, along with the impact of Building Information Modelling. For the present purpose, it is sufficient to say that an efficiently managed professional practice must have adequate copies of the contract documentation (whether in digital or hard copy form) and contract documents should be properly identified by job numbers relating to the job lists (discussed above).

15.2.3 Valuations, certificates and variations

As it ordinarily falls to the professional practitioner to authorise any variations to contracts for the implementation of works; to carry out interim and final valuations; to produce interim and final certificates; to certificate practical completion of the works, the making good of defects and final completion, it should go without saying that a professional practice must retain copies of all such documents, properly linked to job files (whether digitally or in hard copy) by means of job numbers relating back to the job lists discussed above.

15.2.4 Correspondence

Professional practice tends to generate a considerable amount of correspondence, whether in the form of letters, emails, specialist reports, notes of telephone conversations, minutes of meetings or copies of variations and certificates (discussed above).

The professional practitioner will need access to such correspondence whether when planning a project; during implementation of a project; or possibly long after the project's completion. For example, if an allegation of professional negligence is made (discussed in Chapter 3).

Correspondence with the client is likely to concern the initial appointment of the professional practitioner (discussed in Chapter 7); approval of a project budget (discussed in Chapter 11); input as necessary to the preparation of contract documentation (discussed in Chapter 12) and conditions of contract (discussed in Chapter 13); obtaining quotations/tenders and selection of contractor(s) (discussed in Chapter 14); setting-up of agreement(s) for implementation of the works in which the client will have to make a number of decisions (discussed in Chapter 13); and keeping the client informed of the progress of the works (discussed in the current chapter).

It is important the professional practitioner is able to refer to correspondence with contractors in the event problems arise. It may be necessary for the professional practitioner to be able to substantiate what was said, agreed or what instructions were given. For example, to refer to the method statement (discussed in Chapter 4) indicating the contractor would wear a safety harness for climbing the tree he just fell out of!

It is important the professional practitioner is able to refer to correspondence with suppliers, in particular nominated suppliers of goods or services (discussed in Chapter 13) as it may be necessary to substantiate what was agreed in terms of product quality, price and delivery lead time. For example, the contractor may be seeking to claim additional time and money because the nominated supplier requires six weeks to provide goods it previously indicated could be available within two weeks.

The professional practitioner may need to refer to correspondence with the local planning authority to substantiate that written approval was obtained where necessary before works commenced. For example, that authority was obtained to carry out tree surgery operations on a tree protected by a Tree Preservation Order (discussed in Chapter 8).

The professional practitioner is likely to want to refer to correspondence with specialists and/or related professionals in the making of judgments and later defending those same judgments if the need arises. For example, the advice obtained from a Structural Engineer in the event a wall collapses during the progress of works.

It is vital that the professional practitioner is ordered and up-to-date with correspondence. It is pointless having piles of filling waiting to be filed when turning up on site, or dealing with a telephone call, with a file woefully out of date. It is much more effective and professional to have the information readily to hand and, if necessary, to employ administrative support to ensure this is so.

15.2.5   Practice timesheets and invoices

Practice timesheets enable the professional practitioner to keep an accurate record of the time spent on each job and expenses incurred in order to accurately invoice the client for their professional fees.

During the course of an average day in a busy practice the professional practitioner is likely to deal with numerous projects. And during the course of a project handled by a medium or large practice there are likely to be different grades of practice personnel involved.

It is vital that each project has a dedicated job costing (whether digitally or in hard copy) linked back to the job lists discussed above and that each member of the practice team can be individually identified. Most importantly, it is vital the professional practitioner is disciplined in recording each member's time and doing so honestly and accurately.

In picking up a telephone call in relation to one project while working on another, it is very easy for the professional practitioner to inadvertently record the time spent on the telephone as time spent on the project s/he was working on at the time the call came through, thereby charging the wrong client for the time, or not to record the time spent on the telephone call at all, thereby failing to charge anyone for the time.

Recourse to accurate practice timesheets will also be vital as and when the professional practitioner is asked to explain to the client where they were and what they were doing at a given date and time or why a particular aspect of their commission took as long as it did.

Practice timesheets should also record chargeable expenses and disbursements (discussed in Chapter 7) including travel and hotel expenses, vehicle mileage, printing and reprographic costs, project specific stationery, and postage costs. All of these are easier to reconcile if they are recorded alongside the time spent.

Without the information contained on timesheets the professional practitioner has no basis on which to calculate or substantiate their invoice and is very likely to forget to charge for something. It is important that practice timesheets record all the time spent on a project, even that which is non-remunerative (discussed in Chapter 7) or time spent on bidding for projects the practice fails to obtain. Such information is vital for practice administration; to understand how much time is spent on such matters as administration, travelling, quoting for projects and initial meetings, as this information needs to be built-in to the calculation of the professional practitioner's hourly rate (discussed in Chapter 7).

> CHAPTER SUMMARY
>
> - In order to properly monitor and control projects the professional practitioner is required to certificate performance at pre-determined stages of contract implementation including practical completion and final handover to the client
>
> - It is often necessary for the professional practitioner to vary the content of a contract or the sequence and/or season in which the project is implemented
>
> - In order to maintain a successful practice and properly administer contracts the professional practitioner must be diligent and methodical in the keeping of drawing office records

16

Alternative Dispute Resolution Procedures

> THE AIMS OF THIS CHAPTER ARE TO:
>
> - Introduce the major forms of alternative dispute resolution procedures
> - Explain the impetus for and the use of alternative dispute resolution clauses in contracts
> - Evaluate the advantages/disadvantages of different forms of alternative dispute resolution procedures as opposed to civil litigation

Apart from expensive, time-consuming and potentially highly stressful civil litigation, that is to say the resolution of disputes through adversarial court procedures, there are a variety of forms of alternative dispute resolution procedures according to Brown & Marriott (1999, p. 12) 'generally involving the intercession and assistance of a neutral and impartial third party'.

Aiming to overcome the weaknesses of adversarial systems, alternative dispute resolution procedures seek to encourage more openness and better communication and are intended to lead to swifter, more cost-effective dispute resolution.

The fundamental basis of alternative dispute resolution procedures is the ability of the parties to pursue what is important to them in the particular circumstances, often an outcome not available through litigation. Bevan (1992, p. 2) uses the analogy of an orange in suggesting that litigation generally results only in division, whereas alternative dispute resolution procedures enquire what the parties seek and attempt to 'tailor' an agreement; one party perhaps requiring the 'fruit' whilst the other seeks the 'peel'.

According to Brown & Marriott (1999, p. 13), 'There is a view of alternative dispute resolution as a forum in which parties are helped to adopt a problem-solving approach in order to find a "win-win" outcome'. For example, a mediated group action against the National Health Service which according to Lewis (2003, p. 24) resulted in Alder Hey Children's Hospital not only paying £5000 compensation per child but, perhaps more importantly, formally apologising to the parents of children whose organs were wrongly retained; pledging to erect a commemorative plaque; to donate £100,000 to charity; and to push for reforms in the law regarding organ retention. According to solicitors acting for the group claimants in the Alder Hey proceedings, mediation was considered the most appropriate option because the threat of litigation meant parents were having difficulties obtaining the non-financial remedies they sought.

16.1 MAJOR FORMS OF ALTERNATIVE DISPUTE RESOLUTION

According to Goldberg, Sander and Rogers (1992, p. 1) 'negotiation', 'mediation' and 'adjudication' are frequently cited as the major forms of alternative dispute resolution procedures.

Brown and Marriott (1999, p. 12) describe dispute resolution as a continuum, with negotiation at one end, litigation at the other and many forms of alternative dispute resolution procedure found along its length according to the degree of control exercised by the parties. Negotiation is seen by Brown and Marriott (1999, p. 12) not as an alternative form of dispute resolution but as the most fundamental method of resolving differences, a thesis supported by Bevan (1992, p. 3).

According to Brown and Marriott (1992, p. 12), 'While negotiation is invariably one of the main components of ADR [alternative dispute resolution] ... it is only when ... accompanied by neutral intercession and a more structured process ... it becomes ADR'. For this reason, Brown and Marriott (1992) consider the major forms of alternative dispute resolution procedures to be arbitration, mediation and adjudication, although there is debate concerning the inclusion of arbitration.

MAJOR FORMS OF ALTERNATIVE DISPUTE RESOLUTION (ADR):

- Arbitration
- Mediation
- Adjudication

According to Goldberg, Sander and Rogers (1992, p. 1) the legally binding nature of arbitration sets it apart from other form of alternative dispute resolution procedure. However, on this basis, adjudication would similarly be excluded, as the intermediary in adjudication also has the power to bind the parties.

Bevan (1992, p. 6) suggests the legitimate view of alternative dispute resolution procedures is that they should encompass binding and non-binding processes and it is irrelevant if the inclusion of arbitration can be seen as something of an anomaly.

Arbitration, mediation and adjudication will therefore be considered in some detail (in particular their merits relative to litigation) in order to illustrate how alternative dispute resolution procedures are able to resolve problems in a way litigation cannot. Before doing so, it is worth considering a non-exhaustive list of alternative dispute resolution mechanisms drawn from a review of literature sources:

- Early neutral evaluation, in which a neutral professional, commonly a lawyer, hears a summary of the case, giving a non-binding assessment of its merits. This may lead to settlement or further negotiations.

- Expert determination, in which an independent third party, expert in the particular subject, is appointed to decide the dispute. The decision is binding on both parties.

- Conciliation, which is akin to mediation but the 'conciliator' takes a more interventionist role by suggesting possible solutions.

- Med-Arb, which is a hybrid process whereby the parties agree to mediate and, in the event of failure to resolve the dispute, the third party changes position from non-binding facilitator to binding evaluator.

- Neutral fact-finding, which is a non-binding procedure involving the appointment of a neutral expert to investigate the facts in dispute, including complex technical issues, and to make an evaluation of their merits.

- Ombudsmen who are independent office-holders investigating and ruling on complaints from members of the public concerning abuses in public or private sector services, such as the privatised utilities. Most ombudsmen are able to make recommendations. Very few make decisions legally enforceable through courts.

16.1.1 Mediation

The most common alternative to civil litigation is mediation, so much so that the term 'mediation' seems to be used interchangeably with 'alternative dispute resolution' in much of the literature (for example Dodd and Rees [2004] and Genn [2003]).

According to Lord Justice Lightman (2004, p. 189), 'Courts will now enforce agreements … to proceed to mediation … unless there are compelling reasons to the contrary'.

Mediation involves a neutral, frequently specially trained, intermediary (whether legal or non-legal) aiming to facilitate parties finding their own agreement. Mediation meetings are 'without prejudice' to future litigation. That is to say, whatever is discussed or offered at mediation cannot be used against either party in subsequent litigation, if litigation should eventually be unavoidable.

Mediation may be 'evaluative' such that the mediator assesses the strength of the case, or it may be 'facilitative' in which case the emphasis is placed on assisting the parties to define the issues.

Importantly, the intermediary in mediation cannot bind the parties or impose solutions. A mediated settlement once arrived at can however form the basis of a legally binding contract the courts may enforce.

The courts have discretion to award costs against a party who refuses to partake or withdraws from alternative dispute resolution procedures. Exercising this discretion in the cases of *Dunnett v Railtrack PLC* [2002] and *Royal Bank of Canada v Secretary of State for Defence* [2003] the courts declined to award costs to the parties refusing to mediate even though their cases were successful.

According to Lord Justice Lightman in the case of *Hurst v Leeming* [2001]:

> *Case law ... means that a party must have a very good reason for rejecting ADR and show there was no realistic prospect of any mediation succeeding ... Mediation is not in law compulsory ... but ADR is at the heart of today's civil justice system.*

The High Court decision in *Corenso (UK) Ltd v Burnden Group PLC* [2003] held that refusal to mediate will not lead to an automatic costs penalty where there is no fault and the parties are willing to negotiate without going to court. The case follows *Hurst v Leeming* [2001] in which Lord Justice Lightman, stressing refusal to mediate was a 'high risk course', decided mediation was inappropriate 'Where one of the parties was incapable of participating in a rational discussion'.

Legitimate reasons for rejecting mediation, that is to say reasons that have proven acceptable to the judiciary, include that the offer to mediate came too close to trial, as in the case of *Corenso (UK) Ltd v Burnden Group PLC* [2003]; because the offer to mediate was tactical or made in an attempt to apply unreasonable pressure, as in the case of *Socit Internationale de Telecommunications Aeronautiques SC v Wyatt Co (UK) Ltd* (Costs) [2002]; because other appropriate methods of alternative dispute resolution had been attempted without success, as in the case of *Valentine v Allen* [2003]; and because the subject of the dispute meant there was no scope for compromise, as in the case of *McCook v Lobo* [2002].

In the opinion of Flannery (2003, p1415) the cases cited above represent a 'long-called for response by the courts to arguments that a party refusing mediation should always be penalised in costs'. The courts instead take into account a party's conduct and, where litigation succeeds and costs are sought, do not always consider a party's refusal to mediate unreasonable.

CHARACTERISTICS OF MEDIATION

- Most common alternative to civil litigation
- Neutral intermediary aims to facilitate parties finding their own agreement
- Without prejudice to subsequent litigation if required
- Non-binding on the parties
- A party may be penalised in costs for a failure to mediate

16.1.2 Arbitration

According to Newman (1999, p. 2), arbitration is a 'no-nonsense' form of alternative dispute resolution procedure relying on technical assessment by persons with particular expertise (whether lawyers or lay) rather than the nuances of randomly selected judges and juries; what Michaelson (2003, Part I, p. 101) refers to as a form of 'privatised litigation with the judge and venue paid for by the parties'.

According to Bevan (1992, p. 7) the longevity of arbitration testifies to its merits in practice as well as in theory, particularly its 'finality'. That is to say, whereas the third party in mediation is purely a facilitator and has no power to bind the parties, arbitrators impose legally binding awards enforceable by the courts.

However, finality is a 'two-edged sword' since the grounds on which a court will set aside an arbitrator's 'award' (other than issues of law) are limited by the Arbitration Act 1996 to situations where the tribunal lacked 'substantive jurisdiction', for example where an arbitrator was appointed without waiting for expiration of the prescribed period of negotiation (Arbitration Act 1996, s.67); and situations of 'serious irregularity' such as the arbitrator's failure to conduct proceedings in accordance with appropriate procedures, in which case the challenging party must demonstrate 'substantial injustice' (Arbitration Act 1996, s.68).

It is worthy of note that under section 29(1) of the Arbitration Act 1996 an arbitrator is not liable 'for anything done or omitted in discharge or purported discharge of his functions' and, as noted by Densham and Bradford (2004, p. 130), the arbitrator cannot be required to appear as a witness in any court challenge to the arbitration procedures.

Arbitration decisions, being based purely on the evidence presented, frequently require submissions; counter-submissions; formal hearings; deliberation on complex legal issues; and interrogation of witnesses, just as in litigation. As a result, Newman (1999, p. 2) claims arbitration is considered by some to be legalistic and expensive, and Bevan (1992, p. 7) states that 'Despite being less formal than litigation and being private (until litigated) arbitration is most like litigation and can be something of a misfit within ADR'.

Arbitration is widely used in international disputes, where a major advantage is the ability of the parties to nominate the substantive law of a neutral jurisdiction and agree procedures between themselves and the arbitrator. In addition, awards of international arbitration are more 'transportable', that is to say they potentially have greater significance between disparate legal jurisdictions than do the judgments of national courts, as noted by Michaelson (2003, Part II, p. 147) when referring to the New York Convention simplifying reciprocity procedures whereby arbitral awards may be enforced in over 120 countries.

> **CHARACTERISTICS OF ARBITRATION**
>
> - Technical assessment by person with particular expertise
> - Arbitrators impose legally binding awards enforceable by the courts
> - Entirely reliant upon evidence presented
> - Can be legalistic and expensive
> - Private until litigated
> - Parties may nominate substantive law of neutral jurisdiction
> - Awards of international arbitration are potentially transportable

16.1.3 Adjudication

Adjudication is often used as a generic term for litigation but is also a specific form of alternative dispute resolution procedure developed for construction contracts. Construction contracts are so significant in English law they have a specialist court – the Technology and Construction Court.

Aimed at ensuring construction projects are not inordinately delayed by disputes, adjudication arose from work by Sir Michael Latham in the 1990's focusing on the poor payment practices, adversarial and claims-conscious attitude of the construction industry. According to Burns (2003, p. 110):

> Litigation and arbitration processes were criticised as often incurring more costs than the amounts in dispute. Among Sir Michael's 13 recommendations was the statutory implementation of a quick and affordable means for resolving disputes by an independent adjudicator.

Either party has the right to refer disputes to adjudication at any time. Once initiated, the other party cannot prevent adjudication proceeding, although adjudicated decisions are only temporarily binding. According to Bevan (1992, p. 11), at the end of the project, if either party is dissatisfied, other forms of alternative dispute resolution procedure such as mediation or arbitration may be invoked. Alternatively, adjudicated decisions can be reviewed and set aside by application to the courts but this rarely happens. As Burns (2003, p. 111) put it:

> In practice, most adjudicator's decisions resolve the dispute once and for all. One reason is the adjudicator is generally required to explain his conclusions. These often reveal enough to convince a losing party that there would be little merit in taking the dispute to litigation or arbitration.

If either party fails to comply with an adjudicator's decision, the other may obtain an enforcement order from the courts. According to Burns (2003, p. 111), circumstances in which courts will refuse to enforce adjudication decisions include where adjudicators have acted 'contrary to the rules of natural justice', for example where communication with the adjudicator has been available to one party and not the other.

According to Bevan (1992, p. 11) adjudicators may take the initiative in ascertaining facts and relevant law, as opposed to the courts and arbitrators who consider only the evidence put before them. An adjudicator need not be a lawyer and are often industry professionals – a fact which Smulian (2003, p. 22) states some consider a 'lottery', owing to the potential variety of individual knowledge and expertise.

Since May 1998 all contracts for construction, civil engineering and related professional services, as well as construction, project and facilities management, have been required to make provision for adjudication as a first instance dispute resolution procedure. Contracts failing to make provisions for adjudication have such provisions implied by the Scheme for Construction Contracts (England and Wales) Regulations 1998.

CHARACTERISTICS OF ADJUDICATION

- Specialist form of alternative dispute resolution developed for construction contracts
- Involves independent adjudicator with industry expertise
- Quick and affordable means of resolving disputes
- Either party may refer dispute to adjudication at any time
- Adjudicator may take the initiative in ascertaining facts
- Only temporarily binding
- If either party dissatisfied, other forms of alternative dispute resolution may be invoked
- Adjudicated outcomes enforceable by the courts

16.2 CHANGES IN CIVIL LITIGATION

According to Brown and Marriott (1999, p. 534) civil litigation changed considerably in the wake of the Lord Chancellor's commission to the Master of the Rolls, Lord Justice Woolf, in 1994:

> Lord Woolf's reforms of civil litigation are based on collaborative case management with a view to streamlining procedures and facilitating settlement before litigation begins and if it starts, at the earliest possible stage thereafter. Legal aid ... is being abolished in the form in which it has previously operated and a new system of funding and administration is being put in place. The object is to cap expenditure, to ensure better value for money and a more efficient allocation of resources between different forms of civil dispute resolution.

Concerned with improving access to justice and reducing the costs of litigation, from Lord Woolf's report came the Civil Procedure Rules 1998. The Civil Procedure Rules emphasise that litigation must be a last resort when resolving disputes.

According to Pemble (2004, p. 95), there is no express requirement, either in the Civil Procedure Rules or elsewhere, for parties in dispute to make use of alternative dispute resolution procedures. However, under Civil Procedure Rule 1.3:

> Parties are obliged to help the court further the overriding objective. That in turn requires the court to ensure the case is dealt with expeditiously, fairly and with an appropriate share of the court's resources.

Meanwhile, Civil Procedure Rule 1.4 requires the court to:

> Further the overriding objective by actively managing cases. This includes encouraging the parties to use Alternative Dispute Resolution procedures if the court considers that appropriate.

Whilst there is no legal requirement to engage in alternative dispute resolution procedures, since Lord Justice Woolf's report and introduction of the Civil Procedure Rules, there has been considerable emphasis on parties attempting some form of alternative dispute resolution procedure before embarking upon civil litigation. As stated in the case of *Cowl v Plymouth City Council* [2002]:

> Insufficient attention is paid to the paramount importance of avoiding litigation whenever this is possible ... The case will have served some purpose if it makes it clear the lawyers on both sides of a dispute ... are under a heavy obligation to resort to litigation only if it is really unavoidable.

16.3   ALTERNATIVE DISPUTE RESOLUTION CLAUSES

Encouragement towards alternative dispute resolution procedures in advance of and in preference to civil litigation is reflected in commercial contracts by the inclusion of clauses relating to the forms of alternative dispute resolution that must be undertaken before the parties seek resolution in the courts.

The case of *Cable & Wireless PLC v IBM United Kingdom Ltd* [2002] addressed the issue of the enforceability of alternative dispute resolution clauses in contracts. Distinguishing the judgment in *Courtney & Fairbairn Ltd v Tolaini Bros (Hotels) Ltd* [1974] in which Lord Justice Denning held agreements to 'negotiate' were unenforceable for lack of certainty, the judgment in *Cable & Wireless PLC v IBM United Kingdom Ltd* [2002] held that a clause requiring disputes to be subjected to the Centre for Dispute Resolution's mediation procedures provided a sufficiently certain basis for contractual obligations unlike 'a mere undertaking to negotiate a contract or settlement agreement'.

With the impetus of Lord Woolf's reforms and the introduction of the Civil Procedure Rules, the judgment in *Cable & Wireless PLC v IBM United Kingdom Ltd* [2002] made clear that English courts will give every encouragement to attempt alternative dispute resolution procedures in advance of litigation.

In the case of *Channel Tunnel Group Ltd & Another v Balfour Beatty Construction Ltd & Others* [1993], Lord Justice Mustill held the court had inherent power to stay proceedings brought before it if these proceedings were in breach of a contractually agreed alternative dispute resolution procedure, noting:

> *Where large commercial enterprises had agreed a dispute resolution procedure it was in the interests of the orderly regulation of international commerce for the court to exercise its discretion and uphold the clause.*

The decision in *Cable & Wireless PLC v IBM United Kingdom Ltd* [2002] was also on public policy grounds, His Honour Judge Colman stating:

> *For the courts now to decline to enforce contractual references to ADR on the grounds of intrinsic uncertainty would be to fly in the face of public policy as expressed in the Civil Procedure Rules and as reflected in the judgment of the Court of Appeal in Dunnett v Railtrack.*

Use of public policy arguments to defeat contractual uncertainty confirms how strongly the English courts support the use of alternative dispute resolution procedures. Indeed, explaining his conclusion in *Cable & Wireless PLC v IBM United Kingdom Ltd* [2002] His Honour Judge Colman stated his decision would have been the same without reference to the Centre for Dispute Resolution's mediation procedures, provided that the 'obligation to mediate was expressed in unqualified and mandatory terms.'

16.4   ALTERNATIVE DISPUTE RESOLUTION V LITIGATION

Having considered the most common forms of alternative dispute resolution procedures and the courts' encouragement that such procedures should be used before commencing civil litigation, both through the introduction of the Civil Procedure Rules and by upholding alternative dispute resolution clauses contained in contracts, there remains the question of whether alternative dispute resolution procedures can be more effective than litigation. There follows a comparative analysis of the strengths and weaknesses of both systems in each of the following respects:

- Predictability
- Reliability
- Expediency
- Public Scrutiny
- Future Relations

- Expense

- Desired Outcomes

- Sociology

16.4.1 Predictability

The outcome of civil litigation is unpredictable, with experienced litigators never giving clients greater than an 80 per cent chance of success. According to Lord Justice Lightman (2004, p. 185), 'Litigation is a high risk gamble with both financial and human costs ... the outcome is unpredictable with no necessary relationship to the merits.'

There are numerous reasons for this unpredictability; documents emerging at any time before judgment may have a decisive influence on the litigation outcome; the evolution of common law by means of judicial decisions addressing changing perceptions and re-dressing past errors; and judicial decisions, though theoretically introducing only 'incremental' developments in common law, according to Lord Justice Lightman (2004, p.189), 'afford scope for the judge to reflect his evaluation of the justice of the case before him.' In Lord Justice Lightman's opinion (2004, p. 189) the outcome of litigation may be prone to the foibles of individual judges, whilst the effectiveness of individual advocates may also impact upon the outcome of individual cases.

Whilst these factors diminish the predictability of civil litigation, it is difficult to see how alternative dispute resolution procedures fare any better in this regard. Since alternative dispute resolution procedures actively promote early exchange of information between the parties, this may serve only to strengthen the arguments presented by 'the other side'.

As for the unpredictability of advocates and the judiciary, alternative dispute resolution procedures rely just as much on advocates as does litigation, with the added uncertainty of the choice of intermediary, which Smulian (2003, p. 23) sees as 'a lottery ... some are truly excellent but some are barking mad and think they are exercising the judgment of Solomon'.

16.4.2 Reliability

Witnesses in litigation can prove unreliable when subjected to the rigors of the courtroom. Anxiety, fright and cross-examination by advocates may make listening to and answering questions a difficult experience for the witness. According to Lord Justice Lightman (2004, p. 185):

> Witnesses have been known to 'misfire' in the witness box. They can be disconcerted ... lose their way ... fail to make the most of themselves and their evidence. They may exaggerate and 'over-egg' the pudding ... Further, estimates of their credibility and the weight to be afforded to their evidence can vary significantly ... Indeed, the assessment of witnesses is, in my view, the hardest task of a trial judge.

Expert evidence on behalf of each litigant may, at worst, be 'bought' and, at best, even taking into account pre-trial procedures, require the judge (a non-expert in the particular discipline) to decide the relative merits of two conflicting expert opinions.

Alternative dispute resolution procedures take place in surroundings that are generally less intimidating to witnesses. On the other hand, it can often be people rather than places that intimidate a witness. The formality of a courtroom may arguably offer a form of protection to vulnerable parties who may feel 'safer' coming face to face with the other party in a courtroom than meeting in close proximity during mediation.

As regards Lord Justice Lightman's concerns as to the reliability of witnesses and their evidence (expressed above), although intermediaries engaged in alternative dispute resolution procedures may have expert knowledge of the facts, it is reasonable to question whether industry luminaries have sufficient breadth of experience to make them 'experts' in the field of witness evaluation.

16.4.3 Expediency

A common thread running through the literature is that alternative dispute resolution procedures have the potential to be quicker and more effective than litigation. According to Professor Genn (2003) only five per cent of cases attempting alternative dispute resolution end up going to trial. This compares with 15 per cent of those cases that decline alternative dispute resolution procedures.

Professor Genn's 2003 survey sample consisted only of cases in which courts made orders in respect of alternative dispute resolution procedures. The survey sample is therefore not representative of cases generally. That is to say cases in which no orders were made in respect of alternative dispute resolution procedures – procedures that may or may not have been attempted without such orders.

The findings of Professor Genn's 2003 survey also leave unanswered how the 85 per cent of cases that did not attempt alternative dispute resolution procedures and did not go to trial were *actually* resolved. The assumption has to be that the parties in these cases came to some sort of negotiated agreement.

If Brown and Marriott's view of negotiation as the most fundamental method of resolving differences (1992, p. 12) is accepted – a thesis supported by Bevan (1992, p. 3) – and if it is assumed that the majority of parties in dispute are likely to seek some form of advice from a 'neutral' intermediary, then, leaving aside any requirement for formally structured procedures, it might be argued a far greater number of cases are resolved by alternative dispute resolution procedures in their most fundamental form than Professor Genn's 2003 research findings indicate.

16.4.4 Public scrutiny

Litigation is a very public means of resolving disputes. Corporate entities often prefer to avoid such publicity, either because it is potentially damaging to commercial reputations or because an organisation's dealings are themselves commercially sensitive. By contrast, alternative dispute resolution procedures are conducted in private, away from public scrutiny, and any agreements reached may be subject to a privacy agreement.

There are, however, situations in which the public nature of litigation is exactly what is required. For example, one of the required outcomes of intellectual property disputes is generally to deter future infringement. In such circumstances the aggrieved party is likely to be intent upon obtaining the full publicity of a litigated outcome.

The same is true of defamation actions, where the aggrieved party is likely to be looking for its besmirched reputation to be vindicated, although in such cases alternative dispute resolution procedures can be an effective means of negotiating a public apology.

16.4.5 Future relations

The confrontational nature of litigation tends to jeopardise any possibility of future relationships between the parties. In commerce this may be more costly than a court action. The confidential nature of alternative dispute resolution procedures can enable parties to 'save face' and thereby facilitate the best-case scenario of resolving disputes while enabling continuity of the business relationship. The privacy of alternative dispute resolution procedures and their 'conciliatory' rather than 'confrontational' nature clearly being positive benefits.

16.4.6 Expense

Litigation is expensive and thereby denies justice to those unable to countenance the expense. Expressed more cynically, litigated justice is only available to those who can afford it.

According to Lord Justice Lightman (2004, p. 189), litigation costs have increased to an 'all time high' since the introduction of the Civil Procedure Rules and pre-action protocols, suggesting civil litigation's efforts to embrace the principles of alternative dispute resolution have failed to meet the objectives of Lord Woolf or the Civil Procedure Rules, that is to say better value for money. Against this background there is broad agreement that alternative dispute resolution procedures, when successful, represent cost effective dispute resolution.

When alternative dispute resolution procedures are unsuccessful, expense incurred is additional to the subsequent costs of litigation although, according to Brown and Marriott (1999, p. 14): 'there is often some value added by virtue of the ADR [alternative dispute resolution] process such as helping to gather information and clarify or narrow issues.'

16.4.7 Desired outcomes

One key advantage of alternative dispute resolution procedures is the ability to facilitate dialogue. Through dialogue, as in the Alder Hey example quoted above (Lewis, 2003), parties may bring to notice what it is they *actually* want. This potentially enables provision to be made that would be beyond the scope of litigation; the civil courts generally being restricted to monetary awards. According to Lewis (2003, p. 26):

> Through the medium of ADR, patients may get the opportunity to meet the doctor or hospital risk manager, which presents a 'huge benefit'. They can see what steps are being put in place to prevent the situation happening again.

Unfortunately both litigation and alternative dispute resolution procedures are time consuming and therefore, particularly in medical negligence cases, the result may come too late for the claimant to benefit directly.

16.4.8 Sociology

As demonstrated in the Alder Hey mediated settlement quoted above (Lewis, 2003), alternative dispute resolution procedures give claimants a 'voice' and enable them to make sense of what has happened. According to Lewis (2003, p. 26), in being heard and aware their feelings have been acknowledged, parties are better able to move to agreement.

These positive outcomes contrast starkly with the commonly held belief that litigation has no winners. Because the real costs of litigation are so great, success can never be anything more than a pyrrhic victory.

16.5 CONCLUSIONS

Though intended to reduce costs and deal with cases expediently alternative dispute resolution procedures may actually have had the opposite effect. According to Lord Justice Lightman (2004, p. 189), pre-action protocols, presentation of evidence, over-complication of cases, and the input of experts and mediators have all substantially increased costs.

Alternative dispute resolution procedures provide an opportunity for the experienced professional practitioner to employ their expert skills and knowledge in the resolution of contractual disputes.

Arguably civil litigation is fair and transparent, whereas 'private law' remedies provided by ADR procedures may be more open to abuse. The aggrieved party who agrees to a mediated settlement outside the courtroom may be doing so under coercion, intimidation or, at the very least, for fear of incurring the costs associated with litigation.

Whilst the courts should perhaps be doing more than simply 'rubber stamping' agreements reached by alternative dispute resolution procedures, the professional practitioner too, who finds him or herself involved in dispute resolution, must do all they can to ensure a fair, even-handed, just and expedient outcome, as far as they are able.

The Civil Procedure Rules sought to encourage alternative dispute resolution procedures and parties succeeding in civil litigation are being penalised in costs for not attempting alternative dispute resolution. The professional practitioner then should advise their client of the availability of alternative dispute resolution procedures and encourage the client to at least explore such alternatives before embarking upon civil litigation.

Mediation can be unpopular because of its non-binding nature and its encouragement towards early disclosure of evidence which can be disadvantageous to one or other party. In relation to landscape contracts, which generally involve sums easily outweighed by legal fees, suitably trained and experienced professional practitioners can cost-effectively mediate settlement of disputes and preserve ongoing contractual relationships.

Bevan (1992, p. 7) and Newman (1999, p. 2) each consider arbitration to be legalistic and expensive. Nonetheless, arbitration has a place in dispute resolution, not least because of its frequent inclusion in standard forms of contract. Here, too, the appropriately trained and experienced professional practitioner potentially has a role to play.

Smulian (2003, p. 22) considers adjudication to be a 'lottery' owing to the professional rather than legal status of its proponents. Again an appropriately trained and experienced professional practitioner has the opportunity not only to serve as the expert adjudicator but, in so doing, to improve the overall regard in which adjudication is held by acting even-handedly and justly as well as professionally.

In comparison to litigation, alternative dispute resolution procedures better protect working relationships, reduce expense, are more likely to achieve desired outcomes and have distinct sociological benefits. In terms of predictability, reliability and expediency, it is questionable whether alternative dispute resolution procedures are any more effective than litigation.

The suggestion that alternative dispute resolution procedures might resolve problems litigation cannot is spurious. According to Brown and Marriott (1999, p. 15), the two processes working together, though flawed, seem to provide the most effective solution:

> *ADR compliments litigation ... providing processes which can either stand in their own right or be used as an adjunct ... ADR gives parties more power and greater control over resolving the issues between them, encourages problem-solving approaches, and provides for more effective settlements ... it also tends to enhance cooperation and to be conducive to the preservation of relationships. Effective impartial third party intercession can help to overcome blocks to settlement and by expediting and facilitating resolution it can save costs and avoid the delays and risks of litigation. Sometimes ... it can help to heal ... underlying conflicts between parties. ADR processes have advantages and disadvantages which make them suitable for some cases but not for others.*

Procedural reform intended to produce more effective case management seems not to have resulted in cost savings but may actually have increased the overall burden of costs. According to Brown and Marriott (1999, p. 535):

> *In deciding how to reform civil dispute resolution it is essential that we adopt the basic approach of trying to manage efficiently and fairly the transition from one relationship to another. For it is then that we can properly deploy the various methods which may produce the best results.*

The way forward appears to be in combining different methods within the same process. The introduction of a court-based, fixed-fee, judicial mediation service such as that available in Employment Tribunals, could perhaps offer much earlier, informal and affordable 'without prejudice' meetings to determine how far apart the parties are. In effect a form of court-sponsored Early Neutral Evaluation in which suitably trained and experienced professional practitioners might again play a part.

Meanwhile, where disputes are resolved by litigation, suitably trained and experienced professional practitioners, proficient in alternative dispute resolution procedures, might at the very least more expediently and cost effectively resolve issues of damages and costs – the litigation process, with its reliance upon expert witnesses, being arguably less well-suited to do so.

CHAPTER SUMMARY

- The major forms of alternative dispute resolution procedures involve the intercession and assistance of a neutral and impartial third parties and include arbitration, mediation and adjudication

- Aiming to overcome the weaknesses of adversarial systems, alternative dispute resolution procedures seek to encourage more openness, better communication and are intended to lead to swifter, more cost-effective dispute resolution

- Encouragement towards alternative dispute resolution procedures in advance of and in preference to civil litigation is reflected in commercial contracts by the inclusion of alternative dispute resolution clauses

- In comparison to litigation alternative dispute resolution procedures better protect working relationships, reduce expense, are more likely to achieve desired outcomes and have distinct sociological benefits.

- In terms of predictability, reliability and expediency, it is questionable whether alternative dispute resolution procedures are any more effective than litigation.

List of References

Bennett, R.J., 1997. The Relation between Government and Business Associations in Britain: An Evaluation of Recent Developments. *Policy Studies*, Vol. 18, No. 1, pp. 5–33. Policy Studies Institute.

Bennett, R.J., 1998. Business Associations and Their Potential to Contribute to Economic Development: Re-exploring an Interface between the State and Market. *Environment and Planning*, Vol. 30, pp. 1367–87. Great Britain: Pion Publishing.

Bolton, J.E., 1971. Small Firms: Report of the Commission of Inquiry. Cmnd 4811. London: HMSO. Quoted in Bennett, R.J., 1997.

BBC News, 21 October 2007. Population at Least 75m by 2051. [Online] Available at: <news.bbc.co.uk/2/hi/uk_news/7055285.stm> [Accessed 18 September 2013].

BBC News, 30 June 2011. UK Population Sees Biggest Increase in Half a Century. [Online] Available at: <www.bbc.co.uk/news/uk-13975481> [Accessed 18 September 2013].

Bevan, A., 1992. *Alternative Dispute Resolution: A Lawyers Guide to Mediation and Other Forms of Dispute Resolution*. Sweet & Maxwell.

The British Standards Institution, March 2013. PAS 91:2013 Construction Prequalification Questionnaires. BSI Standards Limited 2013. Available at: http://shop.bsigroup.com/en/Navigate-by/PAS/PAS-91-2013/ [Accessed 24 April 2014].

Brown, H. and Marriott, A., 1999. *ADR Principles and Practice*. Sweet & Maxwell.

Burns, M., 10 May 2003. Stop Arguing and Get Back to Work. *Estates Gazette* pp. 110–11.

The Cabinet Office, May 2011. Government Construction Strategy. [Online] Available at: <https://www.gov.uk/government/uploads/system/uploads/attachment_data/file/61152/Government-Construction-Strategy_0.pdf> [Accessed 13 January 2014].

Chua, W. F. and Poullaos, C., 1998. The Dynamics of 'Closure' Amidst the Construction of Market, Profession, Empire and Nationhood: An Historical Analysis of an Australian Accounting Association, 1886–1903. *Accounting, Organizations and Society*, Vol. 23, No. 2, pp. 155–87. Great Britain: Pergamon Press.

Clamp, H., 1999. *Landscape Professional Practice*. 2nd ed. Hampshire and Vermont: Gower.

Clamp, H., Cox, S., Lupton, S. and Udom, K., 2012. *Which Contract: Choosing the Appropriate Building Contract*. 5th ed. London: RIBA Publishing.

Committee of Plant Supply and Establishment, 1995. *Code of Practice for Handling and Establishing Landscape Plants*. 2nd Ed. Berkshire: Joint Council for Landscape Industries.

Densham, W. and Bradford, K., 13 March 2004. Movement on Arbitrators' Awards. *Estates Gazette*, p. 130.

Department for Communities and Local Government, March 2012. National Planning Policy Framework. Crown Copyright.

Dodd, A. and Rees, G., 2004. The Cost of Refusing To Mediate. *New Law Journal*, Vol. 154, No. 7113, p. 124.

Finch, R., 2011. *NBS Guide to Tendering for Construction Projects*. London: RIBA Enterprises Ltd.

Flannery, L., 2003. The Retreat from Mediation? *New Law Journal*, Vol. 153, No. 7079, p. 1415.

The Forestry Commission, April 2007. Tree Felling – Getting Permission. Edinburgh: The Forestry Commission.

Fraser, G.R., 1998. The Future Role of the Joint Council for Landscape Industries: A Strategic Review. Master of Business Administration Integrative Dissertation. University of Brighton Business School.

Genn, Prof. H., 2003. Reported in Alternative Dispute Resolution: Too Little Too Late. *Construction and Engineering Law*, Vol. 8, No. 1, p. 5.

Goldberg, S.B., Sander, F.E.A., and Rogers, N.H., 1992. *Dispute Resolution: Negotiation, Mediation and Other Processes*. Boston: Little Brown and Company.

The Health and Safety Executive, 2006. Health and Safety in Construction. 3rd Ed. Leaflet No. HSG150: The Health and Safety Executive.

Helios Software Ltd., 2013. National Plant Specification Background. [Online] Available at <http://www.gohelios.co.uk/nps/background.aspx> [Accessed 22 September 2013].

HM Government, 1995. Competitiveness: Forging Ahead. Cm 2867. London: Her Majesty's Stationery Office.

Her Majesty's Revenue and Customs, January 2013. Construction Industry Scheme: Guide for Contractors and Subcontractors. Her Majesty's Revenue and Customs: Crown Copyright.

Heseltine, M., 1993. Speech on Trade Associations. Delivered to the Confederation of British Industry (CBI) 17 June 1993. London: Department of Trade and Industry. Quoted in Bennett, R.J., 1997.

The Institute of Civil Engineers, 2011. ICE Conditions of Contract Replaced by Infrastructure Conditions of Contract. [Online] Available at <http://www.ice.org.uk/topics/lawandcontracts/ICE-Conditions-of-Contract> [Accessed 28 September 2013].

Koimn, R., 2011. Professions, Professionals and Traditional Professionals. [Online] Available at <http://www.banderabulletin.com/columnists/article_4113b520-75a1-11e0-9cdc-001cc4c03286.html> [Accessed 6 October 2013].

The Landscape Institute, 2008. Landscape Institute Royal Charter (Revised 2008). London: The Landscape Institute.

The Landscape Institute, May 2012. The Landscape Institute Code of Standards of Conduct and Practice for Landscape Professionals. London: The Landscape Institute.

The Landscape Institute, June 2012. The Landscape Institute's CPD Policy. London: The Landscape Institute.

The Landscape Institute, June 2012. Practice Notes for the 2012 Editions of JCLI Landscape Works Contract (JCLI LWC) and JCLI Landscape Works Contract with Contractor's Design (JCLI LWCD). JCLI Practice Note No. 8 Revision 1. London: The Landscape Institute.

The Landscape Institute, July 2012. Guidelines for Making a Complaint. [Online] Available at <http://landscapeinstitute.sigma.titaninternet.co.uk/PDF/Contribute/Guidelinesformakingacomplaint-July2012.pdf> [Accessed 7 October 2013].

The Landscape Institute, 2013. History of JCLI. [Online]. Available at <http://www.landscapeinstitute.org/knowledge/JCLI.php> [Accessed 25 September 2013].

The Landscape Institute, July 2013. Results of the Employment and Salary Survey 2013. London: The Landscape Institute.

The Landscape Institute, December 2013. Landscape Consultant's Appointment. LI Practice Note 2. London: The Landscape Institute.

The Landscape Institute and Institute of Environmental Management & Assessment, 2013. Guidelines for Landscape and Visual Impact Assessment. 3rd Ed. Oxford, USA and Canada: Routledge.

Larson, M.S., 1977. *The Rise of Professionalism: A Sociological Analysis*. Berkeley: The University of California Press, quoted in Chua, W. F. and Poullaos, C., 1998.

Lewis, J., 2003. Meet The Middleman. *Law Society Gazette*, Vol. 100, No. 18, pp. 24–6.

Lightman L.J., 2004. Litigation: The Last Resort. *New Law Journal*, Vol. 154, No. 7114, pp. 185–9.

MacDonald, K.M., 1985. Social Closure and Occupational Registration. *Sociology*, Vol. 19, No. 4, pp. 541–56.

McKinstry, S., 1997. Status Building: Some Reflections on the Architectural History of Chartered Accountants' Hall, London, 1889–1893. *Accounting, Organizations and Society*, Vol. 22, No. 8, pp. 779–98. Great Britain: Pergamon Press.

McLeod, T.I., 2002. *Legal Method*. 4th ed. Hampshire and New York: Palgrave Macmillan.

Michaelson, J., 2003. The A–Z of ADR – Pt I. *New Law Journal*, Vol. 153, No. 7064, pp. 101–5.

Michaelson, J., 2003. The A–Z of ADR – Pt II. *New Law Journal*, Vol. 153, No. 7065, pp. 146–7.

Murphy, R., 1988. *Social Closure: The Theory of Monopolization and Exclusion*. Oxford: Clarendon Press. Quoted in Chua, W. F. and Poullaos, C., 1998.

Newman, P., 1999. *Alternative Dispute Resolution*. CLT Professional Publishing.

Newmark, C., 2002. In Praise of ADR. *New Law Journal*, Vol. 152, No. 7060, p. 1896.

The Office of National Statistics, 29 March 2012. National Population Projections, 2010-based Reference Volume: Series PP2, Chapter 2.

Olson, M., 1971. *The Logic of Collective Action: Public Goods and the Theory of Groups*. 2nd Ed. Cambridge, MA: Harvard University Press. Quoted in Bennett, R.J., 1997.

Parkin, F., 1979. *Marxism and Class Theory: A Bourgeois Critique*. London: Tavistock Publishing. Quoted in Chua, W. F. and Poullaos, C., 1998.

Pemble, S., 17 January 2004. It Aint Necessarily So. *Estates Gazette*, p. 95.

Preddy, S., 1997. *How to Market Design Consultancy Services*. Hampshire and Vermont: Gower.

Rogers, W., 2011. *The Professional Practice of Landscape Architecture*. 2nd Ed. New Jersey and Canada: Wiley.

The Royal Institute of Chartered Surveyors, 1998. *SMM7 – Standard Method of Measurement for Building Works*. 7th Ed. The Royal Institute of Chartered Surveyors.

Slack, N., Chambers, S., Harland, C., Harrison, A. and Johnston, R., 1995. *Operations Management*. London: Pitman Publishing.

Smulian, M., 2003. Building Blocks. *Law Society Gazette*, Vol. 100, No. 40, pp. 22–3.

Spedding, L.S., 2003. Aspects of Dispute Resolution. *Advising Business: Law & Practice*. Vol. 2, No. 2, p. 6.

Stone, R., 2003. *The Modern Law of Contract*. 5th Ed. London, Sydney and Portland, OR: Cavendish Publishing Limited.

Streeck, W. and Schmitter, P.C., (Eds), 1985. *Private Interest Government: Beyond Market and State*. London: Sage Publishing.Van Doorn, J. A.A., 1966. Conflict in Formal Organisations, quoted in De Reuck, A. V.S. and Knight, J., (Eds), 1995. *Conflict in Society*. London: J & A Churchill, quoted in Walker, S. P., 1995.

Walker, S. P., 1995. The Genesis of Professional Organization in Scotland: A Contextual Analysis. *Accounting, Organizations and Society*, Vol. 20, No. 4, pp. 285–310. Great Britain: Pergamon Press.

Weber, M., 1968. *Economy and Society: An Outline of Interpretative Sociology*, Ed. Roth, G. and Wittich, C., New York: Bedminster Press. In Chua, W. F. and Poullaos, C., 1998.

Wilmott, H., 1986. Organising the Profession: A Theoretical and Historical Examination of the Development of the Major Accounting Bodies in the UK. *Accounting, Organizations and Society*, Vol. 11, No .6, pp. 555–80. Great Britain: Pergamon Press.

Worthington, I. and Britton, C., 1994. *The Business Environment*. London: Pitman Publishing

Index

acceptance of offer 27, 29–30
accounting 83–7
Adams v Lindsell 30
Addis v Gramophone Ltd 36
adjudication 194, 230, 234–5, 242
administration of contract. *see* contract administration
advertisements 19, 28
Advertising Standards Authority 19
agency 34
agreement. *see* contract
Alderson, Judge 43
alternative dispute resolution 6, 229–43
   civil litigation changes and 235–6
   civil litigation compared 237–41, 242
   clauses for 194–5, 236–7
   confidentiality of 239–40
   dialogue facilitated with 240–41
   expediency of 239
   expense of 240
   forms of 230–35
   future relations salvaged with 240
   predictability of 238
   reliability of 238–9
   voices heard with 241
Anglia Television Ltd v Reed 36
approximate all-in costs 161
arbitration 195, 230, 233–4, 242
Arbitration Act 1996 233
Ashton v Turner 49
associations, professional 2–4, 11–23. *see also* Landscape Institute
Atkin, Lord Justice 42

balance sheet 85
Barnett v Chelsea & Kensington Hospital Management Committee 44–5
BBC News online 72

Bennett, R.J. 2, 3–4
bespoke form of agreement 189
Bevan, A. 229, 230, 233, 234, 235, 239, 242
Bill of Quantities 160, 212
Blyth v Birmingham Waterworks 43
Bolam v Friern Hospital Management Committee 44
Bolton v Stone 44
Bourhill v Young 42
Bradford, K. 233
British Standards Institution 178, 207, 208
Brown, H. 229, 230, 235, 239, 240, 242–3
budgeting. *see* estimation
Building Information Modelling 171, 183
Building Information Modelling Execution Plan 171
Burns, M. 234
business environment 70–73
   economic environment 71
   legal environment 70–71
   political environment 71
   social environment 72
   technological environment 72–3
business management. *see* management of business
business performance
   analysis of performance 66–70
   competitor benchmarking 69–70
   goods 65–6
   historical performance 68
   performance criteria 66–8
   services 65–6
   target performance 68–9
   transformation process model 63–5, 66
business promotion 75–6
Byrne v Van Tienhoven 28–9

Cable & Wireless PLC v IBM United Kingdom Ltd 236, 237

Caparo Industries v Dickman 43, 50
Carlill v Carbolic Smoke Ball Co. 28, 29, 30
cash flow forecasting 85–7
central government departments 82
central government trading organisations 82
Certificate of Making Good 216, 222–3
Certificate of Practical Completion 200, 216, 221–2
Channel Tunnel Group Ltd & Another v Balfour Beatty Construction Ltd & Others 237
Chaplin v Hicks 36
Chappell & Co. v. Nestle Co. Ltd 31
charitable incorporated organisation 80
Charities' Commission 80
Chartered Member of the Landscape Institute 12, 127
Chaudry v Prabhakar 50
Civic Amenities Act 1967 114
civil litigation 195
  alternative dispute resolution compared 237–41, 242
  changes to 235–6
  Civil Procedures Rules 1998 236, 240, 242
  confrontational nature of 240
  expediency of 239
  expense of 240
  predictability of 238
  public scrutiny with 239–40
  reliability of 238–9
  remedies available 240–41
Civil Procedure Rules 1998 236, 240, 242
Clamp, H. 190
client
  definition of 143
  domestic 143–4
  responsibilities of 123–5, 143–5, 146
  role of 123–5
Code of Practice for Handling & Establishing Landscape Plants 183–4
Colman, His Honor Judge 237
Committee of Plant Supply and Establishment 183
Common Arrangement of Work Sections 5, 161, 164, 173–7, 181, 210. *see also* materials and workmanship specifications; preliminaries/general conditions
Companies Acts 192, 203
company limited by guarantee 81

competence 17, 151–2
Competitiveness White Paper 3
Computer Aided Design 72, 158, 171, 183
conciliation 231
Conditions of Appointment and Memorandum of Agreement 91
conservation. *see* development control
conservation areas 114
Conservation (Natural Habitats, &c.) Regulations 118
consideration 27, 31–2
Construction Clients' Board 190
construction contract 130, 234. *see also* JCLI Landscape Maintenance Works Contract 2012; JCLI Landscape Works Contract 2012; JCLI Landscape Works Contract with Contractor's Design 2012
Construction Design and Management Coordinator 143, 145–6, 149, 151–2, 193
  appointment of 143, 144, 147, 148, 150
  competence of 151–2
  obligations of 145–6
Construction Design and Management Regulations 1994 141, 144, 145, 148
Construction Design and Management Regulations 2007 5, 141–53, 193, 194, 197. *see also* Construction Design and Management Coordinator
  Approved Code of Practice 142, 151, 152
  client obligations 143–5, 146
  competence requirement 151–2
  Construction Phase Health and Safety Plan 143, 144, 145, 148, 149, 150
  designers/professional practitioners obligations 146–8
  Health and Safety File 143, 144, 145, 146, 147, 149, 150
  notification requirement 142–3
  planning period 197
  Principal Contractor 143, 144, 148–9, 193–4
  self-employed obligations 149–50
  training requirement 151–2
Construction (Health, Safety and Welfare) Regulations 1996 142
Construction Industry Council 91
Construction Industry Scheme 195–6
Construction Phase Health and Safety Plan 143, 144, 145, 148, 149, 150

consumer co-operative society 81
Consumer Credit Act 71
continuing professional development (CPD) 4, 17–18, 22–3
contract
　acceptance of offer in 27, 29–30
　administration of *see* contract administration
　agency 34
　alternative dispute resolution clauses in 235, 236–7
　breach of 34–5
　conditions of 187–204
　consideration in 27, 31–2
　with contractor *see* construction contract
　discharge of 34–5
　elements of 27–32
　forms of 189–91
　invitation to treat in 28
　legal principles for 27–39
　misrepresentation in 37–8
　offer in 27, 28–9
　postal rule 30
　privity of contract 33, 125, 130, 189
　with professional practitioner 89–99
　remedies for breach of 35–7
　roles in 123–8
　sub-contracts 188–9
　terms of 32–3
contract administration 215–27
　certificates 225
　certifications required 216–24
　contract documentation 225
　correspondence 225–6
　distribution of certifications 216
　drawing office records 224–7
　invoices 226–7
　job lists 224–5
　responsibility for 128. *see also* Landscape Architect/Contract Administrator
　timesheets 226–7
　valuations 225
　variations 217–18, 225
contract documentation 169–70, 187, 188, 225. *see also* drawings; specifications
　Bill of Quantities 160, 212
　conditions of contract 187–204
　Schedule of Operations 158–61
　Schedule of Rates 160

contractor. *see also* construction contract; Principal Contractor
　definition of 195
　liability insurance of 202
　payment of 200–201, 218–20, 223–4
　prequalification of 207–8
　responsibilities of 125–6, 131, 149–50
　role of 125–6, 136, 138
Contracts (Right of Third Parties) Act 1999 33
Control of Substances Hazardous to Health Regulations 2002 (COSHH) 57–8
Coordinated Project Information 173
Corenso (UK) Ltd v Burnden Group PLC 232
correspondence 225–6
cost plus rates 162
Courtney & Fairbairn Ltd v Tolaini Bros (Hotels) Ltd 236
cover pricing 209–10
Cowl v Plymouth City Council 236
Cox, S. 190

damages
　liquidated 197–8, 220, 224
　restitution 35–6, 49
dangerous occurrences 59
death of person 58–9
Denning, Lord Justice 45, 48, 236
Densham, W. 233
Department for Communities and Local Government 104
design and build procurement 133–7, 139, 191
designer. *see* professional practitioner
development control 103–19
　conservation areas 114
　Environmental Impact Assessment 107–12
　forestry regulations 114–16
　habitats regulations 118–19
　Hedgerows Regulations 1997 116–18
　permitted development 105–7
　Tree Preservation Orders 112–14, 115
development project, defined 108
Dickinson v Dodds 29
disbursements 98–9
diseases, work related 59
dispute resolution. *see* alternative dispute resolution; civil litigation
domestic gardens 134, 139
domestic sub-contract 188

Donoghue v Stevenson 42
drawings 169, 170, 174
Dunnett v Railtrack PLC 232, 237

early neutral evaluation 231, 243
Employers Information Requirements 171
endangered species 118–19
engagement of professional 89–99
 fee 93–9
 form of agreement 90–91
 scope of services 89–90, 91
Engaging a Landscape Consultant – Guidance for Clients on Fees 93
Ennstone Breedon Limited 184
Entores v Miles Far East Corporation 30
environment control. *see* development control
environment for business. *see* business environment
Environmental Impact Assessment 107–12
Environmental Impact Assessment (Forestry) Regulations 1999 116
estimation 155–67
 fundamentals of 155–7
 measurement 158
 rate attribution 161–2
 schedule formulation 158–61
 sources of rates 162–7
European Protected Species 119
European Union Directive 2011/92/EU *The Assessment of the Effects of Certain Public and Private Projects on the Environment* 108–11
 Annex I 108–9
 Annex II 109–11
 Annex III 111
exchange of letters, agreement by 90–91, 189
expenses 98–9
expert determination 231
extra over rates 162

Fairchild v Glenhaven 45
Farley v Skinner 36
fee setting 93–9
 calculating 93–6
 expenses 98–9
 lump sum fee 97–8
 percentage fee 96–7
 time charged fee 97
Felthouse v Bindley 30

Final Certificate 201, 216, 223–4
financial accounting 83–7
 balance sheet 85
 cash flow forecasting 85–7
 profit and loss accounts 83–5
Finch, R. 206, 210
Fisher v Bell 28
Flannery, L. 232
Forestry Act 1967 115–16, 119
Forestry Commission 114–16, 118
forestry regulations 114–16
Framework Agreement 196
Froom v Butcher 48
frustration, doctrine of 35
Future Role of the Joint Council of Landscape Industries: A Strategic Review, The 184

general conditions. *see* preliminaries/general conditions
Genn, Professor H. 239
Glasbrook Bros. v Glamorgan County Council 31
Glasgow Corporation v Muir 43
Goldberg, S.B. 230
Government Construction Client Group 171

Habitats and Species Regulations 2010 119
habitats regulations 118–19
Hadley v Baxendale 36–7
Hadley v London Electricity Board 42
Hartley v Ponsonby 31
Health and Safety at Work Act 1974 54–5
Health and Safety Executive 53, 151
 accident report form 59
 disease report form 59
 enforcement 59–60
 guide 53
 Incident Contact Centre 58
 notification requirements 58–9, 142–3, 193
Health and Safety File 141, 143, 144, 145, 146, 147, 149, 150
health and safety legislation 53–61
 Control of Substances Hazardous to Health Regulations 2002 (COSHH) 57–8
 enforcement 59–60
 Health and Safety at Work Act 1974 54–5

Management of Health and Safety at
    Work Regulations 1999 55–6
  method statements 57
  Reporting of Injuries, Diseases and
    Dangerous Occurrences Regulations
    1995 (RIDDOR) 58–9
  risk assessment 55–6
health and safety policy 54
Hedgerows Regulations 1997 116–18
Hedley Byrne & Co v Heller & Partners Ltd
  38, 50
Helios Software Ltd 182
Her Majesty's Revenue and Customs
  Construction Industry Scheme 195–6
  for Value Added Tax 157, 193
*Hilder v Associated Portland Cement
  Manufacturers* 44
Holwell Securities v Hughes 30
Housing Grants, Construction and
  Regeneration Act 1996 194–5, 216
Hughes v Lord Advocate 46
Hurst v Leeming 232
Hyde v Wrench 29

ICE Conditions of Contract 190
income statement 83–5
Infrastructure Conditions of Contract 190
injury to person 58–9
Institute of Civil Engineers 190
Institute of Environmental Management
  and Assessment 107
Institute of Landscape Architects 4, 11
insurance
  contractor's 202
  professional indemnity 20–21, 51,
    127–8
  of works 202–3
Interim Payment Certificate 216, 218–20
International Federation of Landscape
  Architects 4, 11
invitation to tender 210–11
invitation to treat 28
invoices 226–7

Jarvis v Swan Tours 36
JCLI Contracts Forum 190, 191. *see also*
  JCLI Landscape Maintenance Works
    Contract 2012; JCLI Landscape Works
    Contract 2012; JCLI Landscape Works
    Contract with Contractor's Design 2012
JCLI Landscape Maintenance Works
  Contract 2012 191, 198, 199, 201, 222

JCLI Landscape Works Contract 2012 5–6,
  191
Articles
  — Article 2 192
  — Article 3 193
  — Article 4 193, 194
  — Article 5 193–4
  — Article 6 194
  — Article 7 194, 195
  — Article 8 194
Conditions of Contract 191–203
  — attestation 203
  — certification forms 216–24
  — Construction Industry Scheme
    195–6
  — contract documents 192
  — contract sum 192–3
  — contractor's liability insurance 202
  — defects 198–9
  — dispute resolution 194–5
  — documents to contract
    administrator 201
  — duration of works 197
  — establishment maintenance
    198–9
  — insurance of works 202–3
  — interest 224
  — interim payments 218–20
  — liquidated damages 197–8
  — malicious damage 199
  — parties 192
  — planning period 197
  — professional practitioner 193
  — Rectification Period 199
  — regulations governing 193–4
  — retention 200–201
  — supplemental provisions 196–7
  — tax changes 201
  — theft 199
  — variations 217
  — works, nature and location of 192
Contract Particulars
  — clause 1.1 197
  — clause 2.1 197
  — clause 2.2 197
  — clause 2.8 197–8, 220, 224
  — clause 2.10A 198, 199, 201, 221,
    222
  — clause 2.10B 198, 199, 201, 221,
    223
  — clause 2.12 222
  — clause 2.13 199

— clause 3.6 217
— clause 4.3 218, 219
— clause 4.3.1 200–201, 218
— clause 4.4.1 200–201, 221
— clause 4.5.2 218, 220
— clause 4.5.4 219, 220, 221, 224
— clause 4.6 219
— clause 4.7 219
— clause 4.8.1 201, 223
— clause 4.8.2 224
— clause 4.9 224
— clause 4.11 201
— clause 5.3.2 202
— clause 5.4 202
— clause 6.8 219
— clause 7.2 194
Recitals
— First Recital 192
— Second Recital 192
— Fourth Recital 195–6
— Fifth Recital 194
— Sixth Recital 196
— Seventh Recital 196–7
Schedules
— Schedule 1 194, 195
— Schedule 2 201
— Schedule 3 196–7
JCLI Landscape Works Contract with Contractor's Design 2012 132, 191, 198, 216
JCT Intermediate Building Contract 2011 191
JCT Minor Works Building Contract 2011 191
job lists 224–5
Joint Committee for Landscape Industries 184
Joint Contract Tribunal 190
Joint Council of Landscape Industries 183, 184
Jones v Livox Quarries Ltd 48

Koimn, R. 1–2

Landscape 12
landscape architect. *see* professional practitioner
Landscape Architect/Contract Administrator 193, 201, 216–23
certifications by 216–23
— Certificate of Making Good 216, 222–3

— Certificate of Practical Completion 200, 216, 221–2
— distribution of 216
— Final Certificate 201, 216, 223–4
— Interim Payment Certificates 216, 218–20
— Landscape Architect's Contract Administrator's Instruction 216, 217–18
— Payless Notice (Type 1) 216, 218–19, 220, 224
— Payless Notice (Type 2) 216, 218–19, 220–21
as Construction Design and Management Coordinator 193
Landscape Architect's Contract Administrator's Instruction 216, 217–18
Landscape Consultant's Appointment 91–2, 96
Landscape Design 12
Landscape Institute 4, 11–12, 94, 107, 151, 184
Code of Practice *see* Landscape Institute Code of Standards of Conduct and Practice for Landscape Professionals, The
construction work definition 142
contract administration forms 216–23
divisions of 11–12
Education and Membership Committee 22, 23
'Elements and Areas of Practice' 12n1
Engaging a Landscape Consultant – Guidance for Clients on Fees 93
Insurance Services 51
Landscape Consultant's Appointment 91–2, 96
objects of 12
Pathway to Chartership 4, 12
standards of conduct and practice 13–21
Landscape Institute Code of Standards of Conduct and Practice for Landscape Professionals, The 13–21
Standard 1 13
Standard 2 14
Standard 3 14–15
Standard 4 15
Standard 5 15–17, 136
Standard 6 17
Standard 7 17–18, 22
Standard 8 18, 92

Standard 9 18–19
Standard 10 19
Standard 11 20
Standard 12 20–21
Standard 13 21
Latham, Sir Michael 234
Law Reform (Contributory Negligence) Act 1945 48
Lewis, J. 229, 241
Lightman, Lord Justice 231, 232, 238, 239, 240, 241
limited company 79
liquidated damages 197–8, 220, 224
litigation. *see* civil litigation
local authorities 82, 103–5
Local Democracy, Economic Development and Construction Act 2009 216
lump sum contract 133, 137
lump sum fee 97–8
Lupton, S. 190

McCook v Lobo 232
McKew v Holland 45
MacKinnon, Lord Justice 33, 46
McKinstry, S. 3
Macmillan, Lord Justice 42, 43
McNair, Judge 44
McParland Finn Ltd 51
management of business 77–87
   financial accounting 83–7
   not-for-profit organisations 80–82
   private sector organisations 77–80
   public sector organisations 82–3
Management of Health and Safety at Work Regulations 1999 55–6
management procurement 137–9
Marc Rich & Co v Bishop Rock Marine Co Ltd 42–3
market appraisal 73–5
   competitors 74–5
   customers 74
   resource markets 74
   resources 73–4
marketing 75–6
Marriott, A. 229, 230, 235, 239, 240, 242–3
materials and workmanship specifications 177–80
   British Standards 178
   finished effect 180
   materials 177
   method 180
   minimum standards 179

proprietary name 179
   quality assurance 178
   supplier 179–80
   type 178
   workmanship 177
measured works 162, 164
measurement contract 133
Med-Arb 231
mediation 230, 231–2, 242
method statements 57
Michaelson, J. 233
misrepresentation 37–8, 50–51
Misrepresentation Act 1967 38
Mullin v Richards 44
Murphy v Brentwood District Council 49
Mustill, Lord Justice 237

National Insurance Scheme 72, 94
National Planning Policy Framework of 2012 103–5
National Plant Specification 181–3
Natural England 119
NBS Landscape 173, 181, 210
negligence 41–52
   breach of duty 43–4
   causation 44–5
   contributory negligence 46, 48–9
   defences 46–9
   duty of care 41–3
   'egg-shell skull' rule 46
   exclusion of liability 46, 47
   general standard of care 43
   negligent misrepresentation 50–51
   neighbour principle 42
   'ordinary skilled man' test 44
   'reasonable foreseeability' test 46
   'reasonable man' test 43
   remedies 49
   remoteness of damage 45–6
   unforeseeable victim 42
   willing assumption of risk 46, 47
negligent misrepresentation 50–51
negotiation 197, 230
neutral fact-finding 231
New Engineering Contract 190
New York Convention 233
Newman, P. 233, 242
nominated sub-contract 131, 188
not-for-profit organisations 80–82

offer 27, 28–9
Office of National Statistics 72

Olson, M. 2
ombudsmen 231
Owens v Liverpool Corporation 46

Parsons v Uttley Ingham 37
partial possession 222
partnership 78–9
Partnership Act 1890 78
Partridge v Crittenden 28
PAS 91:2013 Construction Prequalification Questionnaires 208
Pathway to Chartership 4, 12
Payless Notice (Type 1) 216, 218–19, 220, 224
Payless Notice (Type 2) 216, 218–19, 220–21
Pemble, S. 236
percentage fee 96–7
performance criteria 66–8
performance of business. *see* business performance
Pinnel's Case 32
Plan of Work 91
planimeter 158
Planning and Compulsory Purchase Act 2004 103
planning authorities 103–5
Planning (Listed Building and Conservation Areas) Act 1990 114
Planning Supervisor 141, 143, 145
Plant Health (Forestry) (Great Britain) Order 1993 116
platometer 158
Powell v Lee 30
practical completion 221–2
pre-qualification questionnaire 207–8
Pre-Tender Health and Safety Plan 141
Preddy, S. 75–6
preliminaries/general conditions 174–7
  conditions of contract 175
  description of work 174
  drawings 174
  facilities/temporary work/services requirements 176–7
  management of works requirements 175–6
  project particulars 174
  quality standards/control requirements 176
  security/safety/protection requirements 176
  site/existing buildings 174
  tendering sub-letting and supply requirements 175
preliminary enquiry 209–10
prime cost (PC) 162
Principal Contractor 141, 193–4
  appointment of 143, 144
  obligations of 148–50
private sector organisations 77–80
  sole trader 203
privity of contract 33, 125, 130, 189
procurement strategies 129–39
  design and build procurement 133–7, 139
  management procurement 137–9
  traditional procurement 130–33, 139
professional associations 2–4, 11–23. *see also* Landscape Institute
professional indemnity insurance 20–21, 51, 127–8
professional negligence. *see* negligence
professional practitioner
  associations for *see* Landscape Institute
  contract administration by *see* Landscape Architect/Contract Administrator
  contract with 89–99
  fee setting by 93–9
  indemnity insurance for 127–8
  responsibilities of 126–8, 146–8, 155, 171
  role of 126–8
  standards of conduct *see* Landscape Institute Code of Standards of Conduct and Practice for Landscape Professionals, The
  titles for 127
  workspace for 54–5
professional privilege 3
professionalism 1–2
  character and quality of environment, preserving 13
  code of conduct, promoting 14–15
  competency 17
  complaint resolution 21
  continuing professional development 4, 17–18, 22–3
  finances, management of 20
  indemnity insurance 20–21, 51, 127–8
  integrity, acting with 15–17
  misleading or untrue statements 19
  objectives of Landscape Institute, promoting 15

organisation of work responsibly with clients 18, 92
record keeping 224–7
reputation of profession, upholding 14
standards, adhering to 18–19
standards of conduct and practice 13–21
profit and loss accounts 83–5
promotion of business 75–6
provisional sums 162
public corporations 82
public limited company (PLC) 79–80
Public Sector Clients' Forum 190
public sector organisations 82–3

Quantity Surveyor 138, 160
quantum meruit 35
quasi autonomous non-governmental organisations 82
questionnaire, pre-qualification 207–8

R v Clarke 29
rates
   attribution of 161–2
   schedule of 160
   sources of 162–7
      — indicative quotations 163–4
      — previously quoted schemes 163
      — *Spon's Landscape and External Works Price Book* 164–6, 167
      — supplier's costs 163
records, drawing office 224–7
Rectification Period 199, 201, 221, 222, 223
regional bodies 82
Reid, Lord Justice 50
relationships, contractual 123–8
remedies
   for breach of contract 35–7
   for professional negligence 49
Reporting of Injuries, Diseases and Dangerous Occurrences Regulations 1995 (RIDDOR) 58–9
responsibilities of parties 123–8
retention 200–201, 221, 223
risk assessment 55–6, 147–8
Road Traffic Act 1998 47
Roe v Minister of Health 44
Rogers, N.H. 230
roles of parties 123–8
Roscorla v Thomas 31
Routledge v Grant 28

Royal Bank of Canada v Secretary of State for Defence 232
Royal Institute of Building Architects 91
Ruxley Electronics & Construction Ltd v Forsyth 35–6

safety legislation. *see* health and safety legislation
Sale of Goods Act 1979 33, 71
Sander, F.E.A. 230
scale rule 158
Scammell v Ouston 28
Schedule of Operations 158–61
Schedule of Rates 160
Scheme for Construction Contracts (England and Wales) Regulations 1998 235
Schmitter, P.C. 2
Shirlaw v Southern Foundries 33
Simons, Viscount 46
Smith v Eric S. Bush; Harris v Wyre Forest District Council 47
Smith v Leech Brain & Co. Ltd 46
Smulian, M. 235, 238, 242
Society of Garden Designers 92
Socit Internationale de Telecommunications Aeronautiques SC v Wyatt Co (UK) Ltd (Costs) 232
sole trader 77–8, 203
Somervell, Lord Justice 31
Spartan Steel & Alloys Ltd v Martin & Co 45
specifications 170–85. *see also* Common Arrangement of Work Sections
   general conditions 174–7
   materials 177–80
   preliminaries 174–7
   standard clauses 180–84
   structure of 171–3
   worksmanship 177–80
Spon's Landscape and External Works Price Book 164–6, 167, 173, 178
Standard Method of Measurement 160, 173, 177, 192
Stevenson v McLean 29
Steyn, Lord Justice 42–3
Stilk v Myrick 31, 32
Stone, R. 28, 30, 35
Streeck, W. 2
sub-contracts 131, 188–9
suppliers 130–31
sustainable development 104
'SWOT' analysis 73, 74, 75

Technology and Construction Court 234
tendering 28, 205–13
  cover pricing 209–10
  decision 213
  errors in tenders 212
  evaluation of tenders 211–13
  invitation to tender 210–11
  negotiation in 205, 212
  omissions in tenders 212
  pre-tender evaluation 206–8
  preliminary enquiry 209–10
  quality/price balance 206
  references 208
time charged fee 97
timesheets 226–7
torts. *see* negligence
Town and Country Planning Act 1990 103, 112, 115
Town and Country Planning (General Permitted Development) Order 1995 105–7, 113
Town and Country (Tree Preservation) (England) Regulations 2012 112–13
traditional procurement 130–33, 139
transformation process model 63–5, 66
Tree Preservation Orders 112–14, 115

Udom, K. 190
Unfair Contract Terms Act 1977 47
Unfair Terms in Consumer Contracts Regulations 1994 195

Valentine v Allen 232
Value Added Tax 157, 164, 193, 219, 224
variations 132, 217, 225

Wagon Mound (No. 1), The 46
Walker, S.P. 2
Wieland v Cyril Lord 45
Williams v Cowardine 29
Williams v Roffey Bros & Nicholls (Contractors) Ltd 31–2
Wilmott, H. 3
Woolf, Lord Justice 235, 236, 240
word of mouth agreements 189
workers co-operative 81
workmanship specifications. *see* materials and workmanship specifications
Workplace (Health, Safety and Welfare) Regulations 1992 147, 152
W.S. Atkins PLC 80

Yates v Pulleyn 29